W9-BPP-792

ONLINE PRIVACY

Selected Titles in ABC-CLIO's
CONTEMPORARY WORLD ISSUES
Series

Animal Rights, Clifford J. Sherry
Autism Spectrum Disorders, Raphael Bernier and Jennifer Gerdts
Climate Change, David L. Downie, Kate Brash, and Catherine Vaughan
DNA Technology, David E. Newton
Domestic Violence, Margi Laird McCue
Education in Crisis, Judith A. Gouwens
Environmental Justice, David E. Newton
Gay and Lesbian Rights, David E. Newton
Genocide, Howard Ball
Global Organized Crime, Mitchel P. Roth
Global Refugee Crisis, Mark Gibney
Identity Theft, Sandra K. Hoffman and Tracy G. McGinley
Lobbying in America, Ronald J. Hrebenar and Bryson B. Morgan
Modern Piracy, David F. Marley
Modern Sports Ethics, Angela Lumpkin
Obesity, Judith Stern and Alexandra Kazaks
Same-Sex Marriage, David E. Newton
Sentencing, Dean John Champion
Sexual Crime, Caryn E. Neumann
Sexual Health, David E. Newton
Substance Abuse, David E. Newton
U.S. Border Security, Judith A. Warner
U.S. Space Policy, Peter L. Hays, Ph.D.
U.S. Trade Issues, Alfred E. Eckes, Jr.
Women in Combat, Rosemarie Skaine

For a complete list of titles in this series, please visit **www.abc-clio.com**.

Books in the Contemporary World Issues series address vital issues in today's society, such as genetic engineering, pollution, and biodiversity. Written by professional writers, scholars, and nonacademic experts, these books are authoritative, clearly written, up-to-date, and objective. They provide a good starting point for research by high school and college students, scholars, and general readers as well as by legislators, businesspeople, activists, and others.

Each book, carefully organized and easy to use, contains an overview of the subject, a detailed chronology, biographical sketches, facts and data and/or documents and other primary-source material, a directory of organizations and agencies, annotated lists of print and nonprint resources, and an index.

Readers of books in the Contemporary World Issues series will find the information they need to have a better understanding of the social, political, environmental, and economic issues facing the world today.

ONLINE PRIVACY

A Reference Handbook

Robert Gellman and Pam Dixon

CONTEMPORARY WORLD ISSUES

Santa Barbara, California • Denver, Colorado • Oxford, England

Library of Congress Cataloging-in-Publication Data

Gellman, Robert.
Online privacy : a reference handbook / Robert Gellman and Pam Dixon.
p. cm. — (Contemporary world issues)
Includes bibliographical references and index.
ISBN 978–1–59884–649–2 (hard copy : alk. paper) — ISBN 978–1–59884–650–8 (ebook) 1. Privacy, Right of—United States. 2. Data protection—Law and legislation—United States. 3. Internet—Law and legislation—United States. I. Dixon, Pam. II. Title.
KF1263.C65G45 2011
342.7308′58—dc23 2011019243

ISBN: 978–1–59884–649–2
EISBN: 978–1–59884–650–8

15 14 13 12 11 1 2 3 4 5

This book is also available on the World Wide Web as an eBook. Visit www.abc-clio.com for details.

ABC-CLIO, LLC
130 Cremona Drive, P.O. Box 1911
Santa Barbara, California 93116-1911

This book is printed on acid-free paper ∞

Manufactured in the United States of America

Contents

Preface

Privacy is a much discussed and timely subject on which there is little agreement. There are few subjects on which there is so much interest and so little consensus, even as to the definition or scope of the basic idea. The number and breadth of academics that define, study, and debate privacy illustrate the point best. Lawyers, ethicists, economists, sociologists, historians, physicians, communications professionals, philosophers, political scientists, computer scientists, technologists, and others write about privacy from a wide range of perspectives and standards. Even within particular disciplines, there may be widespread disagreements about the definition, value, scope, relevance, and proper course of study of privacy. To make matters even more complex, the definition and value of privacy also differs across nations and cultures.

However, unlike many complex social and technical issues, privacy is something that affects everyone, and everyone may have an opinion about what is acceptable or not acceptable. One may need a high level of expertise to have a meaningful view on the best way to do a heart transplant or to develop a new standard for Internet Protocol addresses, but no expertise is necessary to decide if a particular online practice invades your own privacy. Still, the more that you know about the background, law, and history of privacy, the more informed your opinion will be. This book will help readers better understand privacy, conduct their own research about online privacy topics, and ultimately make up their own minds about what society should and should not do to protect online privacy.

Privacy can be as simple as a locked door on a bathroom stall and as complicated as a judicial procedure regulating government surveillance of a foreign national who is a suspected terrorist. Privacy is as narrow as an individual's ability to control the disclosure of an identification number assigned to that individual and as disparate as the rules governing the invisible tracking of an individual's online activities for behavioral advertising purposes. Privacy relates to an individual's preference for an ice cream flavor and to an individual's need to protect her physical location from a stalker.

When it comes to privacy, there is much to discuss and often much disagreement about its scope, definition, purpose, best practices, and even how to talk about it. Nevertheless, it is possible and indeed necessary to be able to talk about privacy even in the absence of consensus on what privacy is and what privacy protections are supposed to accomplish, and that is what this book is about. The rapid spread of online activities since 1990 has intensified both the importance of these discussions and the number of participants.

It is important to note that some significant privacy issues related to offline privacy issues (e.g., legal privileges, bodily privacy, and autonomy issues) fall outside the scope of this book. While Internet technology and its importance to personal and business activities make online privacy a major subject of concern, debate, and regulation, the history of privacy in the offline world remains a significant factor in defining online privacy. Online and offline privacy issues cannot be separated completely, nor should they be. What happens offline affects what is done online and vice versa.

What this book does encompass is privacy as it applies to the online world. The discussions in this book describe online privacy, and much of the focus will be on legal rights and other standards that address the protection of online privacy.

Online privacy as an issue is relatively new. As online technologies grew into widespread use, the issue of online privacy also grew with it in urgency and importance. Before 1986, privacy was certainly a focus of some debate and occasional legislation. However, these early privacy laws rarely if ever recognized the existence of the online world. The growth of interest in online privacy in particular—and to some extent privacy in general—parallels the growth of the Internet as an element in modern life.

Online privacy generally has a different dynamic than offline privacy. Online activities do not respect traditional national or conceptual borders. Online technologies have a greater capacity for "memory" via longer retention of and easier access to information. Online activities challenge traditional concepts of information ownership and control, with variable implications for online privacy. Online technologies also make it harder to discern or enforce distinctions among individuals (e.g., age) that are clear in person or even on the telephone. Online actors may reside in jurisdictions that are not easily reached by national regulations or judicial process.

The general pattern of online information persisting for extended periods has led to a new phenomenon sometimes called the *modern permanent record*. The modern permanent record is not the paper file maintained on each high school student in former years. Today's modern permanent record consists of all the information that online marketers, social networking sites, other online businesses, schools, government agencies, social networks, and others can and do compile on individuals, plus other offline information. This new kind of record provides a powerful memory of the purchases, Web browsing activities, physical location, and general history and activities of an individual, a household, or a family. The modern permanent record has a significant commercial value to companies, but it is often be beyond the knowledge or control of the subject of the record.

The modern permanent record is just one example of how—because of the differences in the online space—online privacy poses new, different, and uncertain risks for individuals, businesses, and governments. Most of these new risks have not yet been addressed by any meaningful changes in the law because of the rapidity of the technological advancements and the comparative slowness of policy and legislative processes. There are some notable exceptions, however, and these are discussed in this book. Nevertheless, where the legal or policy process has developed standards, however, those standards are often out of date before they take effect.

This book reviews the current status of online privacy in the United States and elsewhere in the world. Chapter 1 provides a background and history of privacy. This background review explains how privacy is generally defined and provides a legal, social, and cultural context for the topic. Chapter 2 focuses on some of the most fundamental problems, controversies, and solutions in the area of online privacy. An important feature of this chapter is a discussion of self-regulation versus regulation and "opt in" versus "opt out"—concepts that run through many online privacy discussions in this book. Chapter 3 expands this discussion to the European Union and beyond, explaining how the issue of online privacy is similar to and yet different from the privacy debate in the United States. One of the core discussions in this chapter is how privacy law in the United States differs substantially from privacy laws in other countries, particularly Europe.

The remaining chapters of the book provide background and resource information on the issue of online privacy. Chapter 4 provides a chronology of key events in the history of online privacy. Chapter 5 includes brief biographical sketches of important individuals in the history and development of online privacy. Chapter 6 contains documents important to the issue of online privacy and information that is useful in understanding core privacy concepts, such as Fair Information Practices. There are also documents about key issues in online privacy, such as cloud computing and documents outlining key rights, such as the Council of Europe Convention for the Protection of Human Rights and Fundamental Freedoms. Chapter 7 provides a listing of capsule descriptions of organizations that work on issues related to online privacy, including privacy groups, civil liberties groups, consumer groups, and others. Chapter 8 contains an extensive resource list of print and online resources on the topic. A glossary of key terms used in discussions of online privacy is also included.

1

Background and History

What Is Privacy? The Social, Cultural, and Legal Context of Privacy

Privacy is a right, a human right, a legal right, a moral right, a property right, a positive right, a negative right, a value, an economic interest, a personal interest, a societal interest, and other things. Privacy addresses one's physical body, personal information, communications, dignity, relationships, autonomy, and more. Privacy protects individuals and groups, limits governments, regulates business conduct, establishes rules for Internet activities, and accomplishes more. Privacy focuses on the interests of individuals, groups, social networks, societies, and communities of various types. Privacy always covers living individuals, sometimes covers legal persons such as corporations, and may even cover those who are dead as well as their relatives.

Different religions, cultures, nations, regions, states, communities, and individuals take different approaches to privacy. Different professions—doctors, lawyers, clergy, police, and others—take different approaches to privacy. In the United States, different types of records containing personal information (e.g., records containing information relating to health, credit, bank, video rental, and electronic mail) have varying degrees of privacy protection. In other countries—including Canada and member states of the European Union—most records about individuals are subject to the same broad, general privacy standards. Policies, practices, and activities that address privacy vary over time and technologies.

Academics in different disciplines study and define privacy. Lawyers, ethicists, economists, sociologists, physicians, philosophers, political scientists, historians, technologists, and others write about privacy from a wide range of perspectives and standards. Even within particular disciplines, there may be widespread disagreements about the definition, value, scope, relevance, and proper course of study of privacy.

Privacy is as simple as a door on a bathroom stall and as complicated as a judicial procedure regulating government surveillance of a suspected terrorist. Privacy is as narrow as an individual's ability to control the disclosure of an identification number assigned to that individual and as disparate as the rules governing the invisible tracking of an individual's online activities for behavioral advertising purposes. Privacy relates to an individual's preference for an ice cream flavor and to an individual's need to protect her physical location from a stalker.

When it comes to privacy, there is much to discuss and often much disagreement about its scope, definition, purpose, best practices, and even how to talk about it. Nevertheless, it is possible and indeed necessary to be able to talk about privacy even in the absence of consensus on what privacy is and what privacy protections are supposed to accomplish. The discussion here is perhaps simpler because the goal of this book is to describe online privacy and because much of the focus will be on legal rights and other standards that address the protection of online privacy. However, online activities have become so broad and all-encompassing that limiting the discussion to online privacy no longer simplifies the discussion that much. Some important privacy issues (e.g., legal privileges, bodily privacy, and autonomy issues) fall outside the scope of this book. Whether online privacy rights and standards satisfy some broader purpose or objective is an exercise left to the reader.

Online privacy has been an issue that has grown in urgency and importance since the decade of the 1980s. Before 1986, privacy was the focus of some debate and occasional legislation. However, these early privacy laws rarely if ever recognized the existence of the online world. The growth of interest in online privacy—and to some extent privacy in general—parallels the growth of the Internet. While Internet technology and its importance to personal and business activities have made online privacy a major subject of concern, debate, and regulation, the history of privacy in the offline world remains a significant factor in defining online privacy. Online and offline privacy issues cannot be separated completely or for long.

What Does *Online* Mean Today?

In the early 1990s, *online* meant what is now considered to be the old-fashioned *Internet*. The Internet back in that time was essentially a network not of Web pages but of interconnected computers that displayed screens of text. Instead of Web pages, early Internet users surfed bulletin boards, Usenet discussion groups, and pre-websites called *Gophers*. Desktop computers connected to the early Internet primarily via dial-up modems. Today, *online* has much broader connotations. High-speed access to the Internet via cable and DSL connections has become much more common, as has access to the Web via mobile phones and other handheld gadgets, including iPods, tablets, and other devices equipped with wireless access capabilities. Essentially, today, *online* means connections to the Internet in very broad terms. The old model of a person sitting at a desktop computer surfing websites has been overtaken by a much more complex, mobile, and fast-moving landscape.

In its most technical sense, online refers to computers or devices that connect to the Internet and the World Wide Web. That is how this book generally refers to "online." As touched on earlier, there are many flavors and varieties of how a device can be online in this sense. Desktop and laptop computers can be online via modems, broadband, cable, DSL, or wireless connections. Mobile phones and smart phones can also be online. Additionally, there are open wireless connections that are essentially public online spaces that anyone with a device capable of wireless communications can use to connect. For example, some devices designed primarily to play music come equipped with wireless capability that can connect at wireless hot spots.

Online can also refer to sophisticated proprietary networks that ride on top of the Internet or the Web. For example, a hospital may offer patients that ability to view medical records online over encrypted networks that the hospital tightly controls. Online may also refer to *cloud computing*, or the ability to store or work with information on computers owned by third parties with connections via the Internet. Google's Gmail and Yahoo!'s email are examples of this kind of activity—essentially people are using Google's and Yahoo!'s email servers instead of their own devices to store and manage email. Cloud computing can be used for documents, photos, spreadsheets, and almost any activity that can be done on a computer. Social networking sites provide another flavor of cloud computing.

Online may also mean the actual activities people undertake. Websites, blogging, Twittering, Facebooking, emailing, geotagging, videoconferencing, voice-over-Internet Protocol phone calls, instant messaging, Skyping, and many other activities are inherently online activities. Over time, the range of these activities will expand and evolve further. It is safe to say that online activities will make up a greater and greater proportion of peoples' daily lives both now and for the foreseeable future.

Additionally, it is important to recognize that online and offline arenas have merged to some degree already. Brick-and-mortar retailers may offer online coupons to customers who visit physical stores in person. These coupons may even be downloaded via a customer's mobile phone while at a store. Businesses may offer special *apps*, or applications, that work on iPhones and other mobile phones. These apps connect to the Web and to the individual's phone. Some information gathered exclusively online may affect a person's offline experience. For example, a person who fills out an online survey may receive more telemarketing calls at home or more junk mail.

How Is Online Privacy Different?

Online privacy differs in both broad and narrow ways from offline privacy under traditional views. As described earlier, privacy is already difficult to quantify and define; online privacy adds another dimension. The boundaries of online privacy are changing as rapidly as technology, and this makes it hard to establish a firm concept of what online privacy looks like or should be. Views of online privacy may be different in some ways now from a few years ago before social networking exploded in use. However, even though online privacy is a moving target, some things are readily discernible.

Online privacy has a different dynamic than offline privacy. Online activities do not respect traditional national or conceptual borders. Online has a greater capacity for "memory" via longer retention of and easier access to information. Online activities challenge traditional concepts of information ownership and control, with variable implications for online privacy. Online technologies make it harder to discern or enforce distinctions among individuals (e.g., age) that are clear in person or even on the telephone. Because of these differences in the online space, online privacy poses new, different, and uncertain risks for individuals, businesses, and governments. Most of these new risks have not yet been addressed by any meaningful changes in the law because of the rapidity of the technological advancements and the comparative slowness of policy and legislative processes. There are some notable exceptions, however, and these are discussed later in this chapter.

Changed Focus and Dynamic

Online privacy relates only to online activities. In one sense, this may seem like online privacy is a limited sphere. However, that may not be the case for teenagers who have grown up with the Internet as a presence throughout their entire lives. Some teens now live much of their life in some type of online environment. For them and for others, as more and more daily activities occur online in whole or in part, the sphere of activities affected by online privacy standards rapidly expands in a way that touches most aspects of peoples' lives, sometimes in surprising ways.

A good example of this is the developing smart grid.[1] More and more households are being transitioned to smart meters, which are electrical meters that can be read and controlled remotely and that can report more information than simple energy use. An electric utility can use a smart meter to control how much electricity is flowing to a residence and to set different prices for power at different times of the day. However, smart meters are also part of an overall modernization process to move homes to a smart grid environment that would allow most if not all appliances in a residence to be monitored online and be turned on and off remotely. The reasons for the smart grid are improved cost efficiency and greater ability to map, target, and regulate power usage. The smart grid offers many benefits to consumers, to utility customers, and otherwise.

There are, however, privacy implications that flow from the increased amount of information that could be available about how individuals live their lives within the confines of their own homes.[2] The smart grid will monitor home life and activities in ways that were not possible even a decade ago and will collect data that were never available before. Any appliance that draws power could share data about its use and about its owner through the smart grid. The grid will know what appliances you have, when you replace them, when you are home, when you leave your house, when you take a shower, when you cook a meal, when you go to sleep and awaken, which rooms you are in, when you watch television, and so on. This information will have value to marketers and profilers seeking more and more details on every aspect of a consumer's life.

Individuals may be able to access their own smart appliances over the Internet, which may be a new and valuable capability. However, a consequence of that may be an increased sharing of their information with third-party companies that facilitate the access. The result is the creation of a new pool of personal information in the hands of a third party that is not subject to any privacy law or regulation. The new data may be yet another source of data for marketers, the government, private litigants, or others to exploit for their own purposes.

Online privacy also intersects with an individual's physical location in new ways. In the offline world, many activities occur that most people do not give much thought to or leave any permanent record behind. For example, when people park a car to go to a doctor's office or a medical clinic, most people have not considered *online* privacy as they lock the car doors and head into the facility. Cars may have Global Positioning System or other devices that are capable of reporting location through wireless connections. Today, smart phones have cameras and potentially geolocation capabilities built in. These devices and others can and have been used to take pictures and post them online nearly instantaneously, sometimes with unpleasant privacy consequences, especially when sensitive, identifiable photographs of individuals are dated and *geotagged*. New forms of digital advertising signage increasingly used in retail locations capture images of consumers and record their clothes, companions, and activities.[3] As a result, online privacy is expanding in its definition to include things that traditionally were never recorded at all and that may not have been thought of as having an online component.

Longer Memory

Computers have long memories. Computers connected online have the potential for permanent storage because information may be shared with numerous other computers also connected with the Internet and to offline storage devices. Complete deletion of data becomes a near impossibility. Nowhere is this phenomenon more apparent than in social networking. Some teens who have posted messages about their health conditions on Facebook were famously denied insurance. Others have lost job opportunities because potential employers see postings that they think make individuals unattractive employees. Others who simply used new technologies without a lot of caution have found themselves *outed* when information contained in their profiles was inadvertently made public. When Facebook launched its now-infamous *Instant Personalization* tool, it revealed the contacts of at least one public official who later encountered a barrage of criticism for the personal contacts the tool exposed. Celebrities and others who have sent reckless Tweets on Twitter have discovered that once sent, these words have a way of lingering on indefinitely.

The general pattern of online information persisting for extended periods has led to a phenomenon sometimes called the *modern permanent record*. The modern permanent record is not the high school paper file maintained on each student in former years. Today's modern permanent record is all the information that online marketers, social networking sites, other online businesses, schools, government agencies, social networks, and others can and do compile on individuals, plus other offline information. This new kind of record provides a powerful memory of the purchases, Web browsing activities, physical location, and general history and activities of an individual, a group, or a family. The modern permanent record has the potential to include everything you do, everything you click, everything you see, and every place you go. (For more on the modern permanent record, see the expanded discussion of the topic in this chapter.)

Privacy issues and risks relating to the persistence of online activities are just now becoming more apparent. One of the most common impacts on individuals is that they find it impossible to erase all traces of themselves online. At some point, especially if a person has been actively involved in social networking, erasing all past online activity becomes impossible. Some information may be permanently available online as a result, with privacy consequences that can vary as years go by.

Further, offline activities, whether occurring in public or private spaces, are more likely to be recorded through an online facility, making even more information that was rarely available in the past part of that modern permanent record. Another consequence is the blurring of the difference between the physical world and the online world. A camera in a public park that broadcasts pictures on an Internet site turns a physical space into an online one. If the pictures are saved, a transitory activity in the real world that traditionally left no traces may become available permanently online.

Lack of Borders

Online privacy, like many online activities, does not recognize or accommodate national jurisdictions or borders readily or well. This makes controlling information or privacy even messier and less predictable. Consider an individual whose financial records are protected by certain laws in the United States. If those records are, for example, placed in an online storage area (e.g., cloud computing) and the actual physical servers that hold the information are based in another country, those legal protections may be lost.[4] It is also possible that legal protections may be enhanced as a result of data storage in a jurisdiction with stronger privacy laws. Questions about what information is regulated in which legal jurisdiction when the information is stored online and moved from server to server have not yet been answered with any clarity. Simply put, online privacy, like many online activities, does not have borders—however, national and state laws do. And that is a problem that has not been solved.

New Risks

The online world introduces a bevy of new privacy risks with consequences of varying types and degrees. Some risks include being exposed to additional criminal activity. For example, phishing and pharming, hacking, data breaches of online information, and other computer intrusions that take advantage of online security flaws, carelessness, and ignorance often fall into this category. Typically, these online attacks seek to gather sensitive information from individuals as they use online tools, such as financially oriented Web pages or sites. Social Security numbers and account numbers are of particular interest to criminals who use the information for committing identity theft or other forms of fraud. Stealing information is not a new crime. Phishing and pharming, though, are relatively new risks that exist only in the online environment. Concerns about identity theft have done much to increase public concern about privacy.

Other online privacy risks create the potential for privacy mischief and other problems, even if there is no criminal behavior involved. Some privacy challenges relate to the sheer volume of online information being stored and how that information is subsequently used, exchanged, or disclosed. Broadly speaking, as people move more of their lives online, they lose the protection of *privacy through obscurity* that has been a feature of the offline, paper-based world.[5]

In the past, individuals could live their lives, take action, and make mistakes in relative obscurity because of the limits of paper-based record-keeping systems. No one sought to track most individuals as they moved through their daily lives because tracking and linking of data were impossible or too expensive to consider. Paper records were stored in disparate locations, held by independent record keepers, forgotten, and discarded from time to time. As more and more records are created and stored digitally and as people live more of their lives through digital media, privacy through obscurity is quickly disappearing. The ability to track individuals casually and after the fact has increased, and the costs of collecting and retaining information have been reduced dramatically. For example, search engines allow anyone to locate information on a particular individual from a nearly unlimited number of sources. Some limits exist today because old records are still offline, but that will change over time. We will soon live in a world where some individuals have lived their entire lives in a digital environment, and all records about their activities, transactions, and movements may be both digital and online.

This risk can be readily seen in online social networking. For example, recently, the Library of Congress announced that it plans to archive years of Twitter messages, thanks to Twitter's donation of its archive to the library. (Twitter is an online service that allows users to send very short messages known as Tweets to each other through the Twitter website.) The Library of Congress announced that every Tweet since Twitter's inception in March 2006 will be archived digitally at the Library of Congress.[6] That's a *lot* of tweets by the way: Twitter processes more than 50 million Tweets every day, with the total numbering in the billions. The rationale for archiving these messages was to store a slice of history, a snapshot of time that would be invaluable to researchers in the future.

There was an immediate backlash against the planned archive, with some expressing concern about the preservation of private communications. The Library of Congress backtracked a bit, restricting its collection to public Tweets and limiting the database to researchers. Whether you see the preservation of these materials as a good or bad idea, you must recognize how easily online information can be saved or repurposed without prior notice to those who posted the information or to data subjects. A Tweet by a teenager may well come back to haunt that same individual as a middle-aged candidate for political office, something that the teenager never gave a thought to when writing the message in the first place.

Stored information that is sensitive—like health care and financial data—is especially at risk for reuse, misuse, or snooping. Some sensitive information is necessarily shared with insurers, physicians, schools, or family members or as a result of a transaction. Other sensitive information may be disclosed through user groups (e.g., a spina bifida support group). This information may leak out, be inadvertently made public, or even be actively sought by marketers or fund-raisers.

Information that individuals share with companies and third-party websites online may be eventually requested by government agencies or by civil litigants and used in ways that come as a surprise to a website user. A request by a third party for information from a website may not be focused on a particular user, but that user's information may still be disclosed and perhaps used in a way that is embarrassing or otherwise harmful to that user. Any information collected online has the risk of also leaking out online or offline. Data breach laws that have been enacted in many states attempt to address some of the risks introduced by some types of leakage, but these laws will not protect against all the consequences of disclosures.

Another area of risk is data profiling. As people live more and more of their lives online, it becomes easier and less expensive for companies and marketers to compile large quantities of data about individuals, their surfing habits, search requests, and other online activities. These compilations are often called *profiles*. One example is the use of personal information collected and compiled from an individual's Web browsing habits. Information such as gender, interest areas, career information, and potentially even medical conditions can be gleaned from Web surfing patterns. Over time, a much more detailed picture can be drawn using information that was never before available for commercial exploitation. One use of this data is for creating targeted marketing and advertising based on each individual's interests as revealed by Web activities. This kind of advertising, called behavioral advertising, is controversial because information may be collected, compiled, stored, used, and disclosed without the knowledge or consent of the consumer. Additionally, the data may be compiled with other information about consumers gleaned from other sources, including offline sources, to create a rich and subtle history of activities and transactions.

Whether a data profile compiled from online activities is accurate is just one concern. For example, an individual's interest in information about venereal disease may be the result of a recent diagnosis or a school assignment. Another concern is that some harm might result from someone else's use of a data profile. This is a type of risk that has been around for a long time. In 1970, Congress enacted a law called the Fair Credit Reporting Act[7] because credit reports were inaccurate and incomplete and used to affect individual's lives in important ways that were often both unfair and secret. The same effects can happen with an online profile collected by a marketing firm that is invisible to a user. The potential content and scalability of online data profiles raise significant concerns. A consumer profile could be used to affect an individual's ability to obtain employment, insurance, or housing or to otherwise affect an individual's opportunities in the marketplace. The Fair Credit Reporting Act establishes privacy rights for credit reports, but there are no statutory privacy protections covering the broad swaths of data collected about consumers online. These are problems that lawmakers are just now beginning to debate.

Online Privacy and the Modern Permanent Record

Teachers used to tell their students, "Study hard, because these grades will go on your *permanent record*!" Those dread words—*permanent record*—are still enshrined in many people's minds as the ultimate warning to be cautious about the impact of current activities on future outcomes. But today's *modern permanent record* looks nothing like the old-fashioned permanent record of even just 10 years ago.

In the past, credit bureaus held most compiled consumer information, which covered adults with some credit history. The Internet has been a major factor in spreading data collection activities about consumers to other, unregulated consumer data. These newly evolved data collection activities merge online and offline data collections to form an informational picture of the modern consumer that is detailed and comprehensive and may be used to determine a great deal about a consumer's experience and activities. This is especially true for today's teens and children, who leave behind a vast quantity of clicks, patterns, and data that others invisibly compile into consumer profiles and can exploit for decades.

Compiled consumer data may offer benefits. Advertisers argue that they can serve individuals ads that are more relevant, and some but not all consumers agree that more focused advertising is preferable. However, the same information may also be harmful to consumers. For example, a consumer may fill out a survey online with little awareness of the intended use. A seemingly casual question about medical status may result in that consumer ending up on a marketing list aimed at those with specific medical ailments, and that information may remain in that consumer's profile for a lifetime.

Noncredit, unregulated consumer profiling is a well-established business model. Most consumers find out about these profiles only accidentally, if at all. These databases often contain robust and sensitive consumer information, such as financial, employment, and transactional data. The information is often supplemented with other nonpersonal data that relies on census tract or neighborhood data. For example, an individual's income can be modeled using publicly available statistics covering the individual's ZIP code, neighborhood, or block. These profiles are largely unregulated. None of this is new, but the addition of online data may vastly expands the scope, depth, and dangers of the profiles.

What is new and has changed within the past decade is the ease of implementing and expanding this data collection model. Collecting, compiling, and manipulating data have gotten easier and less expensive. In the past, consumer information that was based on noncredit, unregulated reporting was limited to some degree by expense of obtaining and using the data and the challenge of managing the databases. Technological advances have lowered many of the barriers.

Now there are more noncredit consumer databases in use, the databases are being used in new ways, and some are even accessible to other consumers as well as to businesses and advertisers. One can see this phenomenon on websites such as Zabasearch.com. There (and at other similar websites), anyone can purchase online a file with detailed personal information about almost any individual at minimal cost. Often based primarily on public record information, these files provide basic identity, location, and history information about individuals (e.g., former addresses, roommates, neighbors, and so on). This modern permanent record, with varying degrees of granularity or personalization, is now readily available to anyone, anywhere in the world, with a credit card, not just the subject of the record. These databases are a major piece of the consumer data profile picture.

Other important pieces are databases containing detailed consumer behavior patterns and transactions. When combined with basic demographic information, these databases yield a three-dimensional and longitudinal picture of an individual. Online activities such as grocery shopping, browsing books at a bookstore, and Internet searches provide more data points for consumer profiles.

Technology makes it easy for these activities to be captured, stored, classified, and cataloged into behavioral profiles. If you buy a book, visit websites, travel, or buy at many online stores, all of your activities may contribute to the modern-day version of your modern permanent record.

Lack of Remedies

Finding legal remedies for privacy violations has been difficult for offline activities. It is even harder for online activities. In the offline world, much privacy tort law has derived from work done by William Prosser in 1960.[8] Prosser categorized existing law into four types of privacy torts: (1) intrusion on an individual's seclusion or solitude, (2) public disclosure of private facts, (3) placing an individual in a false light highly offensive to a reasonable person, and (4) an unpermitted use for private commercial gain of a person's identity.[9] This categorization had a major influence on the law, and many states enacted statutes codifying the so-called Prosser torts.

Many have always doubted that these torts provide meaningful protections for privacy—and now even more so in the modern online era. Tort remedies do not necessarily match up with the realities of current online activities or with modern data collection and processing activities. Many online commercial data collection and use activities are hidden, and consumers are often unaware of the extent to which their personal information is collected, stored, or shared. The need to prove damages is another barrier. In data breach cases, for example, the courts have been reluctant to recognize an increased risk of identity theft as a harm weighty enough to support litigation. While some class-action lawsuits involving online privacy have succeeded, it is often because online companies are sometimes motivated to settle cases to avoid further adverse publicity. Tort actions have some inherent limits. The scope of relief available through lawsuits will often be narrow (i.e., monetary damages) and may not establish substantive privacy standards that would serve as a guide for others. Improvements or changes in privacy practices are not directly attainable through litigation. A jury verdict may provide damages, but the classic privacy torts are not likely to oblige a record keeper to publish descriptions of record systems, limit collection practices, meet data quality standards, allow individual access and correction, or restrict internal uses of data. Some of these results have been achieved through settlements, however.

A second potential shortcoming with current tort remedies relates to their occasional reliance on expectations and reasonableness as a standard for judging behavior. Technology can easily erode societal expectations of privacy, and those eroded expectations may not be enforceable through the courts. For example, some point to the popularity of Facebook as evidence that young people no longer care about privacy. While polls suggest otherwise, it is apparent that the technology allows individuals to do things with their information that were impossible a generation ago. Some privacy standards have been changed by technological capabilities and their adoption by consumers.

Finally, the online environment creates additional barriers to legal challenges of commercial privacy practices. Because of its multistate and international environment, the Internet readily brings together companies and consumers from different jurisdictions. The courts are not nearly as adept in accomplishing the same feat. Consumers may not be able to find privacy remedies because of judicial limits on jurisdiction, because cases may be expensive to pursue, because violators may be in other countries, and because of an absence of lawyers willing to represent them. These barriers are not unique to the online world, but they are exacerbated by the borderless Internet.

Consumers have been aided by attention to online privacy by data protection authorities in the European Union and in other countries around the world. The importance of the Internet has also drawn more attention in the United States from legislators and the Federal Trade Commission. These developments have, to some extent, counterbalanced the difficulties that consumer find in the courts.

Is Privacy Still Important?

Scott McNealy, chairman of Sun Microsystems, said in 1999, "You already have zero privacy anyway. Get over it."[10] More recently, Mark Zuckerberg, the founder of Facebook, uttered a similar sentiment when he said in January 2010 that privacy was no longer a "social norm."[11] Some agree with these statements, especially those who do not value privacy at all, those who seek to exploit personal information for profit, and those who seek simple solutions to complex problems. It is certainly undisputed that government and business computers today have more personal information about individuals than ever existed in the past. That information is used for a wide variety of purposes that may benefit individuals in some ways (e.g., faster credit decisions) and that may harm individuals (e.g., more monitoring and discrimination) in other ways.

While it is apparent that the Internet and other late twentieth-century developments have undermined the privacy of individuals, it is also true in the beginning of the twenty-first century that there are more privacy laws, rules, and policies in place than in earlier periods. Most commercial websites today have privacy policies; this was not the case at the turn of the century. Privacy policies on websites have legal significance because the Federal Trade Commission has some ability to hold companies to the promises made in those policies.

The spread of identity theft, particularly through fraudulent online activities, has also spurred public interest in and concern about privacy. Congress and state legislatures responded to public fears about identity theft by enacting numerous laws that place restrictions on public information, create remedies for identity theft victims, and establish new criminal penalties. These laws have added significant regulation to the financial industry and were passed over the objection of many businesses. Nevertheless, the harm to consumers from identity theft was substantial enough to create a fertile environment for privacy laws. New privacy laws that relate to identity theft are still regularly debated and sometimes passed, with data breach notification laws being a good example. These laws typically contain a requirement that a business notify an individual when there has been a breach of personal data. Nearly all states have data breach notification laws.

There is no single yardstick for measuring privacy. Because individuals value privacy in different ways, it is difficult to assess the overall state of online privacy or its importance. Each individual may perceive the privacy consequences of any device, action, or facility differently, and an individual's views may be inconsistent. Still, polling consistently shows strong public concern about online privacy across all age-groups.[12] Yet some post a great deal of highly personal information on social networking sites for others to see. Other individuals actively work to hide their identities online by seeking anonymity, using pseudonyms, employing free or untraceable email accounts, erasing cookies, evading advertising, blocking Java scripts, and using other methods to limit tracking of online activities by websites. None of these actions is necessarily right or wrong from a privacy perspective. Part of privacy is the ability to make decisions about what information to share or withhold. One of the consequences of the online world, however, is a diminution of the ability to exercise control over personal information because so many third-party record keepers maintain and control that information in ways that are not transparent to the data subjects.

Some privacy-invasive practices draw popular outrage. When Facebook started its Beacon service that automatically shared an individual's activities with friends, the public controversy was immediate and forced Facebook to change the service to one that required affirmative consent. Google drew fire from U.S. lawmakers and European data privacy officials when it disclosed in 2010 that it had been capturing information from open wireless networks as part of its Street View product. Even though the company apologized for its actions, lawmakers were upset and vocal about the incident. Later revelations about Google's Street View created even more controversy.[13]

While some privacy issues receive public notice, other privacy issues of equal or greater importance receive little if any attention. Search engines routinely collect, maintain, and utilize all of an individual's search requests without drawing much notice, let alone widespread objections. Government actions can be especially controversial at times. The use of cookies and other tracking technologies on government websites has drawn objections at times from privacy advocates and others. However, many aspects of government surveillance of the travel system and its online records have been less controversial in light of ongoing threats from terrorists.

Adapting the Law to New Technologies

Modern discussions of privacy and technology date from a famous and widely cited 1890 article in the *Harvard Law Review* by Louis Brandeis and Samuel Warren.[14] The article expresses, in significant part, an objection to the intrusions of new technology and new forms of dissemination: "Instantaneous photographs and newspaper enterprise have invaded the sacred precincts of private and domestic life; and numerous mechanical devices threaten to make good the prediction that 'what is whispered in the closet shall be proclaimed from the house-tops.' " In many ways, privacy has been chasing to catch up with the consequences of technology ever since. The chase has grown only more heated since the Internet entered the lives of many ordinary people around the world in the mid- to late 1990s.

Brandeis later served on the Supreme Court, and he participated in an important case about the constitutionality of wiretapping in 1928. At that time, the telephone was still seen as a relatively new technology. In *Olmstead v. United States*,[15] the Court held that wiretapping a telephone line was not a search or seizure within the meaning of the Fourth Amendment so that police did not need a judicial warrant to wiretap a telephone call. Brandeis dissented, arguing that the protections of the Constitution must adapt to a changing world. He found it irrelevant *where* the actual wiretap took place—whether in the home or elsewhere. Wiretapping was an intrusion on the privacy of the individual despite location.

Nearly 40 years later, the Supreme Court overturned its ruling in *Olmstead*, holding that the Fourth Amendment protects people and not places. The ruling brought government wiretapping under the protections of the Fourth Amendment. In *Katz v. United States* (1967),[16] the Court essentially adopted Brandeis's view, although it is noteworthy that it took the Court four decades to adapt to telephone technology. It is also noteworthy that, during the period between the two wiretapping decisions, Congress repeatedly tried and failed to enact legislative rules for wiretapping.

In a concurring opinion in *Katz*, Justice Harlan proposed an influential two-part test for assessing a *reasonable expectation of privacy*. Under the test, a person must exhibit an actual subjective expectation of privacy, and the expectation must be one that society is prepared to recognize as reasonable. A well-recognized problem with the reasonable expectation of privacy test is the ability of technology—and the Internet is a perfect example here—to erode expectations of privacy.

The *Katz* decision led directly to 1968 federal legislation establishing rules and procedures regulating law enforcement wiretapping with court supervision.[17] The law and the courts are adapting to the Internet faster than the 40 years it took the Supreme Court to acknowledge the vital role of the telephone in ordinary life. However, that does not mean that legal and judicial adoption to online technology has been fast, comprehensive, consistent, or complete. A current example of this may be found in the area of online advertising and legislation. Many of the privacy advocates profiled in this book advocate new laws to regulate online advertising practices that create profiles of individuals' purchasing and Web browsing habits. Only time will tell if any legislative efforts keep pace with current online practices.

Core Information Privacy Policy: Fair Information Practices

Fair Information Practices (FIPs) are a set of internationally recognized principles for addressing the privacy of information about individuals. Although information privacy is a subset of privacy, it is a major focus of much privacy legislation in general and of online privacy in particular. FIPs are important because they provide the underlying policy for many national laws addressing privacy and data protection matters. The FIPs principles set out the elements of what is usually meant by the general term *information privacy*.

FIPs originated with a 1973 Department of Health, Education, & Welfare (HEW) advisory committee.[18] The same concepts were later revised and restated by the Council of Europe and by the Organisation for Economic Cooperation and Development (OECD) at the beginning of the 1980s. The eight principles set out by the OECD are the collection limitation principle, data quality principle, purpose specification principle, use limitation principle, security safeguards principle, openness principle, individual participation principle, and accountability principle. (See Chapter 3 for more discussion of international efforts and Chapter 6 for the complete text of the OECD FIPs.)

These principles have been highly influential. The original 1973 principles of the Department of Health, Education, & Welfare were effectively enacted into law as the Privacy Act of 1974, a law that regulates privacy practices of federal agencies.[19] The restatement of FIPs by European institutions strongly influenced privacy legislation in the European Union and elsewhere around the world. While there is broad international consensus on the substance of FIPs, different statements of FIPs sometimes are organized differently.[20]

FIPs are not self-implementing or self-enforcing. Actual implementation of FIPs at the statutory, regulatory, or data controller level can vary widely, depending on the country, data controller, type of data, conflicting goals, and other factors. The actual application of FIPs in any given context requires judgment and skill. Most agree, for example, that the principles should be applied more rigorously to medical records than to pizza delivery records.

To illustrate, the accountability principle can be met through many different mechanisms. They include criminal or civil penalties; national or provincial supervisory officials; other administrative enforcement; various forms of self-regulation, including industry codes and privacy seals; formal privacy policies; compliance audits; employee training; privacy officers at the data controller level; and other methods. Similarly, providing data subjects with access to their own records may have different exceptions, depending on whether the records are maintained for employment, educational, credit, medical, law enforcement, or national security purposes.

Notwithstanding the worldwide recognition and adoption of FIPs, critics can be found on both sides. Some in the privacy community believe that FIPs are too weak, allow too many exemptions, do not require establishment of a national privacy agency, fail to account for the weaknesses of self-regulation, and have not kept pace with information technology. Critics from a business perspective often prefer to limit FIPs to reduced elements of notice, consent, and accountability. They complain that other elements may be unworkable, expensive, or inconsistent with openness or free speech principles. Some version of FIPs advocated by business critics leave out or water down principles deemed inconvenient or too costly to implement.

The continuing importance of FIPs in an interconnected or networked environment is underscored by the 2009 Madrid

Declaration—a civil society document signed by more than 100 worldwide organizations and by more than 100 experts—published concurrently with the thirty-first annual meeting of the International Conference of Privacy and Data Protection Commissioners. Among other things, the Madrid Doctrine reaffirms support for a global framework of FIPs.[21]

How Ideas about Privacy Have Adapted to an Online World

As discussed earlier in this chapter, privacy has many aspects, comes in many flavors, and can be defined differently based on its various contexts. Online privacy is no different—it too comes in many flavors and has multiple definitions. Nevertheless, several key elements of online privacy today may be traced through landmark laws and regulations that touch or impact online privacy.

One of the most noticeable aspects about online privacy is that online technology moves far more quickly than the laws that are passed to govern technological-based impacts on privacy. The technologies leap ahead, and the laws lag behind. There is nothing new about that particular dynamic—the law tends to follow developments, not lead them. However, what is new is the extraordinarily rapid pace of change the Internet has introduced. While the law always used to lag well behind developments, now the lag time is extremely pronounced.

There are some notable exceptions to this, and these exceptions form another observation about how online privacy has developed. When great harm or annoyance to consumers rises above a certain level, the law tends to catch up more quickly to developments in narrow areas, at least in the United States. The Children's Online Privacy Protection Act, the CAN SPAM Act, and data breach legislation are examples of U.S. laws that developed in response either to the prospect of significant harm to consumers or to consumer annoyance. It should be emphasized that these laws cover narrow aspects of online privacy, and in the United States, broad laws that cover online and offline privacy together are rarely contemplated.

Another aspect of how ideas about privacy have adapted online is that transitions are messy as well as delayed. The process of updating old laws written for an "offline" world to laws that reflect the way the Internet has become intertwined into the lives of most businesses and consumers is just beginning, and so far things have not been easy or simple. The best possible example of this messiness is the Electronic Communications Privacy Act. This statute is complicated even for lawyers. But when the law—which was written prior to the mainstream adoption of the Internet—is applied in court cases that deal with online privacy issues, it becomes immediately apparent that old laws about privacy and online technologies do not always mix comfortably. Following are four case studies that outline these ideas in more detail.

Case Study 1: Electronic Communications Privacy Act

The 1986 Electronic Communications Privacy Act (ECPA)[22] is a pioneering piece of legislation, passed to address the privacy of electronic mail at an early stage of the penetration of the Internet into mainstream commerce and everyday life. ECPA quickly became outdated because its model of electronic mail and Internet activity badly trailed current practice and technology. Both of these seemingly contradictory statements are true because of the age of the law and the incredibly rapid pace of change on the Internet.

In general, U.S. law on electronic and communications surveillance is tremendously complex. ECPA added to the complexity. ECPA sought to bring the constitutional and statutory protections against the wiretapping of telephone communications into the computer age. ECPA reflects a legislative recognition that some Internet activities should be excepted from the current legal standard that states that there is no reasonable expectation of privacy in records maintained by third parties.

ECPA has two major parts, or "titles." Title I amends the Wiretap Act, a criminal statute that seeks (1) to protect the privacy of wire and oral communications and (2) to set out the circumstances and conditions under which the interception of wire and oral communications may be authorized. ECPA extended to electronic communications the same protections against unauthorized interceptions that existed previously for oral and wire communications via common carrier transmissions. For example, the 1986 amendments provided another way to prosecute computer intrusions that include real-time capture of information.[23]

Title II of ECPA is the Stored Communications Act, which protects email and similar electronic communications and protects data transfers between businesses and customers.

Distinctions recognized by ECPA include electronic mail in transit, electronic mail in storage for less than or more than 180 days, electronic mail in draft, opened versus unopened electronic mail, electronic communication service, and remote computing service. Case law and scholarly discussions continue to address and debate the proper application of the ECPA's distinctions to current Internet activities. The courts have struggled in applying ECPA to situations not contemplated by the law's drafters. Developments such as cloud computing created models of information transfer and storage that do not fit clearly under any of the law's existing standards.[24]

The precise characterization of an activity can make a significant difference to the protections afforded under ECPA. For example, if an "electronic communications service" holds a text message in "electronic storage," then law enforcement needs a probable cause judicial warrant to obtain access. If a "remote computing service" stores the same text message on behalf of the subscriber, then law enforcement does not need a warrant, and a subpoena is sufficient. Whether a search engine or social networking site is a remote computing service remains in dispute.

As discussed earlier, laws typically lag technological developments, often by many years or decades. ECPA is an example of that phenomenon. There appears to be broad agreement that the law needs to be updated; however, reaching agreement on the particulars may not be easy, especially in the post-911 environment. Still, privacy advocacy groups, communications companies, and other interests began an effort to revise ECPA, an effort likely to take several years at best.[25]

An example of shortcomings with ECPA comes from a 2010 incident involving Google's Street View. Street View collects images of public areas taken from a fleet of specially adapted cars with cameras. The results are available online at no cost to users.[26] The service has produced a series of privacy controversies, especially outside the United States. Google responded to objections by obscuring faces and license plate numbers.

Google revealed in early 2010 that the company's vehicles had also collected samplings of public WiFi facilities for three years across 30 countries. The company collected about 600 gigabytes of data over the years from WiFi networks. Google claimed that the data were collected in error.

After its announcement, Google began deleting the data it had collected. Google said that it deleted data collected in Ireland,

Austria, and Denmark after data protection authorities in those countries requested its deletion. The data deletion was halted after numerous other governments as well as privacy groups asked for investigations into what data Google had captured. Specifically, German Data Protection Authorities wanted to know just what data Google had captured. Initially, the company stated it had collected only identification information for networks as well as MAC addresses that identified specific network hardware devices. But the investigation by the German Data Protection Authorities uncovered that Google had in fact intercepted personal information crossing over the WiFi networks from users, for example, bits of emails that were being sent over the wireless networks.

Google stated that it is keeping data from Belgium, France, Italy, Spain, Germany, Switzerland, and the Czech Republic after those countries requested it be kept. A class-action lawsuit against Google has already been filed in the United States, and this lawsuit seeks to prevent data deletion to halt in the United States as well.

Meanwhile, in the United States, lawmakers requested investigations into the matter. The Federal Trade Commission and the Justice Department are looking into potential actions. There are questions whether any of Google's actions in collecting communications violated ECPA or other communications privacy laws. Even though Google inappropriately took data from WiFi networks, it is not certain that in the United States the data collection violated a law. WiFi networks that are not encrypted or password protected may be seen as "public" and not protected against interception.

This incident—where privacy was clearly violated yet no U.S. laws unambiguously prohibit this kind of data interception—illustrate the some of the difficulties with the current legal regime to protect online privacy in light of new technological capabilities.[27]

Case Study 2: Children's Online Privacy Protection Act

In 1998, the Federal Trade Commission (FTC) conducted a survey of online privacy.[28] The report's conclusions about children's privacy had direct legislative consequences. The FTC found that most children's websites collected personal information from children, that only a bare majority of businesses disclosed their information practices, and that few involved parents when collecting and using information from children. The FTC recommended that Congress pass a children's privacy law. The same year, Congress enacted the Children's Online Privacy Protection Act of 1998 (COPPA).[29] The law applies to children under the age of 13. Interestingly, Congress did not take any action to address the online collection of personal information about individuals aged 13 and higher, and it did not regulate the offline collection of information about children.

The goals of COPPA are (1) to enhance parental involvement in a child's online activities in order to protect the privacy of children in the online environment; (2) to help protect the safety of children in online chat rooms, home pages, and pen-pal services in which children may make public postings of identifying information; (3) to maintain the security of children's personal information collected online; and (4) to limit the collection of personal information from children without parental consent.

COPPA has been sometimes confused with a similarly titled law enacted around the same time. The Child Online Protection Act (COPA) also passed in 1998 with a goal of restricting access by minors to any material defined as harmful to such minors on the Internet. The courts promptly enjoined enforcement of COPA, and after protracted legislation that lasted a decade, the law was finally found to violate the First and Fifth Amendments of the Constitution. COPA is not a constitutional law, but COPPA remains in force.

The law charged the FTC with issuing regulations to implement COPPA. The regulations follow the law by requiring operators of websites directed to children and operators who knowingly collect personal information from children to (1) provide parents notice of the website's information practices; (2) obtain prior verifiable parental consent for the collection, use, and/or disclosure of personal information from children (with certain limited exceptions for the collection of online contact information, such as an email address); (3) provide a parent, on request, with the means to review the personal information collected from his or her child; (4) provide a parent with the opportunity to prevent the further use of personal information that has already been collected or the future collection of personal information from that child; (5) limit collection of personal information for a child's online participation in a game, prize offer, or other activity to information reasonably necessary for the activity; and (6) establish and maintain reasonable procedures to protect the confidentiality, security, and integrity of the personal information collected.

The FTC's COPPA rules took effect in April 2000.[30] In subsequent years, the FTC brought several successful enforcement actions against violators. In 2005, the FTC sought comment on changes in the sliding scale that the rule requires for obtaining parental consent. The sliding scale requires more reliable measures for parental consent if an operator intends to disclose a child's information to third parties or the public than if the operator uses the information only internally. After a review, the FTC concluded that more secure electronic mechanisms and infomediary services for obtaining verifiable parental consent were not yet widely available at a reasonable cost. Because of the lack of generally available authentication technology and methodology, the FTC continued the sliding scale rule indefinitely.[31]

The FTC considers that the requirements of COPPA apply to foreign-operated websites if the sites "are directed to children in the U.S. or knowingly collect information from children in the U.S."[32] How the FTC would enforce the law against a foreign website is not clear. This issue raises some of the problems of regulating the international Internet through national legislation.

Case Study 3: CAN SPAM Act

Spam—an electronic mail message whose primary purpose is the commercial advertisement or promotion of a commercial product or service—has been a feature of electronic mail since email became a tool accessible to the public. Estimates suggest that the overwhelming majority (more than 90%) of email is spam. The costs of spam to Internet service providers, employers, government, business, and the public are measured in the billions of dollars.

In 2003, as the use of the Internet continued to expand throughout the general population, Congress took steps to impose requirements on the use of commercial electronic mail messages. The CAN SPAM Act—formally known as the Controlling the Assault of Non-Solicited Pornography and Marketing Act of 2003—was the result.[33] The act was motivated in part by a desire to limit spam and to hold senders accountable. It was also motivated by a desire to establish uniform national standards for commercial email and to preempt attempts by states to create their own standards and their own enforcement methods.

The act imposes a series of requirements on commercial emailers, including the following (1) header information cannot be false or misleading, (2) the subject line cannot be deceptive,

(3) a commercial message must be identified as an advertisement, (4) a commercial message must include a postal address, and (5) there must be a clear and conspicuous explanation of how the recipient can opt out of future email, and an opt out must be promptly honored.

The CAN SPAM Act can be enforced by the FTC and some other federal agencies, state attorneys general, and Internet service providers. Individual spam recipients have no private right of action. In addition, the law provides criminal penalties for some violations. The federal government has brought both civil and criminal enforcement actions with some success. In addition, some state attorneys general and some Internet service providers have used the act's provisions successfully against spammers.

Critics of the law have several complaints. First, they point out that the law has not reduced the amount of spam. While the act may apply to spammers anywhere, enforcement against senders in other countries is problematic at best. Even with international cooperation, the volume of spam has not diminished. Second, some object that the law does not require marketers to obtain affirmative consent before sending marketing email and that the law prevents stronger remedies under state law. They argue that the law effectively legalizes spam until a recipient takes steps to opt out. In addition, because there is no central opt-out registry, each user must opt out of the receipt of spam from each possible sender. Third, federal preemption prevents states from allowing additional remedies. However, state laws that relate to acts of fraud or computer crime are not preempted, and an occasional state law lawsuit about spam has been allowed.

In sum, the CAN SPAM Act reflects widespread aversion to spam, illustrates the problem of controlling the worldwide Internet with national legislation, and provides another example of conflict between state and federal regulation for privacy protection.

Case Study 4: Data Breach Legislation

The modern collection and maintenance of personal information—especially but not exclusively online—has created or exacerbated a number of unsavory activities. One of the most notable of these is identity theft. The online environment has made it easier for a criminal to collect and utilize personal information to impersonate another person, to access another person's email or other accounts, or to undertake other criminal activities. During the 1990s, identity theft grew on the consciousness of Internet users and other individuals. The loss or stealing of personal information is one source for criminals, although criminals use other methods to obtain information as well.

Fears of identity theft helped to draw popular attention to incidents where large quantities of personal data held by third parties (including both businesses and governments) were lost, stolen, or unaccounted for. In the past, it was unusual for the loss or theft of personal data to be disclosed by record keepers. However, a few highly publicized incidents created a demand by citizens fearful of identity theft for notice of data breaches. State legislators responded with mandatory data breach notification legislation.[34] The first of these laws passed in California in 2002 after newspapers reported on an incident where hackers exploited vulnerabilities in a server that contained a database of personal information on all California state employees. The California law became a model for other states.

A continuing series of similar "horror stories" involving security breaches that resulted in the unplanned disclosure of personal information fueled public and legislative interest. One of the most publicized breaches involved ChoicePoint, a commercial data aggregator with dossiers on most Americans. In 2005, ChoicePoint was found to have allowed identity thieves to open business accounts that gave the thieves access those dossiers.[35] The story received widespread attention. At the time, California was the only state with a data breach notification law, and ChoicePoint agreed to comply with the law by providing notification to California consumers but not to consumers in other states.

When citizens and legislators in those other states asked why they did not receive breach notices, the answer was that it was not required by law. The result was that in the next few years, nearly every state passed a breach notification law. A later highly publicized data breach at the Veterans Administration involving millions of veterans resulted in a federal law applicable to the Veterans Administration.[36] A 2009 federal law required health care providers and insurers to provide breach notification to patients.[37] The same law also required commercial websites containing personal health records to provide breach notification.

A general federal breach notification law has been proposed, but policy disputes have kept it from passing. Industry prefers a single national standard, while privacy advocates generally support a federal floor that allows stronger state laws to remain in effect. These disputes about whether states or the federal government should regulate are typical of privacy laws, and federal privacy legislation takes a wide variety of approaches, from total preemption in some cases to allowing strong state laws to remain in effect.

Another controversial breach notification issue is the proper trigger for a notice, a consistently controversial question. Some favor notice in all cases of data breach, but industry in general prefers notice only if the breach is likely to result in harm. Some breaches (e.g., of encrypted data) are unlikely to result in misuse of data. The argument is that sending notices is expensive and that consumers will learn to ignore notices if they come frequently.

Notes

1. See, e.g., U.S. Department of Energy, *The Smart Grid: An Introduction* (undated), at http://www.oe.energy.gov/1165.htm.

2. See Comments of the Center for Democracy & Technology, In the Matter of Smart Grid Technology before the Federal Communications Commission (2009) (GN Docket Nos. 09-47, 09-51, 09-137), at http://www.cdt.org/privacy/20091002_fcc_smart_grid.pdf; Electronic Privacy Information Center, Testimony before the House Committee on Science and Technology Subcommittee on Technology and Innovation (2010), at http://epic.org/privacy/smartgrid/Smart_Grid_Testimony_2010-07-01.pdf.

3. See Pam Dixon, *The One-Way-Mirror Society: Privacy Implications of the New Digital Signage Networks* (2010) (World Privacy Forum), at http://www.worldprivacyforum.org/pdf/onewaymirrorsocietyfs.pdf.

4. See Robert Gellman, *Privacy in the Clouds: Risks to Privacy and Confidentiality from Cloud Computing* (2009) (World Privacy Forum), at http://www.worldprivacyforum.org/cloudprivacy.html.

5. See *Department of Justice v. Reporters Committee for Freedom of the Press*, 489 U.S. 749 (1989).

6. *Twitter Donates Entire Tweet Archive to Library of Congress* (news release), April 15, 2010, at http://www.loc.gov/today/pr/2010/10-081.html.

7. 15 U.S.C. § 1681 et seq.

8. William L. Prosser, *Privacy*, 48 Cal. L. Rev. 383 (1960).

9. See Restatement (Second) of Torts §§ 652A-652E (1997).

10. Edward C. Baig, Marcia Stepanek, and Neil Gross, *Privacy: The Internet Wants Your Personal Info., What's in It for You?*, BusinessWeek (April 5, 1999).

11. Bobbie Johnson, *Privacy No Longer a Social Norm, Says Facebook Founder*, guardian.co.uk (January 11, 2010), at http://www.guardian.co.uk/technology/2010/jan/11/facebook-privacy.

12. See Chris Jay Hoofnagle et al., *How Different Are Young Adults from Older Adults When it Comes to Information Privacy Attitudes and Policies?* (2010), at http://papers.ssrn.com/sol3/papers.cfm?abstract_id=1589864.

13. See, e.g., Kevin J. O'Brien, *Europe Pushes Google to Turn Over Wi-Fi Data*, New York Times (June 27, 2010), at http://www.nytimes.com/2010/06/28/technology/28google.html.

14. Samuel D. Warren and Louis D. Brandeis, *The Right to Privacy*, 4 Harvard Law Review (1890).

15. *Olmstead v. United States*, 277 U.S. 438 (1928).

16. *Katz v. United States*, 389 U.S. 347 (1967).

17. Title III of the Omnibus Crime Control and Safe Streets Act of 1968, 18 U.S.C. §§ 2510-20.

18. Department of Health, Education and Welfare, Secretary's Advisory Committee on Automated Personal Data Systems Records, Computers and the Rights of Citizens (1973), at http://aspe.os.dhhs.gov/datacncl/1973privacy/tocprefacemembers.htm.

19. 5 U.S.C. § 552a.

20. For a history of FIPs, see Robert Gellman, *Fair Information Practices: A Basic History* (2010), at http://bobgellman.com/rg-docs/rg-FIPShistory.pdf. See also Colin J. Bennett, Regulating Privacy: Data Protection and Public Policy in Europe and the United States (1992) (Cornell University Press).

21. http://thepublicvoice.org/madrid-declaration.

22. Public Law No. 99-508, 100 Stat. 1848 (1986) (codified as amended at 18 U.S.C §§ 2510–22, 2701–12, 3121–27).

23. 18 U.S.C. §§ 2510–22.

24. 18 U.S.C. §§ 2701–12.

25. See Digital Due Process, at http://www.digitaldueprocess.org/index.cfm?objectid=37940370-2551-11DF-8E02000C296BA163.

26. http://maps.google.com/help/maps/streetview/.

27. See, e.g., *EU Regulators Critical of Google Street View, Report Says*, Los Angeles Times (February 27, 2010), at http://latimesblogs.latimes.com/technology/2010/02/eu-regulators-critical-of-google-street-view-report-says.html; Mike Harvey, *Google Admits Its Street View Cars Spied on Wi-Fi Activity*, The Times (London), May 15, 2010, at http://www.thetimes.co.uk/tto/technology/article2513098.ece.

28. See *FTC Releases Report on Consumers' Online Privacy* (press release), June 4, 1998, at http://www.ftc.gov/opa/1998/06/privacy2.shtm.

29. 15 U.S.C. § 6501 et seq.

30. 16 C.F.R. Part 312.

31. *FTC Retains Children's Online Privacy Protection (COPPA) Rule without Changes* (press release), March 8, 2006, at http://www.ftc.gov/opa/2006/03/coppa_frn.shtm.

32. Federal Trade Commission, *Frequently Asked Questions about the Children's Online Privacy Protection Rule*, at question 19, at http://www.ftc.gov/privacy/coppafaqs.shtm.

33. 15 U.S.C. § 7701 et seq.

34. For a list of state security breach notification laws, see National Conference of State Legislatures at http://www.ncsl.org/IssuesResearch/TelecommunicationsInformationTechnology/SecurityBreachNotificationLaws/tabid/13489/Default.aspx.

35. See Federal Trade Commission, *ChoicePoint Settles Data Security Breach Charges; to Pay $10 Million in Civil Penalties, $5 Million for Consumer Redress* (press release), January 26, 2006, at http://www.ftc.gov/opa/2006/01/choicepoint.shtm.

36. 38 U.S.C. §§ 6721 et seq.

37. Section 13402 of the Health Information Technology for Economic and Clinical Health (HITECH) Act, part of the American Recovery and Reinvestment Act of 2009, Public Law 111-5. Implementing regulations are at 45 C.F.R. Part 164, subpart D (Department of Health and Human Services); 16 C.F.R. Part 318 (Federal Trade Commission).

2

Problems, Controversies, and Solutions

Online privacy issues have generated numerous problems and controversies, some of which are new and some of which are extensions of offline privacy issues. Questions about social networking, cloud computing, data retention, health care, and self-regulation versus regulation have generated continuing public debate, spirited discussions, many differing perspectives, and occasional outcomes. This chapter discusses the most important controversies in online privacy today. The chapter concludes with a consideration of the remedies and solutions that have been implemented thus far as well as some actual and potential solutions that are part of the practical, political, and policy deliberations surrounding online privacy.

Key Controversies and Problems

Privacy is a complex subject, and organizing privacy issues for analysis and discussion is similarly complex. This chapter offers a framework for discussing of the major issues in online privacy by focusing on specific topical areas. Online privacy presents both old and new controversies wrapped up with new technology, a specialized vocabulary, and evolving business models. Nevertheless, older and more traditional conflicts between core values, overlapping rights, and different interests remain at the heart of the privacy debate. No matter what technology is employed, privacy is always a discussion about the rights and interests of human beings.

Overview of Privacy and Health Information

The privacy of health information has been a recognized concern since the dawn of medicine. Privacy issues grew more complex as written record-keeping practices developed and expanded, largely during the first part of the twentieth century. The rise of third-party payers (including Medicare and private insurers) during the second part of the twentieth century added to the number and type of health records and record keepers as well as to the complexity of the health privacy issues.[1]

Interest in and development of electronic health records and electronic networks of health records—now generally referred to as health information technology—began in the late twentieth century and accelerated during the twenty-first. The position of the National Health Information Technology Coordinator in the Department of Health and Human Services was initiated by presidential executive order in 2004[2] and established by statute in 2009.[3] The formal duties of the coordinator are to support the development of a nationwide health information technology infrastructure that allows for the electronic use and exchange of information to support a wide variety of purposes in the health care system.

As Congress began to pass legislation that supported electronic health information activities, it also recognized the threat that electronic records pose for the privacy of patients. The administrative simplification provisions of the 1996 Health Insurance Portability and Accountability Act (HIPAA) included a requirement for administrative privacy rules that resulted in the issuance of a federal rule on the privacy of health records for paper and electronic records.[4] The Department of Health and Human Services issued a HIPAA health privacy rule at the end of 2002, and the rule took effect in 2003.[5] A separate HIPAA security rule covers electronic records.[6]

While experiments with and implementation of electronic health records and networks accelerate, privacy is trailing the technology. The HIPAA health privacy rule generally covers health care providers and insurers regardless of the technology used for record keeping, but the rule largely reflects a paper-based record system.

When records were created and maintained by a single provider, roles and responsibilities were relatively clearer. As records are centralized and shared between health care providers, responsibility for supporting patient rights loses focus. In addition, as actual or potential sharing of patient records expands, it become more difficult to make choices about the proper role for patient consent and to devise methods for patients to express their preferences. HIPAA largely eliminated the need for consent for nearly all routine health care activities, a choice that remains controversial for paper records. As lifetime records and universal access by health care institutions to health information over the Internet becomes commonplace, there will be a need to reconsider the proper role of patient consent in some areas. The challenge here expands because electronic health records will be shared more widely among users other than providers and insurers. The HIPAA privacy and security rules do not extend to third party users. A 2009 change to the law[7] slightly broadened the scope of HIPAA, but many health record keepers and users remain outside current privacy and security regulation. In short, electronic health records and networks exacerbate privacy existing policies that only barely work tolerably for paper records.

Another problem has to do with the level of regulation. Prior to HIPAA, health privacy was the topic of state legislation. Federal privacy rules only covered federal agency health records and federally funded substance abuse treatment. With HIPAA, Congress adopted a policy that stronger state laws—that is, those that did a better job of protecting patient privacy—remained in place above the federal floor.[8] That policy works in an environment where we can tell the physical location of the record and the person responsible for maintaining it. In an electronic environment where records are shared electronically across state borders, it is much more difficult to allow state laws to remain in place. Nevertheless, there are so many state laws affecting health record keeping, health record keepers, and health record users that a fully preemptive federal law could create widespread gaps and disruptions. Any expansion of federal control into areas of the law where the federal government rarely treads would be unwelcome to many. An example here would be the need for a fully preemptive federal law to replace state court rules that govern the sharing of health records in malpractice or workers' compensation litigation.

Online Medical Privacy Issues

Because of some of the complexities of HIPAA and misunderstandings about health care privacy, many people and many health care professionals believe that health information has better privacy protections than other personal information. In the offline world, however, the actual privacy protections applicable to health records are less than most people expect. Online, the differences between expectation and reality are even greater than in the offline world.

Today, many kinds of nontraditional health activities that involve the disclosure and maintenance of personal health information can take place online and outside the familiar health care system. Some examples include the following:

- An individual posts a question on a health website that requires users to register. The question may be about a specific health condition, test result, or drug interaction. An individual may utilize many different types of websites for this purpose, including general purpose health information websites. Even if the individual is not identifiable to other users, the website knows who he or she is.
- An individual participates in discussions on disease-specific or condition-specific websites. These crowd-sourced sites allow individuals to share stories, seek support from others, compare treatment methods, or discuss other aspects of health care. Websites may focus on weight loss, breast cancer, autism, diabetes, and more. Individuals may or may not identify themselves to others, but the websites may know who they are.
- A Web user employs tools, or "apps," provided by a website for assessing the user's weight, cholesterol, fitness, mental health, or any other aspect of well-being. Some may use online-offline tools, such as a Global Positioning System–enabled watch, to upload workout information to a website for storage, analysis, and possible sharing with others. The website requires each user to register as a condition of using the service.
- A subscriber to a health information website, social networking website, or other websites where the user is identified to the website owner participates in a poll, asking what the subscriber ate that day, whether the subscriber cries, or how much exercise the subscriber routinely gets.
- An individual who just received a copy of laboratory test results from her doctor goes to a search engine and enters

> the results one by one in order to learn more about what the numbers mean. The identity of each user may be known to the search engine, which may retain a copy of each search associated with the user's identity for an extended period of time.

In general, none of this information shared online by users is subject to the privacy protections that apply to health records maintained by a health care provider or a health insurer. While traditional health records may have fewer privacy protections than most people expect, many health records created as a result of Internet interactions have no legal protections for privacy at all. Each website is likely to have its own terms of service and privacy policy, but the policies established by websites are rarely read by consumers, are highly variable, may not offer meaningful privacy protections, and may allow the website to use or share identifiable information, allowing the information to slip into consumer data profiles or into the marketing system. In addition, most websites reserve the right to change their privacy policies at will, so an existing privacy protection may evaporate at any time.

In other cases, the applicability of legal privacy protection may depend on facts or circumstances that are not necessarily transparent to the subject of the record. For example, personal health records (PHRs) are a relatively recent development. A PHR vendor collects a patient's health records with the patient's consent from the health care system or other sources. The PHR vendor stores the information online for use by the patient and the patient's designees through the Internet. There are many types of PHRs today, many different types of PHR vendors, and many different services available. If a health care provider offers PHRs to patients, the PHRs are subject to standard federal health privacy protections. However, if the PHR vendor that is not part of the health care system or is not working for a health care provider maintains the PHR, then formal privacy protections are scarce because the federal rules and most state health privacy laws do not apply.

This confusing state of affairs is partly the result of rapidly developing technology and partly the result of the way that the law protects health privacy. As discussed in the previous section, the most important health privacy protections derive from HIPAA.[9] The federal health privacy and security rules issued by the Department of Health and Human Services cover most health care providers and insurers but little other online health information activity. State health privacy laws remain in effect in addition to HIPAA if the state laws offer better privacy protections. However, few state laws have been amended to apply to nontraditional online health records.

Technically, the HIPAA privacy and security rules apply to *covered entities*, which are most health care providers, all health insurance plans, all health care clearinghouses, and the business associates of all these institutions. Because HIPAA applies only to traditional record keepers within the health care community, nontraditional health record keepers are not subject to the HIPAA rules. For example, schools that have health records are not subject to the HIPAA rules, but they are usually covered by another law (Family Educational Rights and Privacy Act). Others with health information—including gyms, banks, state motor vehicle departments, landlords, credit bureaus, home testing labs, massage therapists, nutrition counselors, pharmaceutical manufacturers, and transit companies—are generally not covered by HIPAA, by state health privacy laws, or by any privacy law at all. As discussed above, many websites that obtain or store health information are not subject to privacy laws. However, some PHR records and some other health records are covered by state or federal breach notification laws.

Consider, for example, a mother who posts a note on Facebook that says, "My baby just had a seizure!" Facebook, like other social networking sites, is not subject to HIPAA. The information posted has no privacy protections, and anyone who has access to that Facebook page may be able to copy, store, and redisclose the information. The information, unprotected for privacy, could follow that mother and child for the rest of their lives.

Privacy protections for online health records are likely to become even more important in the future. The Department of Health and Human Services is developing standards for and promoting the adoption of a nationwide health information exchange.[10] The Office of the National Coordinator for Health Information Technology directs these activities. This office is organizationally located within the Office of the Secretary of the US Department of Health and Human Services. The position of national coordinator was created in 2004, through an executive order and legislatively mandated in the Health Information Technology for Economic and Clinical Health Act of 2009.

There are many benefits to electronic health records and a nationwide health information network. However, these technological developments are also likely to make health information more widely accessible through the Internet, and health records may be used by more people and more institutions than today. Updating and creating privacy and security rules for a new electronic environment is a major challenge.

The states are establishing rules for electronic health care exchanges. This work can include developing appropriate privacy guidelines for information that falls outside of HIPAA and other health privacy law protection.[11] Currently, pilot projects on electronic health information exchanges via a network and the Internet exist—and are in some cases even flourishing—in most states. Within the next few years, the expectation is that states will begin enacting new legislation covering health information exchanged over networks.

Electronic health information exchanges may come in many flavors. One example of an exchange is the New York Clinical Information Exchange. In this exchange, 11 hospitals share patient data. If a patient visits the emergency room of one of the exchange hospitals, then all hospitals in the exchange will have access to the same information.[12] Other exchanges may involve prescription records or public health information. Generally, the progress has been slow because of the complexity of the technology, the many choices about how best to share records, and a wide variety of opinion about the proper approach to privacy. One major privacy question is whether a patient can choose to have his or her information included in the states' health information exchange. If patients have a choice, should that choice be affirmative (opt-in) or negative (opt-out)? The way choices are framed and presented makes a major difference in how individuals are likely to exercise their options. People strongly tend to accept default options, whether affirmative or negative.

Cloud Computing

Cloud computing raises privacy concerns when it involves the sharing or storage by users of personally identifiable information on remote servers owned or operated by others and accessed through the Internet or other connections.[13] The precise borders of cloud computing are still debated, but it is clear that it comes in a variety of flavors, such as private, public, internal, external, free, paid, and otherwise. Cloud computing includes software and other services beyond mere storage of data. Cloud computing services exist in many variations, including data storage sites, video sites, tax preparation sites, personal health record websites, photography websites, social networking sites, cell phones, and many more. Activities that once took place on desktop computers in private homes are shifting to the cloud.

In many respects, cloud computing is not new. Third-party storage of information is as old as the mainframe client-server model. Businesses have always stored electronic information about their customers on computers operated by other businesses. Even basic electronic mail can be viewed as a cloud computing function since the mail is held by third parties for a short or a long time. Almost any type of computer or data activity can take place in the cloud.

When information passes from the immediate personal control and possession of the record keeper, privacy becomes a greater concern. The original record keeper may be the data subject, a government agency, or a business that collects, stores, and uses personal information. Each class of record keeper faces a different set of cloud computing issues. A vendor of cloud computing services can be any individual, business entity, government, or other legal person.

A starting point for analysis of the privacy consequences of cloud computing is with the cloud vendor's terms of service and privacy policy. Larger organizations that have the power to negotiate contracts with cloud vendors are much more likely to be able to protect their own interests. Others are more likely to accept standard terms, often without reading or understanding those terms.

A vendor, especially one providing free service over the Internet to individuals or small businesses, may reserve the right to read, copy, publish, or otherwise use a customer's data. Thus, an individual who maintains a remote backup of a computer hard disk may unwittingly expose all of the user's data to exploitation by the vendor.

For a city, state, or government agency that maintains many different types of data (e.g., police reports, attorney work product, health records, welfare files, tax returns, and motor vehicle licenses), casual use of a cloud computing service could violate privacy laws, undermine legal protections, violate security rules, and create other risks. A business using a cloud computing service could expose customer data to a third party in violation of privacy laws or the business's own privacy policy.

Even cloud computing services that promise not to read or use a customer's data may be able to learn useful information by monitoring transaction information that reveals who is sharing data with whom and when. For example, if two competitors begin sharing information with each other and an investment bank, the activity may signal that a merger is under consideration.

Personal data held by third parties may lose significant legal protections. For example, financial records in the possession of an individual may not be available to government without a judicially approved search warrant or a subpoena that includes notice to the individual. However, those same records in the possession of a bank might be readily obtained with a mere request or subpoena that does not require any notice to the bank's customer. A cloud vendor may be viewed as a third-party record keeper similar to a bank. The Electronic Communications Privacy Act provides protections for electronic mail, but the law's application to cloud computing is not clear. There may be weak or no privacy protections to cloud computing customers.

Other risks include the following:

- Litigation consequences. Information that might be covered by the attorney-client privilege or by the doctor-patient privilege could lose its protections if shared with a third-party cloud computing vendor. Information held by a cloud computing vendor may be more readily accessible to private litigants without notice to the owner of the information.
- International exposure. A cloud computing service could operate in another state or country, or it could store data on servers in another country (perhaps more than one). A cloud vendor might even be a foreign government agency or a hacker in another country. Any of these circumstances could make it easier for data to be obtained by foreign government or litigants under legal standards that are looser than in the user's home jurisdiction. On the other hand, storage of customer data in Europe may bring the data under the protection of a European national data protection law. That may be advantageous to customers who may not have similar privacy protections in their home country, but it may be especially troublesome to a

business that did not anticipate that a casual decision to use a cloud computer service would expand its privacy obligations.

- Mandated disclosures. A cloud provider might be obliged under state or national law to search user records to look for fugitives, missing children, copyright violations, child pornography, political dissidents, or other information of interest to government or private parties. Alternatively, a cloud provider could be obliged to report some types of information that it discovered to police or prosecutors.

It remains to be seen whether users of cloud computing providers can or will do a better job of protecting their own privacy interests by paying close attention to the provider's terms of service. Encrypting data placed in the cloud may also protect many privacy interests, but encryption is not compatible with all cloud services. It also unknown if the cloud computing industry will adopt clearer policies and practices to help users assess the risks to privacy. Finally, it is unclear whether laws will be changed to give greater legal protection to personal (and other) data held by cloud computing vendors. The need to change laws to address cloud computing issues is under discussion in many countries.

Social Networking

Modern social networks are at the epicenter of many online privacy debates today. With the spread of social networks, new and intriguing privacy challenges arise alongside them. Some of the privacy issues that social networks present have no simple solutions, leaving many new gray areas in privacy. Some privacy issues surrounding social networks have been addressed and resolved in innovative ways. One thing is certain about social networks and online privacy: social networks are shaping modern notions of what constitutes online privacy. The hundreds of millions of active users of social networking sites means that social networking will endure and evolve for some years to come, with a large and uncertain effect on just what privacy means online.

In the past, scholars generally defined social networks as meaningful linkages among sets of individuals that can include friends, family, neighbors, coworkers, or others.[14] Today, when people use the term "social networks," they usually have online, Web-based social networks in mind. An online social network has many of the same characteristics as an offline social network. Both allow individuals to connect with others. A major difference is that online platforms, tools, and websites facilitate communication among groups of individuals in ways that in-person network cannot accomplish as readily. In addition, the online medium significantly changes the nature of what kind of information is shared, with whom, and how quickly.[15] If an online network is not an entirely different animal, then it is a major evolution from the old idea of a social network.

Social networks come in many variations. Some social networking sites like Facebook, MySpace, or Google Buzz boast an array of features, including integrated email, photos, video, chatting, event calendars, games, and more. Twitter, a social networking site of a different type, offers one-to-one messages and features that allow the creation of lists of friends. Twitter is focused more on short texts sent to followers or subscribers. Some long-term Twitter users—and especially public figures like celebrities—have followers numbering in the tens of thousands or millions.

What the wide variety of social network sites have in common is that they generally allow individuals to create a profile of their interests, establish lists of friends/followers (those in their personal network), and broadly utilize and view their *social graphs*, or web of online connections. Many social networks also allow entities that do not work at the social network sponsor—typically called third-party developers—to create applications for the social network that others may use.[16] As a result, sites may have literally thousands of applications, or "apps," that any subscriber can install and use. Apps can perform such tasks as providing weather forecasts, issuing daily greetings, sending pictures, monitoring news reports, and much more. Additionally, social networking sites may have connections to external websites. For example, a social network *like* button may appear on other websites, such as newspaper sites or online retail sites, allowing users to make their interest in that site more public.

Because of this interconnectedness and facilitation of personal information sharing, social networking sites raise novel privacy challenges. Broadly, the challenges come in several key areas: (1) the definition of what constitutes public versus private information, (2) the role of users' consent and rights to their own information, (3) secondary uses of the data made available on social networking sites, (4) adequacy of notice, and (5) ease of exercising privacy choices. These core issues arise in a variety of ways in the social networking medium. We begin by discussing third-party apps, which raise all these core privacy issues.

Third-Party Apps

Third-party "apps," or applications, are a rich source of online privacy controversy. When using social networks, a user who wants to use an external application, such as a game that runs on the social network, is often required to give the third-party application permission to access the user's personal information. The app typically cannot be used unless a user consents, often by checking a box or a series of boxes. In many cases, the scope, terms, and consequences of information sharing are not readily transparent to an average user, who clicks though quickly to install the app. Any information given to an app becomes subject to the app's privacy policy (if any), and the terms may not be favorable to users. Different social networking sites have varying policies regarding third-party apps and how the developers can access users' information.

Facebook provides a good case study on how this process can work. When Facebook first began offering third-party apps, it allowed them generous access to users' information. Facebook gave notice to its users by providing a pop-up box telling users what information the app was going to access. Over time, as people began to complain about third-party app privacy issues, Facebook tightened requirements for developers' requests for user information. In addition, Facebook began allowing users to determine what specific information could be shared with third-party apps, if any. The end result of the increased privacy controls was that app developers received less access to user data.

Nevertheless, controversy continues over app data sharing and app access to user data. For example, when Facebook decided[17] in 2011 to allow third-party developers to access more user information—specifically users' home addresses and mobile phone numbers—a public controversy arose, and members of Congress questioned Facebook's policy.[18] The congressional involvement in partly a testament to the importance of social networks today and in part a reflection of broader concern about personal data leakage through social networks.

Beyond concern over immediate access to user data, third-party app access raises some additional privacy issues. For example, how may the information be used later (typically called secondary use)? Will the information be sold or shared with others? Will the information be combined with other user data from online or even offline sources? Generally, even the most informed user will not be motivated to read the privacy policy associated with each and every third-party app, raising questions about the actual privacy protections afforded users and the extent to which user choice and consent are meaningful.

Consent and Social Networks

As with other privacy arenas, consent presents a core privacy challenge in social networking use. Some consent issues arise from misunderstandings about what can be done with publicly posted information. Other consent issues are more subtle and may occur when social networks claims data rights, claims that may come as a surprise to users.

Often, if a user has posted information on the site in a public way, that posting can be seen as a form of consent. This is sometimes called "passive consent" in that if a user does nothing to object, the user is considered to have consented. (Passive consent has been called "opt out" in some cases.) After consent has been granted, it can be extremely difficult for a user to dispute later how that information has been used by others. So a college student who posts a vacation photo on his social networking page may have no basis for complaining when a potential employer reviews that photo.

For data posted on a publicly accessible part of a social networking site, typically the privacy policy will state that the site cannot control how material posted in a public area may be used and that the site disclaims liability or responsibility for any issues that may arise. To give users more controls, social sites may permit users to restrict access to allow certain individuals. Sites may also give users options over whether their public information is indexed in search engines. However, information shared even in limited ways can sometimes "escape" the intended controls. For example, data shared only with friends may nevertheless achieve a wider audience when those friends share the data with others.

A more nuanced consent issue arises when a user agrees to a policy without understanding it or realizing what permissions were granted. One example of this has already been discussed in the context of third-party application access to user data. After a user has consented to third-party access to his or her data, retrieving that information can be problematic at best. Another example arises when users post images and other copyrighted material on social networking sites that claim the ability to reuse information as part of the routine terms of service. This may not considered to be a best practice, but it is also not uncommon.

A third type of consent issue in social networking sites arises as a result of targeted and integrated advertising. The social networking site may itself target ads based on a user's behavior, or the site may share user information with other businesses for advertising purposes without additional permission. An exception often arises with geolocation information tagged to a user's activities via social networking activity. So far, geolocation data on social networking sites have been treated generally as sensitive data that typically requires more affirmative consent. Affirmative consent in this context means that the social networking site will not share the geolocation data unless the user specifically agrees that such data be used. Still, not all users recognize the consequences of sharing geolocation. Someone created a controversial website called pleaserobme.com to highlight some of the potential consequences of sharing current location information. The value of location information to advertisers means that battles over access to and use of location information will continue.

Public or Private?

Historically, privacy protections for some types of information depend on whether the information is "public" or "private." A traditional view is that an individual has no reasonable expectation of privacy when walking down a public street, driving down a highway, or shopping in a mall. Technology, such as a cell phone or digital signage[19] that enables universal tracking of individuals in public space, is placing pressure on the traditional view of a lack of privacy in public spaces. Information posted on a social network site can share many characteristics with other activities that occur in public spaces. Debate over privacy in public is ongoing, and social networks—like other new technologies—are now contributing to that debate in new ways.

Twitter's decision, for example, to allow long-term archiving of its users' Tweets was done without asking Twitter users for express permission to do so. The consent was deemed to have been given at the time the original Tweets were sent because the Tweets were substantially public. However, it is not clear that users expect that data posted on Twitter would remain public forever and beyond their ability to change or recall. Privacy policies and terms of service that notify users of the conditions of use often go unread or unappreciated by most users. The fine print protects the social network operator but may not meet the expectations of users.

Some social networking sites have gotten into trouble when they take actions that violate user expectations about making information public. One of the most notorious examples of this in the social networking arena is the Facebook advertising program called *Beacon*. Facebook launched Beacon in November 2007. The program connected Facebook users' activities on outside websites to the user's Facebook news feed. The Beacon ad program launched with 44 external partner websites, including Yelp, eBay, and Fandango. At its inception, Facebook users were automatically opted in for Beacon, and any user who wanted to opt out of Beacon had to learn about it and then take action. Famously, a Facebook user bought a diamond ring at a partner site as a Christmas gift for his wife. The purchase was meant to be a surprise, but it was broadcast on his Facebook news feed, where his wife and all his Facebook friends saw it.[20] Later, Facebook changed the Beacon program to require a participant to affirmatively opt in and provided a tool to allow users to turn off the program entirely. After a class-action lawsuit, Facebook abandoned the program altogether.[21]

Facebook tends to make public access to a user's information a default feature of its service. The extent to which users fully understand the default terms is uncertain, and the ability of users to change the defaults is variable. Beacon illustrates that, even if user privacy expectations are not well defined, those expectations can be violated. In a social network where information sharing of one sort or another is a core feature, finding just what users expect may be difficult, and expectations may change and may do so for each user as time passes and the user ages.

Ease of Exercising Choice

Social networks have generally been innovative in creating user controls for privacy. However, in creating these detailed controls—something generally viewed as a positive development by privacy advocates—the controls may be too cumbersome, leading to a lack of ease of use.

A good case study in this area is Facebook's location privacy control. When Facebook launched a feature called Places that allowed businesses to track Facebook users via mobile phones and wireless computers, some privacy groups complained about the difficulty of opting out of this feature. The Electronic Privacy Information Center wrote:

> Facebook "Places" Embeds Privacy Risks, Complicated and Ephemeral Opt-Out Unfair to Users: The recently announced Facebook service *Places* makes user location data routinely available to others, including Facebook business partners, regardless of whether users wish to disclose their location. There is no single opt-out to avoid location tracking; users must change several different privacy settings to restore their privacy status quo. For users who do not want location information revealed to others, EPIC recommends that Facebook users: (1) disable "Friends can check me in to Places," (2) customize "Places I Check In," (3) disable "People Here Now," and (4) uncheck "Places I've Visited." EPIC, joined by many consumer and privacy organizations, has two complaints pending at the Federal Trade Commission (FTC) concerning Facebook's unfair and deceptive trade practices, which are frequently associated with new product announcements.[22]

This complaint generally outlines the arguments against highly granular privacy controls. Granular controls for privacy can be a double-edged sword: while controls that are too detailed may discourage user choice because of too much complexity, controls that are too broad may heighten ease of use but reduce the overall amount of choice afforded to consumers. How to frame choices for consumers is a significant problem not easily addressed regardless of your views about the value of privacy.

Secondary Uses of Social Networking Information

An important and ongoing area of controversy in social networking revolves around the use of personal information posted online. This is often called "secondary use." There are many examples. In 2009, Massachusetts Institute of Technology (MIT) students conducted a research project for an ethics and law class project in which they "scraped" Facebook's information. Scraping is a technical term that simply means that a technology was used to gather automatically information from websites in digital form in such a way that it could be used for analysis. In this case, the

MIT students wanted to know if the sexual preferences of a Facebook user could be determined based on the user's social graphs and status posts.[23] This is one of the earliest examples of "scraping" social networking content for unforeseen uses.

The project highlights questions about how social networking data could be used and abused. A decision made by a single user to limit the public availability of some data may not be sufficient to protect that user's privacy. Choices made by that user's friends, together with the type of analysis done by MIT students, may nevertheless reveal information (either direct or inferred) about that user. The nature of the social network and the way in which it is used may make it difficult or impossible for any single individual to participate in the network in any substantial way without the possibility that confidential information will nevertheless be revealed as a result of the postings and analysis done by others.

Scraping user data from Facebook and other social networking sites has become a business model. A company called Klout created an analytic method (Klout Score) that broadly aims to measure a person's online influence. The score is based on scraped Twitter data, for example.[24] Anyone who uses targeted social networks can become the subject of a Klout Score without notice or consent.

Another example comes from Rapleaf, a company that was the subject of a *Wall Street Journal* investigation.[25] The *Journal* revealed that Rapleaf was scraping Facebook postings and storing Facebook user IDs.[26] Rapleaf then sold the data to companies, political campaigns, and others to be used to profile customers or to target advertising. Some of the controversy ended when Facebook stopped Rapleaf from scraping data. However, the company continued its activities on other social networking sites, and Rapleaf's general data collection practices remain controversial in other ways. For example, Rapleaf may be able to assess one consumer's creditworthiness based on the creditworthiness of his social network friends.[27]

Many secondary uses of personal information are not described in the social network's privacy policy because it is third parties that use the information and not necessarily the social network. When a user places some information in public on a social network, that user may be unaware of the consequences of making even limited data public. A user may look to find old friends, classmates, and others who share common interests and may not realize that third parties will find and exploit that user's data in unexpected ways. That user may not recognize that participating in a social network shares characteristics with walking down the street, where anyone can watch and record data about people on the street. The pedestrian may be aware that others are watching, but the social networking user may not receive the same clues that others can collect, use, and profit from the user's data. The marriage of personal data, social networks, computer technology, and new business models may be placing new pressure on the old notion that there is no privacy in public space.

Adequacy of Notice

Privacy advocates contend that many social networking sites fail to provide users with adequate notice of privacy practices. In the United States, the primary mechanism for protecting consumer privacy on social networking sites is the privacy policy. Sites that violate their own privacy policies are subject to the FTC Act, a federal law that generally prohibits website operators from engaging in unfair or deceptive business practices. Violating a stated privacy policy generally qualifies as a deceptive business practice. However, enforcement of the law against those who engage in improper trade practices is spotty at best.

Some websites post privacy policies that offer few limits, are hard to find, or that plainly state that the privacy policy can be changed without notice. An easily changed policy offers no real permanent privacy protection. A weak or ambiguous policy may not be much better. Polls show that people mistakenly believe that the presence of a privacy policy means that the privacy protections are significant, and this belief is often wrong.

Some social networking sites, after information has been made public, do not bother to give timely notice about secondary uses of the information beyond what is posted in the general privacy policy. However, some sites, such as Facebook, provide occasional contextual privacy notices. When a user signs up for a third-party app, for instance, the user receives a notice at that time that the app will want to access certain data. That type of notice can make a user's choice more informed.

Best practices for the thorny and complex privacy challenges posed by social networking are still evolving even as standards may be shifting. Currently, there is much discussion of opt in versus opt out as a solution. Other discussions include "do not track" mechanisms and self-regulation. (These options are discussed in detail in this chapter.) Additionally, some states are considering legislation that would restrict information that social networks may utilize. For example, proposed legislation would restrict how Global Positioning System location tagging can be published by social networks. Generally, though, legislation has been proceeding slowly, and substantive legislation in this area has not yet passed. Privacy on social networks is a subject likely to evolve in many different ways as time passes, as users pay more attention, and as policy makers ask questions.

Identity, Reidentification, and Deidentification

Information privacy rules protect personal privacy by regulating the collection, maintenance, use, and disclosure of personal information about identifiable individuals. If personal information cannot be associated with a specific individual, then it should fall outside the scope of privacy regulation. In other words, fully anonymized information no longer has a privacy interest that needs to be protected.

Reality is more complex.[28] While it may appear that the removal of overt identifiers (e.g., name, address, and account numbers) will make personal data no longer identifiable, identification may still be possible. Professor Latanya Sweeney of Carnegie Mellon University has shown that 87 percent of Americans are uniquely identified by birth date, five-digit ZIP code, and gender.[29] The combination of nonunique identifiers is sufficient to support identification of a specific individual in most cases. If you change birth date to birth month and year, fewer individuals can be identified uniquely, but some will still be identifiable.

The volume of personal information about individuals is large and growing. Partly because of an absence of general privacy laws, the United States is the world leader in the commercial collection, compilation, and exploitation of personal data. American marketers and data brokers collect personal information from many sources, including identifiable public records (from state or local government agencies or from the courts), nonidentifiable sources (e.g., census records), commercial data (e.g., transaction records, frequent shopper cards, and warranty cards), and consumer surveys, questionnaires, and quizzes (which are often designed for the primary purpose of obtaining personal information for sale).

All this information may be collected into profiles and dossiers for nearly every individual and household. Information may include name, address, telephone number, email address, education level, home ownership, mail buying propensity, credit card usage, income level, marital status, age, children, and lifestyle indicators that show whether an individual is a gardener, reader, golfer, and so on. Tracking of Internet users through overt and covert means also contributes to the collection and compilation of personal data. Governments have additional sources of personal information that are not public but that may be used to identify information.

Identifiability of data can be enhanced by other factors. For example, unique or unusual data elements (e.g., 95-year-old Native American living in Rhode Island) may allow identifiable of outliers. The ability to identify people from nonunique identifiers has already been mentioned, but other nonunique data elements (e.g., place of birth, elementary school attended, and make of car) may also support identification.

Information that is not identifiable to one individual may be identifiable to another. Much depends on the data already in the possession of the person doing the identification. Most people cannot tie a fingerprint to a particular individual, but a law enforcement agency can. The amount of time, effort, and money devoted to identifying information also makes a difference.

Identifiability is not static. Data that cannot be identified today may be identified tomorrow because of the availability of new data sources or new identification technology. For example, geospatial tracking by cell phone, mobile Internet devices, or automobile transponders may allow for the identifiability of data and tracking of individual consumers that was heretofore not possible or practical.

Legislation tends to treat identifiability as a black-or-white issue, with different laws applying terminology chosen without any appreciation for the complexity of the problem. Perhaps the most sophisticated American law is the Confidential Information Protection and Statistical Efficiency Act of 2002.[30] It defines identifiable form to mean "any representation of information that permits the identity of the respondent to whom the information applies to be reasonably inferred by either direct or indirect means."

The federal health privacy regulations issued by the Department of Health and Human Services under the authority of HIPAA take a different approach. One deidentification standard in the rule calls for the removal of 18 specific data fields. The resulting data set falls entirely outside the zone of regulation.[31] However, that data may still be identifiable in a small fraction of cases.

The Internet and the data sources available though it make the issue of identifiability even more complex. New sources include personal Web pages, social networking sites, search engines, and Internet archives. The use of nonunique identifiers such as mother's maiden name as identifying elements on websites places that information is the possession of additional institutions.

The domain of deidentified personal information has grown narrower and more troubled over the past few decades. Identification and reidentificiation are likely to become increasingly important in the future as people look for ways to balance privacy against legitimate needs for data in conducting research, making policy, and operating businesses.

Data Retention

Privacy is directly affected by the retention or storage of personal data by a third party. Data retention policies can be mandated by formal legal requirements or by commercial activities. Either way, stored data can be used and disclosed for a variety of purposes, with potentially significant consequences for privacy. Erased data typically has few, if any, privacy consequences. Whether information that has seemingly been erased is actually permanently irretrievable can be an issue, as erased information may still be accessible through backup facilities or may be unerased.

Commercial providers of online services take different approaches to data retention. For search engines, some retain the search inquiry along with other information, such as the Internet Protocol (IP) address of the user, a cookie assigned to the user, the time of the request, and the links that the user selected. The privacy consequences of this type of data retention were illustrated in 2006 when America Online released for research purposes a list of searches that included the actual search request.[32] While no names or user IDs were included, the material released assigned unique identification numbers so that requests by the same individual could be linked. Within days, the identities of some individuals were uncovered by reporters or others using the search content to identify the location, interests, possessions, and sometimes name of the requester. The incident illustrated one of the consequences of search data retention for privacy.

Practices of search engines vary tremendously. At least one search engine treats privacy as a feature, advertising that it does not retain IP addresses.[33] Other search engines retain search logs with identifiable elements (IP addresses and cookies) for set periods of time before the logs are anonymized. However, as the America Online research release shows, searches can sometimes be identified from the content of the search even without other identifiable elements. In addition, the extent of anonymization may make a difference to the degree of protection. If an IP address is anonymized by changing 123.123.123.123 to 123.123.123.xxx, the number of possible addresses is 255 since each part of an IP address can hold values from 0 to 255. Combining a truncated IP address with the content of the search request will make identification of the requester easier.

Similar issues arise with electronic mail. Some email services offer unlimited storage, and email can be retained without restriction. Google's Gmail originally did not even have a readily accessible button for deleting a message. A button was eventually added. Other email providers have differing capacities and policies. Similarly, merchants may choose to retain customer information, including purchases, searches, and account information, as long as they please. A merchant may allow customers to restrict use of stored information (e.g., no use for marketing), but the merchant may still retain the information indefinitely if it chooses.

Any personal information, not limited only to search requests and email, retained by a website, merchant or other third party can be used, disclosed, or exploited commercially according to the terms of service and privacy policy of the service provider; be accessed during litigation; or be demanded by the government using different forms of compelled disclosure, including search warrants, subpoenas, or national security letters. Personal information retained by a data subject and not stored in third-party hands is less vulnerable to secondary use and disclosure without notice to the data subject.

Some personal information held by some providers must be retained by law or by contract for a period of time. Records of Internet credit transactions, like those of other transactions, must be kept as required by the credit card company. Telecommunications billing records must also be retained by regulation for a period. However, most records of Internet activity are not required to be retained by service providers in the United States.

The European Union (EU) adopted a Data Retention Directive in March 2006 that requires member states adopt measures to ensure that electronic communications traffic data and location data generated or processed by providers of publicly available electronic communications services (including Internet access, Internet email, and Internet telephony) be retained for not less than six months and not more than two years.[34] It is important to note that the EU requirement does not apply to the *content* of a communication or activity. The adoption of the EU data retention requirement followed the 2004 Madrid train bombings and the 2005 London bombings, where authorities claimed that retained telephony data aided police investigations. The data retention requirement has been controversial in Europe. Similar proposals have been made in the United States.

Privacy versus The First Amendment

The First Amendment to the Constitution limits the ability of laws to abridge the freedom of speech or freedom of the press. Privacy interests can conflict with both of these freedoms at times, although privacy can also be a component of speech and other First Amendment values (e.g., freedom of assembly). The overlap of values is complicated and not always clear. Further, First Amendment jurisprudence is extensive and not easily summarized.

Because the Internet is a global medium, the First Amendment does not always apply. John Perry Barlow, cofounder of the Electronic Frontier Foundation, famously observed that "in Cyberspace, the First Amendment is a local ordinance."[35]

State laws seeking to prevent the publication of names of sexual assault victims highlight a conflict between the privacy interest of the victim and the ability of the press to publish truthful information. When these conflicts arise in tort or criminal cases, free speech values have prevailed in Supreme Court cases and laws limiting publication of information have been overturned. The ability to publish of truthful lawfully obtained is a powerful free speech and free press interest. Even in other cases where the information published was not legally obtained, the right to publish was upheld.

The online world raises new issues. The mainstream print and broadcast media have been relatively easy to identify in the past, but it is now possible for anyone to establish a website, publish a blog, or circulate newsletters. When does Internet activity qualify for constitutional protections afforded to the press? When Wikileaks released classified U.S. government communications in 2010, questions were raised whether the website qualified as the "press."[36] In addition, the Supreme Court has found constitutional limitations on libel actions brought by public officials or by public figures, requiring proof of actual malice. To what extent has the Internet affected the definition of who is a public figure? Is a blogger a public figure? Is an individual who is the subject of a YouTube video a public figure? Does the answer change if the video is popular? These questions are not easy.

Privacy laws often restrict the use and disclosure of personal information held by private companies. Companies often object, arguing that their First Amendment rights are unduly burdened by these laws. In part because commercial speech has lesser protections under the First Amendment, these arguments have not generally been successful. In a case involving the Driver's Privacy Protection Act—where the challenge to the law was brought by a state and not on First Amendment grounds—the Supreme Court upheld the law under the Constitution's commerce clause, finding the sale or release of the personal information in the interstate stream of business was sufficient to support congressional regulation.[37]

Whether the same result would be reached in a First Amendment case is debatable. The Internet has made it easier for companies and for anyone else to obtain these records from government agencies or from the courts, to compile the records, and to disseminate them. In cases involving public records (e.g., voter registers, occupational licenses, property ownership records, and court records), statutory restrictions may create different conflicts. For example, the Fair Credit Reporting Act (FCRA) prevents credit bureaus from disclosing records of bankruptcies, judgments, or tax liens after a term of years.[38] All the underlying information comes from public records. The Maine Supreme Court upheld a First Amendment challenge to a state law with similar restrictions.[39] However, credit bureaus have not chosen to aggressively pursue a challenge to the federal restriction, which remains in force.

State and local government agencies have sometimes responded to the ease of distribution of personal information from public records by removing the records from general public availability. Because First Amendment rights of access to government records are limited and weaker than access rights under freedom of information laws, denial of access to government records once made public has been a successful strategy. In a statutory case under the federal Freedom of Information Act, the Supreme Court denied a request for access to a "rap sheet," a compilation of an individual's arrests, charges, convictions, and incarcerations. Most of the information in a rap sheet is public information drawn from other public sources. The Court found the privacy interest substantial, noting the "practical obscurity" of the information from its original sources.[40] However, with search engines and other Internet facilities allowing for the storage and retrieval of information from obscure sources seemingly without limit, it remains to be seen if the notion of practical obscurity will have continue to have any significance in either statutory or First Amendment litigation over privacy interests.

Overview of Remedies to Privacy Problems

Many challenges arising from privacy problems revolve around the lack of laws and regulations responsive to those challenges. In general, privacy laws—especially in areas where technology intersects with privacy—tend to lag behind the social and technological changes that often lead to privacy challenges. This is also true for most types of regulations. One of the most significant ongoing discussions in the area of privacy remedies has to do with a particular type of regulation, which is called "self-regulation." Self-regulation as well as other privacy remedies such as opt in versus opt out, Do Not Track, and the FCRA model are discussed in more detail below.

A Closer Look at Regulation versus Self-Regulation

Self-regulation can be seen as a middle ground between a wholly unregulated or market approach on the one hand and a regulatory or legislative regime on the other. Self-regulation has been used in many areas, with some widely recognized successful applications that achieve beneficial results. Self-regulation for privacy has been tried with disputed results.

The history of the Controlling the Assault of Non-Solicited Pornography and Marketing Act of 2003—know as the CAN SPAM Act—illustrates some of the complexities.[41] Unsolicited commercial email has been a problem for email users and for email service providers, with the costs of spam measured in the billions of dollars annually. In 1999, the Direct Marketing Association responded to the vocal established an E-Mail Preference Service that allowed consumers to place their names on a list not to receive unsolicited email. This self-regulatory approach was found to be insufficient. States also began to pass regulatory legislation, but, given the absence of geographical borders on the Internet, state legislation was not very effective.

Failures of both state regulation and self-regulation led Congress to enact the CAN SPAM Act in 2003. The federal law sought to preempt state legislation, to require commercial email to include an opt-out mechanism, to establish criminal penalties for some activities, and to provide for private enforcement by Internet service providers (but not by private individuals). The act also gave the FTC authority to create a national do-not-email list similar to the National Do Not Call Registry against telemarketing. The Do Not Call Registry became a highly successful legislative response to the failure of industry self-regulation to limit unwanted telemarketing calls.[42] The FTC has declined to create a do-not-email list, however.

The CAN SPAM Act has been successful in some ways. Large commercial entity compliance with the requirement to include an opt out appears greater than under the self-regulatory regime. There have been some successful criminal prosecutions, civil actions by the FTC, and private lawsuits. Overall, however, it is far from clear that the CAN SPAM Act was successful in significantly reducing the volume of spam. That may have been an unrealistic goal for any type of controls.

In 1997, commercial data brokers responded to political and other criticism about their business operations and privacy practices by establishing the Individual Reference Services Group (IRSG) to promote privacy self-regulation and to head off legislation.[43] The IRSG adopted privacy standards that privacy advocates viewed as weak but that were stronger than used elsewhere. In 2001 following passage of the Gramm-Leach-Bliley Act, IRSG dissolved. Although the act had weak privacy standards for financial institutions and imposed no direct regulation on data brokers, the lack of political support for stronger privacy regulation made the IRSG's mission no longer valuable to its members.

The Online Privacy Alliance was established in 1998, around the time of the enactment of the Children's Online Privacy Protection Act. The alliance had a broad industry coalition of companies and trade associations, and member companies were required to adopt policies for protecting privacy online. The alliance actively promoted self-regulation as an alternative to legislation. With the election of George W. Bush as president, the likelihood of stronger regulatory or legislative action for privacy diminished. The alliance faded away within a few years.[44]

Another business-supported privacy group—the Privacy Leadership Initiative—was established in 2000 with focus on consumer education, research, and privacy standards. Again, the subtext was avoidance of regulation through better industry practices. As with the other business privacy activities, the Privacy Leadership Initiative disbanded in 2002 as the political winds blew more favorably in a pro-business direction.

Another form of self-regulation comes from privacy seal programs that certify that websites meet privacy standards. A number of privacy seals have come and gone over the years, including one from the Better Business Bureau. One long-term privacy seal comes from TRUSTe, an organization founded in 1997. TRUSTe has been criticized by some in the privacy community for having weak standards and for not challenging its seal holders, who are its only source of revenue. The criticism intensified in 2008 when TRUSTe was purchased and became a for-profit company.[45] It is not clear that a self-regulatory program can be operated effectively as a profit-making business.

Another example of an industry self-regulatory effort is the National Advertising Initiative (NAI). The NAI started in 1999 when the FTC showed interest in online profiling activities and invited industry to regulate itself. In a 2000 report to Congress, the FTC recommended the NAI as a self-regulatory solution. As the political interest in privacy regulation diminished with the election of George W. Bush, NAI slowly faded away, losing membership and failing to keep up with browser technology.[46] When the FTC again showed interest in the subject in 2007, the NAI revived in another attempt to avoid regulation. A 2009 report by the staff of the commission continued to call for self-regulation, but one commissioner (who became FTC chairman in 2009) wrote that "this could be the last clear chance to show that self-regulation can—and will—effectively protect consumers' privacy in a dynamic online marketplace."[47]

The same pattern of privacy self-regulation has repeated since the late 1990s. Businesses show interest when there is demonstrable pressure for legislative or regulatory action. They propose or implement self-regulation as an alternative, but the will to self-regulate fades as the pressure diminishes. Privacy advocates criticize the bona fides of the self-regulatory efforts and generally call for more formal government action to establish binding standards.

National codes of conduct drafted by industry are encouraged by the European Union's Data Protection Directive as an acceptable method of self-regulation for privacy. Some differences between Europe and the United States are the presence of national privacy standards that all must meet, the existence of dedicated privacy supervisory agencies, and the requirement for approval of codes by the agencies. These factors have the potential to make European self-regulation more rigorous.

The FCRA Model

The FCRA covers records of credit bureaus (formally known as consumer reporting agencies). There are three national credit bureaus (Equifax, Experian, and Trans Union) and an unknown but large number of specialty credit bureaus. Regulation of national credit bureaus and specialty credit bureaus is different under the FCRA, with stronger consumer protections for national credit bureaus.

The importance of the FCRA is that it was the first real national privacy law (1970), that it has been amended and improved over the years, and that it may offer a model for the protection of privacy online. The FCRA established what became a common pattern for privacy legislation, namely, the use of horror stories to force action. In the case of the FCRA, several members of Congress created a record that demonstrated how credit records were essential to the ability of consumers to engage in basic and important activities, such as acquiring credit, buying houses, and obtaining employment. However, consumers had no right to see or correct the records that credit grantors and employers used when making decisions. The lack of formal and enforceable consumer rights resulted in widespread unfairness. The policy behind the FCRA was that it is unreasonable to burden a consumer with a bad credit record if the consumer's performance has improved or if the record was incorrect, incomplete, or out of date.

The FCRA gave consumers the right to see and correct credit reports, placed limits on the reporting of old negative information, and restricted the permissible purposes for which the records could be used.[48] Although Fair Information Practice principles were not defined until 1973, the FCRA was a reasonable implementation of the principles. The law was far from perfect, however.

By the late 1980s, problems with the law and continuing consumer complaints about credit reporting practices came to public attention because of efforts by consumer groups such as the U.S. Public Interest Reporting Group. Studies showed that credit reports had a high error rate and that consumer complaints about credit reporting agencies led the list of all consumer complaints to the FTC, the federal agency charged with oversight of the FCRA. In 1993, Ed Mierzwinski, a leading consumer lobbyist, called the original FCRA a "piece of prehistoric junk."[49]

The fight to amend the law took many years, with consumers fighting against the credit reporting industry and the broader financial services sector. Changes made by the Consumer Credit Reporting Reform Act of 1996 included expanding the circumstances under which consumers could see credit reports at no cost, new requirements for those who furnish information to credit bureaus, expanded consumer rights when credit reports are used for employment, the ability to opt out from prescreening, and a narrowing of permissible purposes. The compromise law included some things that industry wanted, including expanded federal preemption, weakening of prescreening standards, and broader affiliate sharing.[50]

Another major set of changes came in the Fair and Accurate Credit Transactions Act of 2003.[51] These amendments expanded identity theft protections for consumers, required national credit bureaus to provide credit reports to consumers once a year at no cost, allows consumers to opt out of affiliate sharing, imposed new requirements on furnishers for accuracy of information, and limits the use and sharing of medical information. The law also expanded federal preemption. With these changes, the consumer reporting system because more consumer friendly, but some consumer goals remained unfulfilled. Consumer groups object to federal preemption in the law, want access to credit scores without cost, seek consumer rights for consumer data held by companies outside the credit reporting industry, and press for more help for identity theft victims.

As online consumer data activities increased because of behavioral advertising, social networking, and other Internet developments, some activities that were commonplace in the pre-FCRA period are being repeated. Consumer data from Internet activities are increasingly being collected by companies that have no direct relationship with consumers, and the data are being used to make determinations about what marketplace opportunities are available to consumers. Consumers have no legal rights with respect to these non-credit reporting data profiles, and the companies have no legal obligations to provide access, correct mistakes, or limit the collection and use of the information. While some consumer data companies do provide consumers with limited privacy rights and protections, including some as the result of industry self-regulatory policies, these practices are voluntary and can be readily changed by the companies at will. Whether the same types of privacy protections that the FCRA granted to consumers for credit reporting data will be necessary or appropriate for online data remains to be assessed and determined. A major challenge arises because the Internet makes it difficult to define the universe of consumer data brokers.

Remedies in a Self-Regulated or Regulated World

In the middle of the twentieth century, American courts developed common law remedies for invasions of privacy. These remedies are largely but not exclusively aimed at private rather than governmental actions. A 1960 law journal article condensed the common law cases into four basic privacy torts: (1) intrusion on an individual's seclusion or solitude, (2) public disclosure of private facts, (3) placing an individual in a false light highly offensive to a reasonable person, and (4) an unpermitted use for private commercial gain of a person's identity.[52] In addition, the right of publicity—or the right to control commercial use of an individual's identity—is often recognized as a related right. The Restatement of Torts adopted these torts, and many states followed.[53]

The question, however, is whether these remedies are relevant and responsive to privacy concerns in an online world.

The development and maintenance of many pools of personal data—much of it subject to privacy policies that leave consumers with few, if any, formal rights—makes the classic torts look obsolete or ineffective. The availability of the torts did not stop the creation of offline databases, and the merger of offline and online databases continues today with little fear of tort suits.

A principal problem with privacy lawsuits is the proof of harm. Many plaintiffs and potential plaintiffs have difficulty proving exactly how a disclosure harmed them in a compensable way. A 2004 Supreme Court decision under the Privacy Act of 1974 illustrates the point. The law seemed to provide minimum damages of $1,000 to a successful plaintiff. However, the Court, in *Doe v. Chao*,[54] read the awkward words of the law to require a proof of actual, quantifiable pecuniary loss. Although the decision covered only the specific law in question, the holding had its influence elsewhere. When lawsuits followed a security breach of personal data, courts have not been willing generally to allow the cases to proceed merely on the basis of possible identity theft or other speculative harms. Some class-action lawsuits over online privacy actions have resulted in settlements for nuisance value, but actual damages paid to plaintiffs are rare.

Privacy advocates strongly favor private rights of action, and some older privacy laws include them and provide for minimum statutory damages. Litigants sometime face the problem that a successful case could result in a huge judgment that courts perceive as disproportionate to the violation. The result can be that the courts find ways to dismiss the cases. Newer statutes tend to provide for administrative enforcement. An example is the health privacy rule issued under the authority of HIPAA. The only enforcement under federal law is by the Department of Health and Human Services, and enforcement actions in the first eight years of HIPAA were almost unheard of. Because HIPAA does not allow private lawsuits for health privacy violations, individuals must find a cause of action under state law if they want to sue, and some have been successful.

Administrative enforcement by the FTC provides another remedy, but it rarely results in specific relief for individuals. The Children's Online Privacy Protection Act is one of several laws that allows state attorneys general to bring enforcement actions in addition to FTC actions.[55] The CAN-SPAM Act did not provide a private right of action for an individual who receives unsolicited commercial electronic mail in violation of the law. However, in addition to providing for enforcement by federal agencies and by state attorneys general, CAN-SPAM allows Internet service providers to bring a lawsuit.[56] Some providers have successfully filed lawsuits against spammers.

In the absence of a statute, a company failure to comply with its stated privacy policy can result in action by the FTC, which relies on its authority to prevent unfair or deceptive trade practices.[57] This authority has been used, but the actual number of cases brought is small relative to the large number of commercial websites. The FTC does not normally have authority over noncommercial or governmental websites.

Privacy seal programs also offer some type of remedy to consumers. However, seal programs are generally seen as having a lack of independence from the companies that they oversee.

Effective remedies for most online privacy violations remain broadly elusive, just like effective remedies for many offline privacy violations. Some plaintiffs do win some judgments, but lawsuits only occasionally result in broad changes to a company's privacy practices that have the potential to benefit more data subjects. Nevertheless, lawsuits following highly publicized incidents can result in a willingness by websites and others to improve privacy policies as a way of settling cases and avoiding further publicity.

Consumer Choices: Opt In versus Opt Out

Privacy debates often focus on how to present choices to consumers. The choices may be about how information can be used, shared with other companies, or made public. Whether choices should be opt in or opt out has been a part of that debate. The analysis of opt in and opt out offers a window on the complexity of consumer choice and on privacy in general.

Opt in means that information will not be used unless the record subject affirmatively gives consent. Opt out means that information will be used unless the record subject states an objection. Both opt in and opt out provide guidance to a record keeper in the absence of a clear preference from a record subject.

Typically, consumers accept the default policy, no matter what it is. The general view is that consumers accept the default roughly 95 percent of the time, although there are occasional exceptions.[58] One reason is that consumers often do not read privacy policies at all or with care. In an online environment, those running websites favor opt out because it allows them to use consumer information in the manner the websites want. Privacy policies typically maximize the sharing of information to the benefit of the website operator, and websites may make it hard for consumers to find and exercise choices limiting use and disclosure. Privacy advocates, on the other hand, tend to favor opt in because if consumers take no action, their data are less likely to be used or shared.

However, as simple as those two alternatives may appear, the manner in which options are presented to consumers and in which they are interpreted can be complex in practice. The complexities include the following:

- Is a default rule really needed? If consumer can be required to express a preference, then neither opt in nor opt out is necessary. On a website that asks users to register for access, a registration page can demand that a user make a choice about the reuse of personal information. The user must make a selection in order to advance to the next screen and complete the registration. The result is that each user states a preference, and no default rule is necessary.
- What is the difference between opt in and opt out on a website? Consider a website that asks users to decide whether to allow or prohibit secondary use of their personal information. Suppose that the box indicating one of the alternatives is prechecked. The user who clicks through to the next page without paying much attention gets the default selection. If the box that allows secondary use is prechecked, is that opt out? If the box prohibiting secondary use is prechecked, is that opt in? Whether a box is prechecked and which box is prechecked seems a small difference, especially when consumers are often anxious to move to the next screen. It is difficult to characterize choices presented with prechecked boxes as either opt in or opt out.
- What information does a website user receive when making a choice? If a notice is incomplete, misleading, hard to find, or difficult for the average consumer to understand, the presentation of options may be unfair regardless of other considerations. Privacy notices are often long, complex, hard for the average consumer to

understand, and frequently misinterpreted.[59] If the consumer makes an uninformed choice, regardless of how that choice is framed, is the choice fair?

- Does the type of personal information make a difference? On a social networking site, many consumers expect to share their information with friends and others. However, on a website that collects and maintains health information for consumers, secondary use or sharing of information may not be expected or desired by most consumers. Should consumers be asked to express choices in the same manner for all types of personal information regardless of sensitivity? Is it fair to rely on opt out for both social networking websites *and* health information websites?
- How specific are the choices that consumers have? Does one selection cover all of a consumer's information, or does the consumer have the ability to make more granular decisions about who can see or share which types of data? Giving more choices may be fairer, but studies show that consumers can be overwhelmed if there are too many options.[60] A single choice for all data may be too simplistic, but a two-page, 50-question list of options may be too complicated.

This short discussion shows that finding a fair balance between a website's commercial interest in increased data use and the consumer's interest in privacy is often hard. There are more layers of complexity. Many privacy advocates argue that notice and choice (whether opt in or opt out) has been proved to be a failure.[61] It may be too easy for a website to wheedle the choice it wants from consumers, and a discussion limited to opt in and opt out is too narrow and ignores other alternatives. Advocates argue that websites should first comply with the Fair Information Practices for purpose specification and use limitation and then limit consent within that context.

Consumer Choices: Do Not Track

The online activities of users are increasingly monitored in some fashion by a large variety of companies that collect user data for advertising and other purposes. One major purpose of the monitoring is for *behavioral targeting*, which uses information collected on a user's Web browsing activities to target the ads shown to that user.

On some websites, dozens of different companies may monitor the actions of each user. Whether the methods used to monitor users produce overtly identifiable records, potentially identifiable records, or truly anonymous records is both variable and somewhat in dispute. However, there is little dispute that the monitoring of users can affect privacy in some way.

One of the privacy protection responses to behavioral targeting of Web users is a method that allows users to avoid being tracked. This is generally referred to as *Do Not Track*. The basic idea is to allow users to state a preference about monitoring that will be honored by websites. However, beyond this highest level of generality in describing Do Not Track, there is little agreement on what Do Not Track means or how it would work.

Do Not Track originated in a 2007 at a meeting of privacy advocates convened by the World Privacy Forum in Berkeley, California. The participating advocacy organizations wrote a position paper on behavioral advertising principles.[62] The document was signed by 10 groups and was submitted formally to the FTC as part of its November 2007 Behavioral Advertising Workshop. The document included updated definitions of personally identifiable information and other key ideas applicable to maintaining consumer privacy protections in the behavioral advertising space.

The Do Not Track idea in its original inception called for a registry similar to the FTC's Do Not Call Registry.[63] The FTC Do Not Call Registry allows U.S. consumers to opt out of most telemarketing phone calls by calling or using the Internet to register a telephone number. The idea of Do Not Track was that consumers could have one simple, accessible place where a user could opt out of multiple forms of online tracking, particularly tracking that was targeted to consumer's Web browsing habits.

The proposal stated the following:

> To help ensure that these principles are followed, the FTC should:
>
> Create a national Do Not Track List similar to the national Do Not Call List:
>
> - Any advertising entity that sets a persistent identifier on a user device should be required to provide to the FTC the domain names of the servers or other devices used to place the identifier.

- Companies providing web, video, and other forms of browser applications should provide functionality (i.e., a browser feature, plug-in, or extension) that allows users to import or otherwise use the Do Not Track List of domain names, keep the list up-to-date, and block domains on the list from tracking their Internet activity.
- Advertisements from servers or other technologies that do not employ persistent identifiers may still be displayed on consumers' computers. Thus, consumers who sign up for the Do Not Track List would still receive advertising.
- The Do Not Track List should be available on the FTC Web site for download by consumers who wish to use the list to limit tracking.
- The FTC should engage in public education to disseminate the Do Not Track List information broadly to consumers, along with instructions for its use. The FTC should actively encourage all creators of browsing and other relevant technology to incorporate a facility that will enable consumers to use the list.[64]

In its follow-up report about the November 2007 hearings, the FTC supported the original Do Not Track proposal in broad terms but noted that the idea needed a lot of work on implementation specifics. Over the next few years, various groups, including browser companies Mozilla and Microsoft, worked on the technical aspects of how a Do Not Track mechanism might work. The Do Not Track concept evolved as more individuals became involved with it. The registry idea was eventually joined with other technology-based solutions to limit online tracking.

One of the later solutions relied on Web browsers to "inform" websites of a person's privacy preference regarding tracking. This approach would allow a user to set a Do Not Track preference using the browser's options and for that choice to be conveyed automatically to a website. No central registry would be required. In December 2010, the FTC released a new report on privacy and technology and expressly recognized and endorsed Do Not Track as a viable proposal, taking its support of the Do Not Track idea a step further than in its previous report on online privacy.[65]

Researchers at Mozilla, Stanford University, and elsewhere worked on the specifics of exactly how this conception of Do Not Track would work in a browser. In February 2011, Mozilla formally announced that it had created a Do Not Track mechanism that worked.[66] Mozilla's browser-based approach was called the *HTTP header approach*.[67] The Stanford team that assisted in the development of this particular incarnation of Do Not Track described the "header approach" this way:

> Much like the popular Do Not Call registry, Do Not Track provides users with a single, persistent setting to opt out of web tracking.
>
> Here's how it works: Whenever a web browser requests content or sends data using HTTP, the protocol that underlies the web, it can optionally include extra information, called a "header." Do Not Track simply adds a header indicating the user wishes to not be tracked. Unlike Do Not Call, Do Not Track is not a list; rather, it employs a decentralized design, avoiding the substantial technical and privacy challenges inherent to compiling, updating, and sharing a comprehensive registry of tracking services or web users.
>
> Compliance with Do Not Track could be purely voluntary, enforced by industry self-regulation, or mandated by state or federal law. We do not take a position on these alternatives.[68]

Other companies also added Do Not Track features to their browsers.

During the 112th Congress, Do Not Track became the subject of several legislative proposals.[69] The proposals generally supported the idea of a browser-based mechanism together with a self-regulatory mechanism for enforcement. However, other ideas remained under discussion, including the idea of compiling lists of objectionable websites and allowing users to subscribe to lists created by different organizations. Other controversies about Do Not Track include whether it means that information about a user will not be collected or whether a user will merely not see behaviorally targeted ads. The option of only not showing targeted ads suggests that the creation of consumer profiles for other purposes would continue without limit. Some in the advocacy community worry about monitoring in general, suggesting that the focus on Do Not Track at online activities is too narrow and that consumers are being tracked in the offline world using different technologies that have the same effect of creating unregulated consumer profiles. There are many technical and policy controversies about any implementation of Do Not Track, and even those who support the idea may not agree on the best way to accomplish it.

The debate over Do Not Track offers a good illustration of the interplay between policy and technology. In the middle of the twentieth century, consumer profiles were often limited to postal mailing lists with limited information on consumers. Over time, the ability to collect more information about consumers led to more robust lists and broader consumer profiles. Most of these activities took place outside the view or knowledge of consumers. The online world brings new technology to consumer monitoring activities, more awareness by consumers of these activities, and new capability for consumers to express privacy preferences in real time. Do Not Track is one potential response to some of the new forms of online tracking that pose privacy issues. Whether it is ever adopted or becomes a model for controlling consumer monitoring more generally remains to be seen.

Notes

1. See Robert M. Gellman, *Prescribing Privacy: The Uncertain Role of the Physician in the Protection of Patient Privacy*, 62 North Carolina Law Review 255 (1984).

2. Executive Order No. 13335 (April 27, 2004), 69 Federal Register 24059 (April 30, 2004).

3. 42 U.S.C. § 300jj-11.

4. 42 U.S.C. § 1320d-2 (note).

5. http://www.hhs.gov/ocr/privacy/hipaa/administrative/privacyrule/index.html.

6. http://www.hhs.gov/ocr/privacy/hipaa/administrative/securityrule/index.html.

7. 42 U.S.C. § 17931.

8. 42 U.S.C. § 1320d-2 (note).

9. See the Department of Health and Human Service's HIPAA website for the rules and other related materials at http://www.hhs.gov/ocr/privacy.

10. http://healthit.hhs.gov/portal/server.pt/community/healthit_hhs_gov__home/1204.

11. See, e.g., California Health and Human Services Agency, *California Privacy and Security Advisory Board Interim Guidelines* (October 2009), at http://www.ohi.ca.gov/calohi/LinkClick.aspx?fileticket=yLyFEJ10JNE%3d&tabid=56.

12. See http://www.nyclix.org.

13. See Robert Gellman, *Privacy in the Clouds: Risks to Privacy and Confidentiality from Cloud Computing* (2009) (World Privacy Forum), http://www.worldprivacyforum.org/pdf/WPF_Cloud_Privacy_Report.pdf.

14. See, e.g., Patricia Voydanoff. *Work, Family and Community: Exploring Interconnections* (2006).

15. For a technical definition of online social networks, see Dana M. Boyd and Nicole B. Ellison, *Social Network Sites: Definition, History, And Scholarship*, 13 Journal of Computer-Mediated Communication (2007), at http://jcmc.indiana.edu/vol13/issue1/boyd.ellison.html.

16. See https://developers.facebook.com.

17. https://developers.facebook.com/blog/post/446.

18. For a distillation of the controversy, see *Facebook Letter to Representative Edward Markey* (February 23, 2011), at http://markey.house.gov/docs/facebook_response_markey_barton_letter_2.2011.pdf.

19. Pam Dixon, *The One-Way-Mirror Society: Privacy Implications of the New Digital Signage Networks* (2010), at http://www.worldprivacyforum.org/pdf/onewaymirrorsocietyfs.pdf.

20. Ellen Nakashima, *Feeling Betrayed, Facebook Users Force Site to Honor Their Privacy*, Washington Post, November 30, 2007, at http://www.washingtonpost.com/wp-dyn/content/article/2007/11/29/AR2007112902503.html.

21. See http://www.beaconclasssettlement.com.

22. Electronic Privacy Information Center, Social Networking Privacy, at http://epic.org/privacy/socialnet.

23. Carolyn Y. Johnson, *Project Gaydar: At MIT, an Experiment Identifies Which Students Are Gay, Raising New Questions about Online Privacy*, Boston Globe, September 20, 2009, at http://www.boston.com/bostonglobe/ideas/articles/2009/09/20/project_gaydar_an_ mit_experiment_raises_new_questions_about_online_privacy.

24. http://klout.com/kscore.

25. Emily Steel, *A Web Pioneer Profiles Users by Name*, Wall Street Journal, October 25, 2010, at http://online.wsj.com/article/SB10001424052702304410504575560243259416072.html.

26. http://www.clickz.com/clickz/news/1866122/rapleaf-agrees-leave-facebook.

27. See, e.g., Lucas Conley, *How Rapleaf Is Data-Mining Your Friend Lists to Predict Your Credit Risk*, Fast Company, November 16, 2009, at http://www.fastcompany.com/blog/lucas-conley/advertising-branding-and-marketing/company-we-keep.

28. See Paul Ohm, *Broken Promises of Privacy: Responding to the Surprising Failure of Anonymization*, 57 UCLA Law Review 1701 (2010), at http://papers.ssrn.com/sol3/papers.cfm?abstract_id=1450006.

29. Comments of Latanya Sweeney, PhD, Carnegie Mellon University, on the Department of Health and Human Service's Standards of Privacy

of Individually Identifiable Health Information (2002), at http://privacy.cs.cmu.edu/dataprivacy/HIPAA/HIPAAcomments.html.

30. 44 U.S.C. § 3501 note.

31. 45 C.F.R. §164.514(b)(2)(i).

32. See, e.g., Andrew Kantor, *AOL Search Data Release Reveals a Great Deal*, USA Today (August 17, 2006), http://www.usatoday.com/tech/columnist/andrewkantor/2006-08-17-aol-data_x.htm.

33. See https://startpage.com/eng/protect-privacy.html.

34. Directive 2006/24/EC of the European Parliament and of the Council of March 15, 2006, on the retention of data generated or processed in connection with the provision of publicly available electronic communications services or of public communications networks and amending Directive 2002/58/EC, at http://eur-lex.europa.eu/LexUriServ/LexUriServ.do?uri=CELEX:32006L0024:EN:NOT.

35. http://www.great-quotes.com/quotes/author/John/Barlow.

36. See, generally, Bill Keller, *Dealing with Julian Assange and the Secrets He Spilled*, New York Times, January 26, 2011, http://www.nytimes.com/2011/01/30/magazine/30Wikileaks-t.html.

37. *Reno v. Condon*, 528 U.S. 141 (2000).

38. 15 U.S.C. § 1681c.

39. *Equifax Services, Inc. v. Cohen*, 420 A.2d 189 (Me.1980).

40. *Department of Justice v. Reporter's Committee for Freedom of the Press*, 489 U.S.749 (1989).

41. 15 U.S.C. § 7701-7713.

42. http://www.ftc.gov/bcp/edu/microsites/donotcall/index.html.

43. Some information about the IRSG remains available through the FTC website; see, e.g., http://www.ftc.gov/bcp/privacy/wkshp97/irsdoc1.htm.

44. See http://www.privacyalliance.org. The group may have come back to life in 2010 when new pressures arose to regulate online advertising.

45. http://www.truste.com.

46. See World Privacy Forum, *The NAI: Failing at Consumer Protection and at Self-Regulation* (2007), http://www.worldprivacyforum.org/behavioral_advertising.html.

47. See http://www.ftc.gov/opa/2009/02/behavad.shtm (statement of Commissioner Jon Leibowitz).

48. 15 U.S.C. § 1681 et seq.

49. Quoted in Robert M. Gellman, *Can Privacy Be Regulated Effectively on a National Level? Thoughts on the Possible Need for International Privacy Rules*, 41 Villanova Law Review 129, 141 (1996).

50. Public Law 104-208, the Omnibus Consolidated Appropriations Act for Fiscal Year 1997, Title II, Subtitle D, Chapter 1.

51. Public Law 108-159.

52. William Prosser, *Privacy*, 48 California Law Review 383 (1960).

53. Restatement (Second) of Torts §§ 652A–652I (1977).
54. 540 U.S. 614 (2004).
55. 15 U.S.C. § 6504.
56. 15 U.S.C. § 7706(g).
57. 15 U.S.C. § 45.
58. See, e.g., Federal Trade Commission, *National Do Not Call Registry Tops 200 Million Phone Numbers* (press release) (July 27, 2010), at http://www.ftc.gov/opa/2010/07/dnc.shtm.
59. See Chris Jay Hoofnagle and Jennifer King, *What Californians Understand about Privacy Online* (2008), at http://ssrn.com/abstract=1262130.
60. See, generally, Richard H. Thaler and Cass R. Sunstein, *NUDGE Improving Decisions About Health, Wealth, and Happiness* (2008).
61. See Federal Trade Commission, *Protecting Consumer Privacy in an Era of Rapid Change: A Proposed Framework for Businesses and Policymakers* at 19 (2010) (Preliminary Staff Report), http://ftc.gov/os/2010/12/101201privacyreport.pdf.
62. World Privacy Forum et al., *Consumer Rights and Protections in the Behavioral Advertising Sector* (October 2007), at http://www.worldprivacyforum.org/pdf/ConsumerProtections_FTC_ConsensusDoc_Final_s.pdf.
63. See https://www.donotcall.gov.
64. Ibid.
65. Federal Trade Commission, *Protecting Consumer Privacy in an Era of Rapid Change: A Framework for Business and Policymakers* (December 2010), at http://ftc.gov/os/2010/12/101201privacyreport.pdf.
66. Mozilla, *Mozilla Firefox 4 Beta Now Including Do Not Track Capabilities*, The Mozilla Blog, February 8, 2011.
67. The Do Not Track website maintained at Stanford University provides an overview of the HTTP header approach being pursued by Stanford researchers; see http://donottrack.us.
68. Ibid.
69. Kate Kaye, *House Meets to Discuss Do Not Track, John Kerry to Propose Privacy Bill*, ClickZ (December 2, 2010), at http://www.clickz.com/clickz/news/1929879/house-meets-discuss-track-john-kerry-propose-privacy.

3

Worldwide Perspective

Introduction to International Approaches

Basic Approaches

Personal information in the online world flows routinely without respect to national borders, making online privacy an international issue of some complexity. While some countries successfully impose restrictions—sometimes called censorship—that limit or prevent the flow of personal and other information on the Internet and through other means of digital communications, a great deal of data nevertheless flows freely. Individuals, businesses, governments, and others can usually send, receive, and use personal information regardless of their location in the physical world.

Currently, there are no universal privacy laws that apply throughout the world. Although some cooperative agreements exist between some countries, each nation typically creates its own approach to privacy regulation, including some countries that have chosen to have no privacy laws at all. That being said, most industrialized countries have enacted at least some privacy protections.

Generally, privacy protections fall into two main categories: *sectoral* privacy laws and *omnibus* privacy laws. The United States uses sectoral regulation, whereas the European Union (EU) uses omnibus regulation. The EU privacy approach has significantly influenced the law in many other countries.

The U.S., or Sectoral, Approach to Privacy

The approach of the United States to privacy differs from that taken by much of the rest of the world. No general privacy standards apply in the United States. Instead, the American approach to privacy is usually described as a *sectoral approach*. This essentially means that laws and regulations aimed at protecting privacy apply to particular classes of information or to particular record keepers. Health information is an example of a class or type of information, as is financial information. A credit bureau (consumer reporting agency) is an example of a particular record keeper. American privacy laws are often enacted following *horror stories*, which are highly publicized incidents of privacy invasive activity or breaches.

As a result of the U.S. sectoral approach, the same personal information in the hands of two different American record keepers may be subject to different privacy rules. State privacy laws generally work the same way. A well-known example of this is health records. If a hospital holds a file on a patient, that information is protected by a federal privacy law applicable to most of the health care sector.[1] But if that very same information is given to a marketing company by a patient, that information is not protected under that law or any other.

The interplay of U.S. state and federal laws is complex. Some federal privacy laws preempt state laws, while other federal laws establish minimum levels of privacy protection that states may exceed. California has been the most aggressive state for enacting privacy legislation, with one famous example of high-impact legislation being California's "data breach notification" law.[2] This law influenced other states to pass similar laws.[3] Now, most states now have security breach notification laws that require notice to data subjects when personal information is inadvertently disclosed. In other areas of privacy, state laws are more occasional and more variable.

When there is no privacy law in the United States protecting personal information, there is no mandated privacy protection. For example, the federal Video Privacy Protection Act[4] limits the disclosure of information about a consumer's choices at a video rental store. The law protects privacy and the exercise of First Amendment rights. However, no federal statute limits the disclosure of information about a consumer's choices at a bookstore, even though the interests are nearly identical. The federal Cable Communications Policy Act[5] limits the collection of personal information from subscribers to cable television and disclosure of their viewing habits. Yet no federal law limits collection and disclosure of information about those who watch programming online. Because there is no general federal law regulating records compiled for marketing purposes—records such as consumer profiles and mailing lists—these records have no formal legal protection. Lists of consumers are readily available for marketing uses contain information about a consumer's religion, ethnicity, income, health status, wealth, sexual orientation, and other characteristics that many would consider to be sensitive.[6]

The EU, or Omnibus, Approach to Privacy

Most industrialized countries rely on an *omnibus approach* to privacy legislation. Omnibus privacy laws establish common standards that apply to most public and private activities that involve the processing of personal information. Although there are some limited exceptions, omnibus privacy rules generally apply to all record keepers of personal information. More than 50 countries have adopted some form of national data protection legislation of this type.[7]

The EU's *Directive on the Protection of Individuals with Regard to the Processing of Personal Data and on the Free Movement of Such Data*[8] is a leading example of the omnibus approach to privacy regulation. The EU Data Protection Directive requires that member states enact national laws that meet minimum privacy standards. Many records that have no statutory privacy protections in the United States would, if located in the EU, fall under the privacy protections mandated by the directive. For example, marketing records that are unregulated for privacy in the United States would fall under regulation in the EU.

Differences in national approaches to privacy raise complicated problems because personal information routinely flows between countries as a result of activities undertaken by individuals and as a result of activities undertaken by businesses and governments. Activities that result in what is sometimes called *transborder flow of personal information* include electronic mail, credit card usage, consumer transactions, social networking, Internet usage (e.g., search engines), health treatment, multinational company employment and compensation practices, research, investments and other financial transactions, international travel, law enforcement, and more. For instance, air travel involves the collection, maintenance, and transfer of a *passenger name record* (PNR) containing all data necessary to enable reservations to be processed by participating airlines. PNR data can include sensitive information about health (need for a wheelchair) or religion (food preferences) as well as information about travel plans, hotel reservations, and other activities. The focus on terrorism following the events of September 11, 2001, in the United States highlighted the relevance of PNR records to national immigration controls. A European Commission agreement with the United States that facilitates the transfer of PNR records to the United States has been the focus of much controversy with the EU.[9]

Consider as well the situation when a consumer uses a credit card to make a purchase over the Internet from a merchant in another country. Information about the transaction in the possession of the merchant and any other local parties to the transaction (e.g., credit card processor) will be subject to the privacy law of the country where the merchant is located. The merchant will share some information about the transaction through local intermediaries with the credit card company, which will transmit the information to the consumer's home country so that the consumer can be billed. The information in the consumer's home country will become subject to local privacy laws in that country. In addition, if the record of the credit card transaction were to be routed through a third country, it is possible that the consumer's records could be subject to a third set of national privacy rules.

This single example illustrates some of the complexity of privacy in an international context. The privacy rights of the consumer to the credit card transaction in the country where the merchant is located could be different from the consumer's privacy rights in the consumer's home country. If the case of a dispute about the accuracy of the record or about whether the information may be shared with a third party for marketing purposes, the rights, procedures, or standards in the two countries could be different.

These types of transborder disparities or conflicts are not unique to privacy. They can arise, for example, with international consumer transactions, where a principal threshold question is which consumer protection law applies to the transaction. Is it the law of the nation where the consumer lives or the law of the nation where the business operates? Online activities have made these questions more acute because they make international transactions much easier and more common.

Differing Privacy Rules and Data Exports

Looked at broadly, the export of personal information from a country where it is regulated for privacy to another country where it is not regulated or it is regulated more loosely can create gaps or conflicts. If personal data can flow freely from a country with stronger privacy protections to a country with weaker privacy protections, then an exporting nation that allows those data flows may undermine its own laws that protect the privacy of its citizens. If data exports are unrestricted, then privacy protections that exist at home may be readily evaded by exporting data. Thus, a company that wanted to use personal data for a marketing activity prohibited by its national law could merely export the data to a country where marketing is not restricted. Unlimited personal data exports could conceivably engender a *race to the bottom*, where the country with the fewest privacy restrictions attracts more commercial activity as businesses move personal information to locations where it can be more readily exploited.

One way to protect national privacy standards is to limit personal data exports. However, a flat ban on data exports is not practical for many reasons. For example, credit card usage information must flow back to the home country of the user if credit cards are to be accepted internationally. Travel between countries also requires some sharing of personal information across national borders. Consumers routinely seek health care or investment transactions in other countries. Many other ordinary consumer or commercial activities require transborder data flow of personal information.

Another consequence of personal data restrictions is interference with markets, competition, and free trade. The Internet increasingly supports international consumer transactions. Restrictions in the name of privacy could prevent a merchant in one country from selling goods and services at a lower price than would be available in another country. Privacy rules could prevent a business from offering data processing services in other countries or could limit the ability of multinational companies to move information from country to country in support of internal operations. Yet the right of a country to protect the privacy of its citizens is recognized. In 1994, the General Agreement on Trade on Services, part of the General Agreement on Tariffs and Trade, added a general exception recognizing a nation's right to adopt measures for the protection of privacy of individuals.[10] The breadth and significance of this provision is disputed.

Another problem is that a record keeper operating in more than one country may be obliged to comply with different privacy rules in each country. Even when privacy laws are similar, small variations could create additional compliance problems and expenses. Larger variations could create overt conflicts, foe example, if data use allowed in one country is banned in another. Privacy laws could serve as a barrier to trade, a point sometimes made by businesses opposed to increased privacy protections.

The potential barriers that privacy regulation presents to transborder activities have been recognized since the beginning of the modern data protection movement. In 1980, the Organisation for Economic Cooperation and Development (OECD) issued one of the earliest and most influential documents on international privacy regulation. The title of the OECD document—*Guidelines on the Protection of Privacy and Transborder Flows of Personal Data*—emphasizes the importance of both privacy and international data transfers.[11] The OECD guidelines demonstrate that personal privacy and international transfers of data were viewed as directly related and jointly provided an impetus for regulating the processing of personal information. The guidelines have eight principles: (1) collection limitation, (2) data quality, (3) purpose specification, (4) use limitation, (5) security safeguards, (6) openness, (7) individual participation, and (8) accountability. The Council of Europe adopted a *Convention for the Protection of Individuals with Regard to Automatic Processing of Personal Data* about the same time as the OECD guidelines and with a similar emphasis on both privacy and the free flow of information.[12] (For additional discussion of these guidelines, see the discussion of Fair Information Practices in Chapter 1.)

In 1990, the United Nations adopted *Guidelines for the Regulation of Computerized Personal Files*.[13] The nonbinding guidelines leave it to each state to adopt its own procedures. The UN document, which has not had a major influence in international discussions, also addresses both privacy and transborder data flows. The UN document was the first international data protection standard that included a requirement for an independent supervisory authority.

The 1995 Data Protection Directive also has an emphasis on both privacy and the free flow of information. Its formal title, *Directive on the Protection of Individuals with Regard to the Processing of Personal Data and on the Free Movement of Such Data*, shows the same dual emphasis as the OECD guidelines. One of the principal purposes of the directive was to simplify the burden of complying with multiple national laws within the EU Common Market for a *data controller* (record keeper). The basic policy is that an EU data controller that complies with the national privacy law in one member state cannot be required to comply with the national privacy law of another member state. Compliance with one national regulatory scheme is sufficient for the entire EU. The directive ensures that all national laws meet minimum standards so that there is a sufficient level of protection for privacy interests throughout the EU. Other aspects of data exports to third countries are considered separately later in this chapter.

Privacy and Human Rights

In 1948, the United Nations adopted the *Universal Declaration of Human Rights*.[14] Article 12 provides, "No one shall be subjected to arbitrary interference with his privacy, family, home or correspondence, nor to attacks upon his honour and reputation. Everyone has the right to the protection of the law against such interference or attacks." The UN declaration is not enforceable, but it influenced other international instruments, most notably in Europe.

In Europe, the right of privacy is also considered to be a *human right*. The European *Convention for the Protection of Human Rights and Fundamental Freedoms* is an international convention that defines a wide range of civil and political rights and provides a means for the enforcement of those rights.[15] The convention, which dates back to 1950, was developed by the Council of Europe, an international organization of European states that seeks to achieve a greater unity between its members for the purposes of safeguarding and realizing common ideals and principles and facilitating economic and social progress. The Human Rights Convention is the most famous product of the council.

Article 8 of the European Convention addresses respect for private and family life. It prohibits interference by a public authority only in accordance with law and when necessary in the interests of national security, public safety, or the economic well-being of the country; for the prevention of disorder or crime; for the protection of health or morals; or for the protection of the rights and freedoms of others. These interests that conflict at times with privacy are, of course, not unique to Europe. As a result of the convention, European debates about privacy utilize human rights rhetoric and principles much more than comparable debates in the United States.

The significance of the privacy language in the European Convention is that it establishes a privacy right that has effectively acquired constitutional status and that the right is enforceable ultimately through the European Court on Human Rights. The enforcement process, however, is neither simple nor speedy, with cases taking up to five years to run their course. However, there have been several important cases by the European Court involving privacy and clarifying obligations under the convention.

In December 2008, the European Court upheld a challenge to a British policy of collecting and storing the fingerprints and DNA of criminal suspects, including those found to be innocent. The court found the "blanket and indiscriminate nature of the power of retention . . . irrespective of the nature or gravity of the offence . . . or of the age of the suspected offender" together with the lack of a time-limited retention policy and limited possibilities for an acquitted individual to have the data removed "failed to strike a fair balance between the competing public and private interests." The policy "constituted a disproportionate interference with the applicants' right to respect for private life and could not be regarded as necessary in a democratic society." The court found a violation of Article 8.[16]

EU Data Privacy Directive

As discussed earlier in this chapter, perhaps the most important international privacy regulatory document is the EU's Data Protection Directive. The directive focuses primarily on the privacy of personal information rather than on the many other matters that fall under the broad heading of *privacy*. The term *data protection*, used in Europe and elsewhere abroad, is similar to the concept of *information privacy* more often used in the United States to define a particular subset of privacy interests. *Data protection* terminology was introduced in part because there is no word equivalent to *privacy* in all languages. Some mistakenly think that data protection refers only to security of information.

The EU adopted the directive in 1995 following a lengthy and contentious process that began in 1990 with an initial proposal from the European Commission. However, the Data Protection Directive was not the first European document on privacy. National and provincial laws as well as international instruments helped to set the stage for the EU action. Ironically, they also made it harder to reach agreement on the directive because nations wanted to preserve as much of their existing laws as possible.

The first general data processing regulation—the Data Protection Act—was enacted in 1970 by the German state of Hesse. Sweden passed its Data Act of 1973 establishing a data inspection board. The Swedish law had a significant influence on other European countries in the 1970s. West Germany passed a Federal Data Protection Act in 1977 establishing a data protection commissioner. The French enacted a 1978 Law on Informatics, Data Banks, and Freedoms and established a permanent privacy agency, the National Commission for Data Protection and Liberties. Norway, Denmark, and Austria also passed national laws in 1978. The United Kingdom was a somewhat late actor, passing its Data Protection Act in 1984. The U.K. action—by a conservative government—occurred after pressure from both the civil liberties lobby and industry. The arguments of hardware and software manufacturers and other private sector organizations that their business prospects would be adversely affected in the absence of a privacy law strongly influenced the U.K. government.[17] The economic need for and benefits of privacy laws in a world where some nations regulated activities for privacy is especially noteworthy and reflects the ongoing concern within the EU about harmonization of privacy laws.

The harmonization objective of the Data Protection Directive was an important part of the political and policy debate that resulted in the adoption of the directive. The passage of numerous national laws in Europe created the potential for conflicting or unenforceable privacy regulations. The directive developed as a response to the problems created by widely divergent national privacy laws. Each EU member state had to pass a law meeting the minimum standards of the directive, and each state had to accept the law enacted by the other states. That policy minimized intra-EU conflicts.

In contrast, U.S. privacy legislation has traditionally paid little attention to the international harmonization of privacy laws. An echo of the harmonization problem can be heard, however, in American debates over preemption of state law with federal law. The American concern about interstate commerce has broad similarities to the EU's concern about international harmonization. Although the U.S. internal market is entirely domestic, some constitutional restrictions prevent state regulation that interferes with interstate commerce activities. Preemption of state laws is a familiar and controversial issue in American privacy debates. These federal-state conflicts over privacy regulation reflect some of the same concerns that resulted in the adoption of the Data Protection Directive by the EU. American multinational companies are more attentive to international harmonization of privacy regimes that affect their commercial activities. The executive branch has also become enmeshed in international privacy issues, particularly in the travel, law enforcement, and national security arenas.

The Data Protection Directive sets out a regulatory framework for the processing of personal data that all member states are obliged to enforce through national laws. The directive applies broadly to the processing of personal data by both government and private sector organizations. There are some exceptions. Under Article 3 of the directive, the regulatory scheme does not apply to activities that fall outside the scope of community law and to processing operations for public security, defense, state security, and criminal law activities. These exceptions are increasingly controversial. In addition, the directive does not apply to the processing of personal data by a natural person in the course of purely personal or household activities. Other provisions address potential conflicts with journalistic activities and with artistic and literary expression.

The EU conceived of and drafted the Data Protection Directive before the Internet and the electronic marketplace became an important feature in the daily lives and activities of people and institutions around the world. Applying the directive's terms and concepts to Internet activities results in some interesting and complex problems. For example, a 2009 opinion by the Article 29 Working Party established under the directive addressed the application of privacy principles to social networking.[18] The personal or household exception applies to some activities of individuals on a social networking site. However, the exception does not apply to a company or association that uses a social networking site mainly as a platform to advance commercial, political, or charitable goals. Even the use of a site by an individual may fall outside the exception if the individual user acquires a high number of third-party contacts, some of whom the user may not actually know.

A 2008 Article 29 Working Party addresses application of the EU Data Protection Directive to search engines.[19] Both social networking sites and search engines operate on the Internet and across national borders, making the application of national laws more challenging. These opinions reflect the ongoing struggle to adapt privacy policies in new environments and to new institutions.

Data Exports

The Data Protection Directive included one of the first attempts to control data exports in the interest of privacy protection. Articles 25 and 26 establish rules for the transfer of personal data to third countries. The general standard allows data exports to third countries that ensure *an adequate level of protection*. The directive calls for the assessment of adequacy in light of all the circumstances surrounding a data transfer, including the nature of the data, the purpose of the transfer, and the rules of law, both general and sectoral, in the third country. In order to meet this controversial and much contested EU standard, some nations drafted their privacy laws following the European model so that their national laws would qualify. National privacy laws found to meet the EU standard include Canada, Switzerland, Argentina, and the Isle of Man. Data exports from EU member states to these countries can continue without additional scrutiny or procedure for privacy.

Other provisions of the Data Protection Directive address the possibility of exports of personal data to third countries whose privacy laws have not found to be adequate. Export is allowed (1) with the unambiguous consent of the data subject, (2) if necessary for the performance of a contract and the data subject, (3) if necessary for performance of a contract in the interest of the data subject, (4) on important public interest grounds, (5) to protect the vital interest of the data subject, and (6) from a public register. These grounds for data exports are complex, uncertain, and legalistic, and they create uncertainties for some routine data transfers.

Other methods under the Data Protection Directive that permit data exports to countries without adequate privacy laws include contracts between data exporters and data importers and binding corporate rules for multinational companies. Both of these devices can be complicated, expensive to develop and implement, and not suited to the needs of smaller companies. The EU has offered model contracts to simplify and clarify matters for participants, but the contractual approach may require a multinational company operating in many countries to have a large number of contracts for routine operations.[20]

The data export rules of the Data Protection Directive have been the focus of considerable criticism, especially by companies seeking to send personal data from Europe to other countries. However, another perspective on the directive is that it addresses, if imperfectly, the mechanics of how to function in a multijurisdictional world. If there were no directive, multinational companies would be obliged to resolve independently how to address privacy in each EU member state rather than rely on the harmonization that the directive requires. The lack of harmonized rules could be a barrier to trade of possibly greater dimension than the current harmonized rules.

The United States, which lacks any comprehensive privacy protections, does not meet the EU standards for adequacy, although it is conceivable that specific sectoral legislation could be found to be adequate. Because of the importance of the United States in international trade and especially in business and Internet functions that involve the transfer of personal data, the difficulty of finding a justification for routine data exports presented potentially serious economic problems once the directive took effect.

The U.S.-EU *Safe Harbor Framework* was developed in response to those problems. Some view the Safe Harbor Framework as a political solution to the trade problem and one that had the effect of undercutting the privacy standard established in the Data Protection Directive. The Safe Harbor Framework was negotiated by the Department of Commerce and the European Commission and approved in 2000, two years after the directive became effective.[21]

Under the Safe Harbor Framework, personal data may be exported from Europe to a U.S. company that certifies that it meets the safe harbor requirement for activities covered by the safe harbor certification. The seven safe harbor principles are a subset of data protection requirements compatible with but not identical to the Data Protection Directive's data protection requirements. Enforcement of the commitment of U.S. companies to comply with safe harbor principles generally comes through a combination of dispute resolution and verification procedures adopted by the U.S. company as required by the safe harbor requirements. Additional enforcement may come from the Federal Trade Commission (FTC) or other federal agency that has the ability to enforce a promise made by a U.S. company using authority to prohibit unfair or deceptive trade practices.

Enforcement actions have been rare, but the FTC did take action against several companies in 2010 for representing that they were Safe Harbor participants when they were not.[22] Some question whether scarce U.S. privacy enforcement resources will ever be used to address the protection of European consumers. However, few if any complaints from Europeans have arisen. The lack of meaningful enforcement mechanisms is one of the principal criticisms of the Safe Harbor Framework by European and U.S. consumer organizations, the European Parliament, and others.[23] Following persistent reports that companies in the Safe Harbor were not actually in compliance with the requirements, German data protection authorities (DPAs) in 2010 told companies not to rely on Safe Harbor certification but to verify compliance.[24]

The Safe Harbor Framework provides a relatively simple method that supports the continued export of personal data from the EU to the United States. It is not apparent that the framework provides much real privacy protection to those whose personal data were exported to the United States. In 2009, the Safe Harbor Framework was extended to cover data exports from Switzerland to the United States.[25] Switzerland is not a member of the EU. There is no comparable Safe Harbor instrument covering personal data exports from the EU to any country other than the United States.

Evolution of the Directive

In 2011, the EU began a major review of the data protection directive. Matters likely to receive attention include the need for better harmonization, for clearer controls by users over their information, for simpler administration for companies doing business in more than one country, and for streamlined data export rules. How the directive will change is unclear.

Another issue exacerbated by the Internet and receiving attention especially in Europe is the so-called Right to Forget. The basic concern is that older information about individuals that appears on the Internet has a tendency to remain accessible for a long period and perhaps indefinitely. Search engines make it easier to find and retrieve that information, even when the subject of the data no longer wants it to be available. An example is a college photo being available decades after an individual graduated. The US Supreme Court once referred to the inability to find and retrieve information in a paper world as *practical obscurity*. However, it is not apparent that the concept of practical obscurity is meaningful on the Internet. In Europe, the supposed right of an individual to control his or her data is an element of the Right to Forget.

The basic idea of individual control over personal data has appeal, but it is not clear how a Right to Forget would or could operate. Whether older data would have to be removed after a fixed period or upon the request of the data subject is uncertain. The rights of those who posted data need to be considered, as well as the interests of historians, researchers, and others. Controls over older information may conflict with freedom of speech principles. The mechanism that would enforce the Right to Forget is unknown. Whether and if Europe will seek to address a Right to Forget in any revision of the Directive remains to be seen.

Canada: The Personal Information Protection and Electronic Documents Act and the Canadian Standards Association Standard

Canada took a somewhat different route to establishing privacy standards for the private sector. A law covering federal agencies was enacted in 1983.[26] In 1995, the effort to develop private sector rules began with the Canadian Standards Association (CSA) developing a Model Code for the Protection of Personal Information. The CSA Model Code was drafted by a committee that included representatives of business, consumers, federal and provincial government, labor unions, and others.[27] The committee based its work on principles of Fair Information Practices as defined by the OECD in 1980. The process of developing the code took two years.

Subsequent public consultation by the Canadian government found a consensus that the CSA Model Code should be used as the basis for legislation. The Personal Information Protection and Electronic Documents Act (PIPEDA) was enacted in 2000 and became effective on January 1, 2001, for most Canadian private sector commercial activities involving personal information.[28]

PIPEDA took the unusual step of enacting into legislation what is essentially a management standard for data protection. Section 5 of the act requires every covered organization to comply with the obligation of the CSA Model Code as set out in Schedule 1 of the act. In some places, the legislation specifies deviations from the Model Code.

The Model Code and the act include 10 privacy principles based on internationally recognized Fair Information Practices. The 10 principles address (1) accountability; (2) identifying purposes; (3) consent; (4) limiting collection; (5) limiting use, disclosure, and retention; (6) accuracy; (7) safeguards; (8) openness; (9) individual access; and (10) challenging compliance.[29]

The application of PIPEDA to personal data exports to third countries is not expressly stated in the act. Canada may have deliberately chosen not to address this issue, which created so much controversy in Europe, in order to avoid conflicts with the United States, a major trading partner. PIPEDA provides generally that an organization covered by the law is responsible for personal information in its possession or custody. That organization is also responsible for personal information transferred to a third party for processing. A company that exports personal data from Canada for processing must use contractual or other means to provide a comparable level of protection for the data, including when it exports data to a subsidiary. That means that a third-party processor must provide protection that can be compared to the level of protection the personal information would receive if the information had not been transferred. It does not mean that the protections must be the same across the board, but it does mean that they should be generally equivalent. Unlike the EU, Canada makes no centralized attempt to assess the general level of privacy in third countries, and there is no review of individual contracts that involve the export of personal information from Canada.

The lack of detail about data exports in Canadian privacy law may have contributed in part to a 2004 controversy that arose in Canada over the outsourcing of processing of personal information to the United States. In British Columbia, a public outcry arose because outsourced personal information about Canadians would be accessible to U.S. government authorities because the companies hired to undertake the processing activities were located in the United States. The controversy may have been fueled in part by labor union anxiety about the loss of government data processing jobs to the private sector, but the public reaction reflected a broader concern than any union jobs issue. Public attention focused mostly on the USA-PATRIOT Act, a law that passed following the events of 9/11 and that significantly expanded intelligence and law enforcement access to records. The USA-PATRIOT Act was also controversial in the United States, and advocates in Canada used the U.S. controversy for their own purposes. Public fears were sharp enough to draw prompt responses from legislative and policy officials.[30]

In general, the major privacy concern was that personal data exported to the United States would receive less privacy protection than if the data were processed in Canada. A study showed that the actual legal situation covering law enforcement access to some domestic records and to exported records was quite complex and that possible access by U.S. officials to Canadian government personal information was already subject to other laws and agreements. The legislative response focused on outsourcing by the provincial government in British Columbia. Legislation essentially made outsourcing of personal data processing much more difficult or impossible for provincial agencies.[31]

The provincial limitation in British Columbia (and in Nova Scotia as well) adds another level of regulation to the control of transborder data flows of government information about individuals. Provincial controls over data exports joined national controls. It thereby further illustrates how regulations for the transfer of personal information across national borders may need to consider local demands for privacy protection as well as national demands.

Asia Pacific Economic Cooperative

The Asia Pacific Economic Cooperation (APEC) is an intergovernmental grouping of 21 member economies in the Asia Pacific region.[32] Members are Canada, Chile, Chinese Taipei, Hong Kong, Indonesia, Japan, Malaysia, Mexico, New Zealand, Papua New Guinea, the People's Republic of China, the Republic of Korea, Peru, the Republic of the Philippines, the Russian Federation, Singapore, Thailand, the United States, and Vietnam. APEC operates on the basis of nonbinding commitments, open dialogue, and equal respect for the views of all participants. Decisions made within APEC are reached by consensus, and commitments are undertaken on a voluntary basis.

In 2004, APEC adopted a Privacy Framework after two years of development by a Privacy Subcommittee on the APEC Electronic Commerce Steering Group.[33] The APEC privacy approach appears to be an attempt to establish an international privacy regime as an alternative to the standards established by the EU in its Data Protection Directive. The directive's requirement that the privacy regimes of other countries be "adequate" had the effect of seeking to pressure other countries to adopt privacy laws similar to EU standards. In 2001, the EU declined to find Australian privacy law as "adequate," and this action spurred Australian interest in other approaches to international privacy standards. The business community in the United States has also been unhappy about the spread of EU privacy standards to other countries and has been supportive of the APEC alternative. It is unlikely that the APEC privacy efforts would have progressed without U.S. business pressure and support.

The APEC privacy principles are roughly at the same level of generality as the OECD *Guidelines on the Protection of Privacy and Transborder Flows of Personal Data*. The nine principles of the APEC Privacy Framework are (1) preventing harm, (2) notice, (3) collection limitation, (4) uses of personal information, (5) choice, (6) integrity of personal information, (7) security safeguards, (8) access and correction, and (9) accountability. The APEC alternative model of privacy protection emphasizes self-regulation, self-certification, and trust marks.

While APEC covers some of the same ground as OECD, there are some significant differences. The most important difference is with the first principle: preventing harm. There is no comparable principle in the OECD guidelines or in the Data Protection Directive. The APEC *harm* principle appears to reject the European view that privacy is a universal and fundamental human right. The focus on the principle is not on the rights of data subjects but rather on the prevention of misuse of personal information. In the absence of harm, the APEC principles seem to suggest that privacy interests need little or no protection. This is perhaps the most controversial element of the APEC Privacy Framework. The choice principle also has the potential to allow processing activities with less rigor than the EU directive's equivalent and more limited concept of consent. The APEC Privacy Framework also takes a much less prescriptive approach to transborder data flow issues. The accountability principle appears to leave it to a data exporter to take reasonable steps to ensure protection of exported data.

It remains to be seen how the political battle over international privacy standards will play out. Privacy legislation in the APEC region is variable, with some nations adopting comprehensive EU-style privacy laws and fewer nations pursuing elements of the APEC standards. The United States has taken no action to adopt any overarching privacy framework. It seems highly uncertain that the EU will in the near future recognize the APEC privacy framework as meeting its adequacy standards. However, the EU may recognize privacy laws of individual APEC members as adequate.

Privacy Supervision

Hand in hand with the establishment of privacy laws outside the United States has been the development of privacy supervisory offices to oversee and assist with the implementation of the laws. In the EU and elsewhere, national privacy officials, called Data Protection Authorities (DPAs), have become a force in national and international development and implementation of privacy policies.[34] This is another aspect of privacy where the United States has taken a significantly different approach. There is no American official comparable to the DPAs generally found in other nations with privacy laws. In some jurisdictions (e.g., the United Kingdom and Canadian provinces), data protection responsibilities have been combined with supervision of access to record (freedom-of-information) laws.

Article 28 of the Data Protection Directive requires that each EU member state provide for a public authority to monitor application of national privacy laws. The supervisory authority must be consulted by government when rules are being drafted that affect the processing of personal information. In addition, each authority must have investigatory powers, effective powers of intervention (including the power to ban processing of personal information), and the power to engage in legal proceedings where a national law has been violated.

In the EU, it is an express requirement that the privacy supervisory authority be able to act with complete independence. The effect of this requirement is that national privacy offices have some degree of separation from the government that they oversee. In some instances, the privacy supervisory authority takes the form of a collegial body with 3, 4, 10, or as many as 17 (as in France) members; is appointed by, is part of, or reports to a national parliament; or is headed by a single commissioner appointed for a term of years. Many privacy regulators view independence as essential because a privacy supervisory agency must be able to comment on and criticize its own government's activities that affect privacy.

Once again, the EU's approach has been influential worldwide. Most countries outside the EU with national privacy laws also have privacy supervisory authorities with many of the characteristics established in the Data Protection Directive. In Canada, for example, a national privacy commissioner is appointed for a term of seven years and reports directly to the parliament.[35] Canada also has provincial privacy supervisory authorities.[36]

Other countries with provincial authorities include Germany and Australia. Some states in the United States have privacy offices at the state level. A leading example is California's Office of Privacy Protection, which was established in 2000.[37]

Despite the presence of some state-level privacy offices, the United States stands virtually alone among developed nations in not having a national-level privacy agency. The FTC has jurisdiction over some privacy laws (e.g., the Fair Credit Reporting Act and the Children's Online Privacy Protection Act). The FTC's jurisdiction over unfair or deceptive trade practices has been the closest thing to general privacy authority, although there are significant gaps and limits on that authority.[38] The FTC has little or no jurisdiction over the federal government, state governments, or nonprofits. For some financial sector laws, the FTC shares jurisdiction with numerous other federal agencies responsible for various banking activities. Some FTC jurisdiction will migrate to the newly established Consumer Financial Protection Bureau.

Other federal agencies have jurisdiction over other aspects of privacy, such as health (Department of Health and Human Services), education (Department of Education), and communications (Federal Communications Commission). The Department of Commerce oversees the U.S. Safe Harbor Framework with the EU. The Office of Management and Budget has oversight responsibilities for the Privacy Act of 1974, the main privacy law applicable to federal agencies. However, even these assignments of responsibility blur. For example, most health record privacy jurisdiction is split in complex and uneven ways between the Department of Health and Human Services, the Department of Education, and the FTC. Regulatory and enforcement powers of these agencies vary significantly. In short, privacy supervision in the United States is a hard-to-explain pastiche of powers and responsibilities, with many gaps in oversight and regulation.

Other Formal and Informal Supervisory Institutions

The Data Protection Directive established another important privacy institution beyond the national DPAs. Article 29 of the directive created a Working Party on the Protection of Individuals with Regard to the Processing of Personal Data. Members of the Working Party are representatives of the national supervisory authorities. The Article 29 Working Party has been an influential resource for the interpretation of the directive and for the application of data protection principles to new technologies.[39] Working

Party documents have explored the application of data protection principles to social networking, children's privacy, electronic communications, international transportation, search engines, electronic mail, and many other topics. The Working Party documents have had noticeable impacts on businesses based in the United States. Many American multinational Internet companies (e.g., Amazon, Google, and Yahoo!) are subject to privacy laws in multiple countries. For example, Facebook changed some of its business practices in the EU after the Working Group published its document on social networking.

Another EU institution is the European Data Protection Supervisor (EDPS), an office created in 2000.[40] The EDPS is an independent supervisory authority that addressed personal data and privacy matters in EU institutions and bodies. The EDPS advises the European Commission, the European Parliament, and the European Council on proposals for new legislation and other issues with a data protection impact. The EDPS is another important voice and resource in privacy matters.

Each year, the international data protection and privacy commissioners hold an annual conference. In 2009, the thirty-first annual conference was held in Madrid, Spain, hosted by the Spanish Data Protection Agency.[41] The first conference was held in Bonn in 1979. The international conference has been slow to develop a permanent secretariat or even a permanent website. It was only in 2001 that the conference began to accredit members so that the assembled commissioners could adopt resolutions with legitimacy. A national DPA may be a full member if it is established by law with independent status; if the national data protection law is consistent with international principles in OECD, Council of Europe, UN, or EU standards; and if it has broad substantive authority and jurisdiction. The United States had not been given full membership status at the conferences because of the lack of a national privacy official with independent status. However, the United States was allowed to participate in various ways at the conferences short of having full membership. Finally, in 2010, the FTC was admitted as a member despite its jurisdiction limitations.

The commissioners work together to enhance the independence, status, and powers of DPAs around the world. In recent years, the assembled commissioners passed resolutions on current privacy issues and on organizational issues. It is not apparent that these resolutions had much political or other effect.

The commissioners have also been pressing for a global convention establishing binding data protection rules, so far without any success.

The commissioners have been more successful in supporting cooperation among the national DPAs. Spanish, French, and Portuguese DPAs have undertaken direct initiatives with countries that speak the same language to promote data protection. Several Latin American countries (Brazil, Paraguay, and Argentina) have followed the EU lead on data protection and expanded it using the relatively new legal writ of *habeas data*.[42]

Privacy supervisors have been in place long enough to have been headed, in some countries, by five or more generations of leaders. Leadership of the privacy agencies has passed from pioneers of the privacy movement like Spiros Simitis, the head of the privacy office established under the world's first general purpose Data Protection Act enacted by the German state of Hesse in 1970. Later privacy commissioners came from a variety of backgrounds—legal, technical, governmental, business, and media—some with no particular experience or preexisting commitment to privacy. Privacy offices are subject to the ebb and flow of interest and expertise found in other government regulatory activities. Many privacy supervisory agencies publish annual reports that are often a rich source of information, including detailed reviews of annual activities, for most national and provincial privacy offices. However, there is no recent or definitive analysis of the operation of privacy supervisors. It remains uncertain what characteristics, structures, and powers make a privacy supervisory most effective.

The APEC Privacy Framework does not call for a national supervisory agency. The framework's guidance for domestic implementation accommodates various methods of implementation, including through central authorities, multiagency enforcement bodies, a network of designated industry bodies, or a combination. This appears to be a recognition of the inconsistent American approach to privacy supervision.

The idea of privacy supervision has also spread to private companies and other data controllers. The idea originated with the German Data Protection Act, which requires any company or organization with more than nine employees involved in automated data processing to appoint a data protection officer.[43] Many American and multinational companies now have a chief privacy officer, although the powers and placement of the function vary considerably. Some state and local governments also have privacy officers who are often responsible for implementing privacy policies within government rather than undertaking broader privacy policy supervision activities akin to the functions of national DPAs.

Internet Jurisdiction

Basic Issues

In general, jurisdictional questions about the Internet and national laws are complicated, controversial, and far from settled. International jurisdictional matters are not unique to the Internet, of course. International law establishes rules that determine a country's authority to exercise jurisdiction in cases that affect of nonresidents. The Internet undermines the traditional reliance on territorial borders to establish jurisdiction. The same types of issues that arise with online activities have arisen for years with respect to international commerce and communications.

Precedents from those arenas have been used by the courts in an attempt to resolve Internet jurisdictional questions. However, resolution of these questions has been slow to develop and inconsistent. It can take the courts years to develop coherent approach to novel questions of jurisdiction, and with international interest, courts in different countries can reach different results. The Internet has made the questions more pressing and more relevant to activities of individuals as opposed to activities of governments and businesses. Most of the legal complexities of Internet jurisdiction are beyond the scope of this analysis, but an introduction to basic issues follows here.

Jurisdiction questions are not just international. Even within the United States, jurisdictional questions arise when courts in one state need to determine if they have jurisdiction over Internet activities and websites that originated in another state. Some developing law in the United States looks to whether a website engages in passive activity (display but no response to users), integral activity (conducting transactions, receiving orders online, and sending messages directly to customers), or interactive activity (activities in between passive and integral). This analysis illustrates the types of distinctions that courts sometimes use to resolve jurisdictional questions.

The earlier discussion in this chapter about data exports considered one method of writing legislation so that privacy is protected when data are to be transferred to another jurisdiction. Privacy laws can seek to limit exports to other countries with weaker privacy laws so that privacy violations do not occur, or privacy laws can allow exports only if privacy standards are adequate or other forms of relief are available. These approaches help to only a limited degree.

For privacy matters involving online activities, many types of jurisdictional issues can arise. Few have clear answers, and answers can be different in different countries. For example, national policies may differ on whether a contractual clause determining the choice of law and choice of forum is valid in matters involving consumers. Further, the practicalities of international enforcement of rights may make it difficult or impossible for an individual to pursue privacy rights though the courts or administrative bodies in another country.

Does a National Privacy Law Apply to an Internet Activity That Takes Place in Another Country?

Under the Data Protection Directive, a national law applies to data processing that takes place in an establishment in the territory of the member state. This is not a particularly difficult or controversial result. Laws generally apply to actors within the jurisdiction of the government enacting the law. However, under Article 4(1)(c) of the directive, a national law will also apply to a controller not established in the territory of the EU member state if the processing of personal data uses equipment situated in the territory of the member state. An exception covers the use of equipment solely for purposes of transit. If a company in a third country uses computers in an member state for the processing of personal data, that company may fall under the scope of the directive despite the lack of other operations in that member state.

In an Internet context, the use of equipment situated in another country may include something other than the use of a large data processing facility. In an opinion on the Data Protection Directive's application to search engines, the Article 29 Working Party concluded that the setting of a cookie on a user's computer qualifies as the use of equipment in the territory of the member state so that the directive applies.[44] The setting of cookies and other persistent identification elements on a user's computer is commonplace on the Internet, as is the use of JavaScript programs routinely downloaded to and run locally on a user's browser. The Working Party opinion could bring under the scope of the directive a considerable amount of routine Internet activity initiated by organizations and individuals in third countries. How the Working Party's controversial opinion will be treated by national supervisory authorities and courts remains to be seen.

Privacy laws in the United States are often written without much consideration to their possible international effects. One law that expressly has an extraterritorial effect is the Children's Online Privacy Protection Act, which seeks to limit the online collection of personal information from children under the age of 13 without express parental consent.[45] This law applies to any person who operates a commercial website and who collects personal information about visitors to the website, even a website in a foreign nation. However, it remains unclear how or if the law could be enforced against a website operated by an actor who has no presence or other operations in the United States. Other laws that seek to control Internet activities—such as rules seeking to reduce or prevent the sending of spam[46] (unsolicited commercial electronic mail)—face the same enforcement questions for borderless activities. International cooperation is one method that may allow or enhance enforcement, but differences in national laws may inhibit some cooperative efforts.

Can a National Privacy Law Be Enforced by a National Privacy Authority against Persons Outside the Country?

Determining how Canada's PIPEDA applies to Internet activities that take place in other countries has been contested for several years. When considering a complaint in 2005 against an Internet-based U.S. company (Abika.com) that collected information on Canadians and provided individual profiles to its customers, the Office of the Privacy Commissioner initially decided that PIPEDA did not extend to organizations outside Canada, even those who obtained information on Canadians over the Internet. That decision came as somewhat of a surprise to privacy observers. A Canadian court reached a different conclusion in 2007, deciding that the law gave the privacy commissioner jurisdiction to investigate complaints relating to the transborder flow of personal information. This led to another decision by the office in 2009 upholding parts of the original complaint and finding a violation of Canadian law after all.[47]

While much can be said about what this case suggests about Canadian law and about the aggressiveness of the Canadian privacy commissioner, the case illustrates more generally some of the complexities that can arise when applying national laws to companies and events that take place in other countries or in the virtual space of the Internet. In Canada, at least, the basic question of jurisdiction took a long time to resolve, and the resolution may be far from final. Even if the privacy commissioner has jurisdiction under Canadian law over a foreign company, enforcing a decision or taking action against that company may not be simple or possible. A judgment reached in Canada against a U.S. company may or may not be enforceable in American courts.

In 2009, the FTC brought an action against a U.S. company selling products over the Internet to customers in the United Kingdom.[48] The company had a website address that made it appear that the company was located in the United Kingdom. Its actual location in the United States created shipping, warranty, and import problems that customers did not anticipate. The basis for the action was deceptive practices. The FTC was aided in this case by the U.K. Office of Fair Trading, one of several countries that cooperate in the international enforcement of consumer laws.

While the case focused more on deceptive trade practices that did not include overt privacy violations, one element of the complaint was that the company claimed to be participating in the U.S.-EU Safe Harbor Framework. International cooperation overcame the difficulty that the U.K. office would have faced in pursing and enforcing a judgment against an American company. The same type of cooperation can help to pursue privacy cases, which in the United States are sometimes based on the FTC's jurisdiction over unfair and deceptive trade practices. However, international cooperation against bad actors on the Internet may end at the borders of countries that choose not to participate.

Can an Individual Pursue a Privacy Complaint against a Merchant in Another Country?

Online and other activities by a consumer can give rise to violations of privacy that may be actionable in some way. An activity can be a violation of a privacy statute, a violation of a website's stated privacy policy, a violation of a contract, or a tort (e.g., breach of privacy or defamation). It may be possible theoretically for an individual to pursue a complaint in a variety of ways. These include a lawsuit, a complaint filed with a privacy commissioner, a privacy seal program that a website may have subscribed to, or a complaint made directly with the website operator.

Some of these dispute resolution methods (e.g., a complaint to a website operator) may be accessible to the average consumer. Some may require access to tribunals in other countries or use of local languages that would be difficult for most consumers in other countries to find or use. The U.S.-EU Safe Harbor Framework is greatly concerned with the ability of consumers to find remedies that they can pursue when U.S. firms in the Safe Harbor violate the rights of European consumers. However, there has been virtually no use of the Safe Harbor Framework for the adjudication of individual complaints.

Other EU E-Privacy Directives

This section describes several additional EU directives that bear on online privacy matters beyond the omnibus Data Privacy Directive discussed above. Other activities under way at the EU could lead to changes or additions to these directives. Other issues under debate that have a bearing on privacy (as well as other matters) includes the right of a user to a connection to the public communications network at a fixed location and at an affordable price, additional protections against spam, and the rules and procedures (e.g., the need for judicial involvement) applicable to the imposition of restrictions on the fundamental rights and freedoms of an end user to access the Internet.

Directive on Privacy and Electronic Communications

Another EU directive is particularly important to the protection of privacy for electronic communications. In July 2002, the EU adopted a directive on the processing of personal data in the electronic communications sector.[49] The so-called *E-Privacy Directive* sought to update EU law with respect to electronic communications in light of the importance of confidentiality to communications, advanced digital technologies, and changes in traditional market structures brought about by the Internet. One major goal of the E-Privacy Directive was to provide an equal level of privacy protection for personal data and for privacy for users of publicly available electronic communications services regardless of the technologies used and to harmonize the protection throughout the European Community.

The E-Privacy Directive has a similar implementation scheme as Data Protection Directive. Member states must enact national legislation "to ensure the confidentiality of communications and the related traffic data by means of a public communications network and publicly available electronic communications services." The E-Privacy Directive sets the minimum standards for national laws. As with the Data Protection Directive, the E-Privacy Directive allows restrictions on rights when "necessary, appropriate and proportionate" to safeguard national security, defense, public security, and the prevention of criminal offenses or of unauthorized use of the electronic communication system.

The principal provisions of the E-Privacy Directive oblige member states to do the following:

- Require a provider of a publicly available electronic communications service to take appropriate technical and organizational measures to safeguard security of its services, to ensure a level of security appropriate to the risk presented, and to inform a subscriber of a breach of security
- Prohibit listening, tapping, storage, or other kinds of interception or surveillance of communications and the related traffic data by persons other than users without the consent of the users concerned except when legally authorized
- Place limits on the maintenance and use of traffic data (data processed for the purpose of the conveyance of a communication on an electronic communications network or for billing), including an opt-in rule for the purpose of marketing electronic communications services or providing value-added services
- Provide that subscribers have the right to receive nonitemized bills
- Address the rights of calling parties and called parties regarding calling and connected line identification (caller ID)
- Restrict the processing of identifiable location data (e.g., from cellular phones and other devices that provide location-based services) without the consent of the user
- Ensure that subscribers are informed in advance about a printed or electronic directory of subscribers available to the public and that subscribers are given the opportunity

to determine whether their personal data can be included in a public directory
- Require prior consent for unsolicited marketing messages (spam), whether by electronic mail, facsimile, or automated calling systems, with opt-out rights for electronic mail sent for direct-marketing purposes when an electronic address is obtained by a merchant in connection with a transaction without customer refusal for the receipt of messages

The E-Privacy Directive also calls for users to be able to take an opt-out approach to cookies. Users have been provided with clear and precise information on the purposes of cookies and with the opportunity to refuse them. An amendment to the directive adopted in 2009 and effective in 2011 strengthened the rules on cookies. The new provision appears to require user consent, but much ambiguity remains. Consent "may be expressed by using the appropriate settings of a browser or other application." That language may or may not allow browser acceptance of cookies to qualify as consent. Much will depend on how national laws change to comply with the new language and national implementation appears to be proceeding slowly. Another new provision adds security breach notification requirements.

The E-Privacy Directive's restrictions on traffic and location data have been superseded in part by a later directive, the Data Retention Directive, which is discussed in the next section.

EU Data Retention Directive

In March 2006, the EU enacted a directive calling for the mandatory retention of communications traffic data. The Data Retention Directive expressly amended the E-Privacy Directive.[50]

The newer directive requires that member states adopt measures to ensure that electronic communications traffic data and location data generated or processed by providers of publicly available electronic communications services be retained for not less than six months and not more than two years from the date of the communication. The Data Retention Directive requires the retention of data necessary to do the following:

- Trace and identify the source of a communication
- Trace and identify the destination of a communication
- Identify the date, time, and duration of a communication

- Identify the type of communication
- Identify the communication device
- Identify the location of mobile communication equipment

The retention requirement applies only to data generated or processed as a consequence of a communication or a communication service. It does not apply to the content of a telephone call or of electronic mail.

The data must be made available to competent national authorities in specific cases "for the purpose of the investigation, detection and prosecution of serious crime, as defined by each Member State in its national law." This provision allows each member state to establish its own standards for serious crime and its own judicial or other procedures for access.

The Data Retention Directive has been controversial. A leading argument for the directive was that communication data would be necessary in combating terrorism. Passage of the directive was influenced by the July 2005 London bombings and the March 2004 Madrid train bombings. The privacy community strongly opposed the directive and argued that the data would not prevent terrorist acts. Constitutional challenges against the Data Retention Directive succeeded in Romania and Bulgaria, and challenges are pending in other countries. The future of the Data Retention Direction appears to be uncertain.

The WHOIS Database

The operation of the Internet has created a unique set of privacy issues surrounding the registration of Internet domain names. The focus of the debate is on the WHOIS database.[51] The WHOIS database records and identifies the registrant or assignee of Internet resources, such as a website domain name or an Internet Protocol address. The WHOIS system began as a method for system administrators to obtain contact information for Internet Protocol address assignments or domain name administrators. The database includes a considerable amount of information on registrants, including name, address, telephone number, and email address. For individual registrants, a registration record may include personal information.

The information in the WHOIS database is often public and available to any inquirer, although there are differences from one WHOIS server to another. The information in the database, like other personal and business information, can be used for marketing, spam, and other secondary purposes that a registrant may not welcome. However, the data in the WHOIS database have a variety of uses that support Internet activities and related operations. These include assisting with the security and stability of the Internet; combating abusive uses of the Internet, including child pornography, trafficking in human beings, and child abuse; identifying intellectual property infringement; enforcing national laws and international cooperation; and fighting fraud. Some of these secondary uses are controversial.

Domain name registrars offer a privacy service to registrants who want to protect their identities, addresses, phone numbers, and other contact information from being publicly displayed. With this type of *private registration*, these registrars list themselves as the owner of the domain name, thus shielding the personal information of the real owner. One effect is to diminish the value of the WHOIS database as a resource for other purposes. Other issues arise from the application of national privacy laws to domestic registrars, who must nevertheless operate in an international environment.

The Internet Corporation for Assigned Names and Numbers (ICANN), the nonprofit corporation that manages a number of Internet-related tasks, has been forced to establish a policy that provides guidance for a registrar that is legally prevented by local or national privacy laws or regulations from complying with the provisions of the registrar's contract with the corporation regarding the collection, display, and distribution of personal data via WHOIS.[52]

The conflict over the WHOIS database can be described as a fight between those who want increased privacy protections for individuals who have registered domains and those who want WHOIS information to be available for other purposes, at least some of which are socially beneficial. The battle has continued over many years and has not been clearly resolved. Although WHOIS is a uniquely Internet database, the data protection problems that it has created parallel privacy conflicts that arise in other contexts between privacy rights of individuals and governmental and privacy interests in fighting crime, protecting consumers, preventing terrorism, and the like. These issues can arise over any compilation of personal information regardless of location, purpose, and technology.

Notes

1. The Department of Health and Human Services issued health privacy and security rules under authority granted by the Health Insurance Portability and Accountability Act (HIPAA), 42 U.S.C. § 1320d-2 note (section 164(c)). The rules are at 45 C.F.R. Parts 160–164.
2. Cal. Civil Code §§ 1798.29 and 1798.82.
3. The National Conference of State Legislatures maintains a list of state breach notification laws at http://www.ncsl.org/IssuesResearch/TelecommunicationsInformationTechnology/SecurityBreachNotificationLaws/tabid/13489/Default.aspx.
4. 18 U.S.C. § 2710.
5. 47 U.S.C. § 551. See also 47 U.S.C. § 338(i) (privacy rights of satellite subscribers).
6. See, e.g., Mailing List Finder at http://lists.nextmark.com.
7. See International Privacy Laws at http://www.informationshield.com/intprivacylaws.html.
8. http://ec.europa.eu/justice_home/fsj/privacy/law/index_en.htm.
9. See, e.g., European Union Article 29 Data Protection Working Party, Opinion 2/2007 on information to passengers about the transfer of PNR data to U.S. authorities (WP 151), at http://ec.europa.eu/justice_home/fsj/privacy/docs/wpdocs/2008/wp151_en.pdf.
10. World Trade Organization, *General Agreement on Trade in Services*, Article XIV(c)(ii), at http://www.wto.org/english/docs_e/legal_e/26-gats.pdf.
11. http://www.oecd.org/document/18/0,2340,en_2649_34255_1815186_1_1_1_1,00.html.
12. http://conventions.coe.int/Treaty/en/Treaties/Html/108.htm.
13. http://www.unhcr.org/refworld/publisher,UNGA,THEMGUIDE,,3ddcafaac,0.html.
14. http://www.un.org/Overview/rights.html.
15. http://conventions.coe.int/Treaty/en/Treaties/Html/005.htm.
16. *S. and Michael Marper v. The United Kingdom* (nos. 30562/04 and 30566/04) (2008), at http://cmiskp.echr.coe.int/tkp197/view.asp?action=html&documentId=813409&portal=hbkm&source=externalbydocnumber&table=F69A27FD8FB86142BF01C1166DEA398649.
17. For current citations on national data protection laws, see http://www.informationshield.com/intprivacylaws.html.
18. http://ec.europa.eu/justice_home/fsj/privacy/docs/wpdocs/2009/wp163_en.pdf.
19. http://ec.europa.eu/justice_home/fsj/privacy/docs/wpdocs/2008/wp148_en.pdf.
20. See generally European Union, Frequently Asked Questions Relating to Transfers of Personal Data from the EU/EEA to Third Countries,

at http://ec.europa.eu/justice_home/fsj/privacy/docs/international_transfers_faq/international_transfers_faq.pdf.

21. The Department of Commerce's Safe Harbor Web page is at http://www.export.gov/safeharbor/index.asp. The Safe Harbor documents are at http://www.export.gov/safeharbor/eu/eg_main_018493.asp.

22. Federal Trade Commission, *FTC Settles with Six Companies Claiming to Comply with International Privacy Framework* (press release) (October 6, 2009), at http://www.ftc.gov/opa/2009/10/safeharbor.shtm.

23. See, e.g., Galexia, The US Safe Harbor—Fact or Fiction? (December 2008), at http://www.galexia.com/public/research/articles/research_articles-pa08.html.

24. See Düsseldorfer Kreis, http://cdl.niedersachsen.de/blob/images/C63144076_L20.pdf (April 2010) (in German).

25. The Department of Commerce maintains the Swiss Safe Harbor documents at http://www.export.gov/safeharbor/swiss/eg_main_018498.asp.

26. R.S., 1985, c. P-21. The current text is at http://laws.justice.gc.ca/en/P-21/FullText.html.

27. See http://www.csa.ca/cm/ca/en/privacy-code.

28. R.S., ch. 5 (2000). The current text is at http://laws.justice.gc.ca/PDF/Statute/P/P-8.6.pdf.

29. The text of the Model Code is included in Schedule 1 of PIPEDA at http://laws.justice.gc.ca/eng/P-8.6/page-4.html#anchorsc:1.

30. See British Columbia Information and Privacy Commissioner, *Privacy and the USA Patriot Act Implications for British Columbia Public Sector Outsourcing* (2004), at http://www.oipc.bc.ca/sector_public/archives/usa_patriot_act/pdfs/report/privacy-final.pdf.

31. See Freedom of Information and Protection of Privacy Act, [RSBC 1996] Chapter 165, at http://www.oipc.bc.ca/legislation/FIPPA/Freedom_of_Information_and_Protection_of_Privacy_Act%28April%202010%29.htm#section33.1.

32. See http://www.apec.org.

33. http://www.apec.org/apec/news___media/2004_media_releases/201104_apecminsendorseprivacyfrmwk.MedialibDownload.v1.html?url=/etc/medialib/apec_media_library/downloads/ministerial/annual/2004.Par.0015.File.v1.1.

34. For a list of national data protection commissioners, including EU and non-EU commissioners, see http://ec.europa.eu/justice_home/fsj/privacy/nationalcomm/index_en.htm.

35. The website of the office is at http://www.priv.gc.ca/index_e.cfm.

36. A list of provincial offices and websites can be found at http://www.oipc.bc.ca/index.php?option=com_content&view=article&catid=12%3Acontent&id=138%3Auseful-links&Itemid=62.

37. http://www.privacy.ca.gov.

38. See 15 U.S.C. § 45(a)(1).

39. See http://ec.europa.eu/justice_home/fsj/privacy/workinggroup/index_en.htm.

40. See http://www.edps.europa.eu/EDPSWEB.

41. See http://www.privacyconference2009.org/home/index-iden-idweb.html.

42. See generally http://www.habeasdata.org (in Spanish).

43. Section 4f. For an English translation of the German Data Protection Act, see http://www.bdd.de/Download/bdsg_eng.pdf.

44. *Opinion 1/2008 on data protection issues related to search engines* (2008) (WP 148), at http://ec.europa.eu/justice_home/fsj/privacy/docs/wpdocs/2008/wp148_en.pdf.

45. 15 U.S.C. §§ 6501–6504.

46. See, e.g., the CAN-SPAM Act, 15 U.S.C. §§ 7701–7713.

47. Office of the Privacy Commissioner (Canada), letter released about Abika.com, an online data broker in the U.S. (November 18, 2005), at http://www.priv.gc.ca/legislation/let/let_051118_e.cfm; Office of the Privacy Commissioner (Canada), *Report of Findings Complaint under PIPEDA against Accusearch Inc., Doing Business as Abika.com* (July 31, 2009), at http://www.priv.gc.ca/cf-dc/2009/2009_009_rep_0731_e.cfm; *Lawson v. Accusearch Inc. (F.C.)*, 2007 FC 125, (2007) 4 F.C.R. 314 (February 5, 2007), at http://reports.fja.gc.ca/eng/2007/2007fc125/2007fc125.html.

48. See Federal Trade Commission, *Internet Payday Lenders Will Pay $1 Million to Settle FTC and Nevada Charges; FTC Had Challenged Defendants' Illegal Lending and Collection Tactics* (press release) (September 21, 2009), at http://www.ftc.gov/opa/2009/09/cash.shtm.

49. Directive 2002/58/EC of the European Parliament and the European Council of July 12, 2002, concerning the processing of personal data and the protection of privacy in the electronic communications sector, at http://eur-lex.europa.eu/LexUriServ/LexUriServ.do?uri=OJ:L:2002:201:0037:0047:EN:PDF.

50. Directive 2006/24/EC of the European Parliament and the European Council of March 15, 2006, on the retention of data generated or processed in connection with the provision of publicly available electronic communications services or of public communications networks and amending Directive 2002/58/EC, at http://eur-lex.europa.eu/LexUriServ/LexUriServ.do?uri=CELEX:32006L0024:EN:HTML.

51. http://www.whois.net.

52. ICANN Procedure for Handling WHOIS Conflicts with Privacy Law (January 17, 2008), at http://www.icann.org/en/processes/icann-procedure-17jan08.htm.

4

Chronology of Online Privacy

1791 Reacting to concerns that the Constitution did not do enough to protect fundamental human liberties, the United States adopts the Bill of Rights as amendments to the Constitution. Parts of the First, Third, Fourth, Fifth, and Ninth Amendments relate to privacy protection, with the Fourth Amendment containing the most important single limitation against unwarranted government intrusion and against unreasonable searches and seizures of houses, papers, and effects.

1890 Samuel D. Warren and Louis D. Brandeis publish in the *Harvard Law Review* an article titled "The Right to Privacy." This article marks an early attempt to define privacy, to address the consequences of new technology (in this case, unposed photographs), and to provide a legal remedy.

1914 Congress passes the Federal Trade Commission Act, a major law designed to provide protections to consumers. The act establishes the Federal Trade Commission (FTC), makes unfair or deceptive acts or practices in or affecting commerce unlawful, and gives the commission the ability to enforce the law.

1928 The Supreme Court decides *Olmstead v. United States*, finding that the use of wiretaps by government agents on telephone lines without a judicial warrant does not violate the Constitution's Fourth Amendment

1928 (*cont.*) provision against unreasonable searches and seizures. Justice Louis Brandeis dissents, arguing that constitutional protections must adapt to new technology.

1948 The United Nations adopts the Universal Declaration of Human Rights, with a right to privacy included as part of Article 12.

1949 George Orwell publishes *1984*, a dystopian novel that envisions a world where government surveillance of the population is constant.

1950 The Council of Europe adopts the European Convention for the Protection of Human Rights and Fundamental Freedoms, an international convention that defines civil and political rights of individuals. Article 8 of the European Convention addresses respect for private and family life.

1964 Vance Packard publishes *The Naked Society*, an early, broad, and popular look at the effects on personal privacy of government and business activities.

1967 The Supreme Court decides *Katz v. United States*, deciding for the first time that, under the Fourth Amendment to the Constitution, a judicial warrant is required before a government agent can wiretap a telephone conversation. The decision overturns the 1928 decision in *Olmstead v. United States* and largely adopts the dissenting views of Justice Brandeis from that case.

1968 In response to the Supreme Court's 1967 decision in *Katz v. United States*, Congress ends decades of legislative gridlock and passes a law establishing rules and procedures for the use of wiretapping by the government. The law is the Omnibus Crime Control and Safe Streets Act of 1986.

1970 After a series of hearings documenting how important credit reports have become to an individual's ability to live in modern society and how little control

1970 (*cont.*) consumers have over the information in their credit reports, Congress passes the Fair Credit Reporting Act. This is the first modern information privacy law ever enacted and provides consumers with meaningful rights to see and correct information held by credit bureaus.

1970 The German state of Hesse becomes the first jurisdiction anywhere to enact a general data protection law.

1973 The Advisory Committee on Automated Personal Data Systems at the Department of Health and Human Services issues a report, *Records, Computers, and the Rights of Citizens*. Willis Ware of the RAND Corporation is chair of the committee. The report proposes Fair Information Practices as fundamental principles for personal information record keeping and recommends passage of privacy law for federal agencies, a law that becomes the Privacy Act of 1974.

1974 Congress enacts the Family Education Rights and Privacy Act, a law regulating the privacy of records at schools and colleges that receive federal funds. The law is sometimes called the *Buckley Amendment* after its sponsor, Senator James Buckley.

1974 The Privacy Act of 1974, a law that requires federal agencies and some federal contractors to comply with a specified set of Fair Information Practices, is signed into law by President Gerald Ford. The legislation is based in part on extensive investigations into federal agency record-keeping practices held in the early 1970s by Senator Sam Ervin, chairman of the Senate Committee on Constitutional Rights. The act also seeks to restrict federal, state, and local agencies from requiring the disclosure of Social Security numbers by individuals. The Social Security number provision is the first legislative restriction on Social Security numbers.

1974 *Privacy Journal* is founded by Robert Ellis Smith. *Privacy Journal*, the first publication of its kind focusing

1974 (*cont.*) exclusively on privacy, is a monthly newsletter that has been continuously published since 1974.

1975 Perhaps the first true personal computer (Sphere 1) is marketed by computer pioneer Michael D. Wise. The computer included a keyboard, a number pad, and a monitor.

1976 The Supreme Court decides in *United State v. Miller* that bank customers have no constitutional right to privacy with respect to records held by banks. Therefore, the government can obtain those records without notice to the customer or a search warrant. The case suggests that there is no constitutional right to privacy in personal information held by third-party record keepers.

1977 Inger Hansen is appointed as the first privacy commissioner for Canada following passage of the Canadian Human Rights Act.

1977 The Privacy Protection Study Commission, a temporary study commission established by the Privacy Act of 1974, issues a report titled *Protection Privacy in an Information Society.* The commission recommends establishment of a permanent federal privacy entity and the enactment of numerous individual bills giving individuals privacy rights with respect to records maintained by health care providers, insurers, and others. The report receives some immediate congressional attention, but, like the reports of many similar study commissions, few of its recommendations are adopted.

1978 Reacting to the Supreme Court's 1976 decision in *U.S. v. Miller,* Congress enacts the Right to Financial Privacy Act of 1978. The law gives bank customers limited privacy rights in their banks records by preventing federal agencies from obtaining the records without notice to the customer and legal process. The law gives bank customers narrow grounds to oppose a government demand and, in addition, includes numerous exceptions and limitations.

1980 The Organisation for Economic Cooperation and Development publishes the *OECD Guidelines on the Protection of Privacy and Transborder Flows of Personal Data.* These guidelines recommend that member states adopt national laws based on Fair Information Practices to protect privacy and to remove unjustified obstacles to transborder flows of personal data. More uniform privacy rules are intended to achieve both objectives.

1981 *Privacy Times* began publication in Washington, D.C., with Evan Hendricks as editor. *Privacy Times* is a privacy-focused newsletter that covers privacy and freedom of information activities of federal agencies and private companies.

1981 In 1981, the Council of Europe adopts the Convention for the Protection of Individuals with Regard to Automatic Processing of Personal Data. The convention encourages member states to enact legislation concerning the automatic processing of personal data via computers. The convention relies on Fair Information Practices as core principles for defining information privacy.

1984 Congress includes in the Cable Communications Policy Act of 1984 a provision addressing the privacy of cable subscriber information. The law requires a privacy notice for subscribers and strictly limits disclosure of personal information about subscribers, including information on viewing habits. The law includes a private right of action for subscribers.

1984 Caller ID, which transmits a caller's number to the called party's telephone equipment while the telephone is ringing, is offered for the first time. The new service sparks a widespread debate about the rights of the caller and the called party. The controversy lasts a few years and then dissipates.

1986 Congress enacts the Computer Fraud and Abuse Act of 1986, criminalizing unauthorized access into or theft of computer data. The law applies to computers

1986 (*cont.*) of the federal government, financial institutions, and those affecting interstate and foreign commerce.

1986 Congress enacts the Electronic Communications Privacy Act of 1986, which amends and updates laws on wiretapping. It also establishes for the first time in statute specific rules and procedures regulating government access to electronic communications, including electronic mail. The law makes a distinction between electronic mail in transit and electronic mail in storage.

1987 The nomination of Robert Bork to be a Supreme Court justice generates tremendous controversy. One reporter obtains a list of movies that Bork rented from his local video store. Members of Congress are unhappy about the disclosures and respond by quickly enacting the Video Privacy Protection Act of 1988. The law prevents videotape service providers from disclosing the names of videos rented or purchased by any individual.

1988 After hearings documenting due process abuses of the results of computer matching activities that involve the automated comparison of records about individuals, Congress enacts the Computer Matching and Privacy Protection Act of 1988. As an amendment to the Privacy Act of 1974, the matching law regulates some but not all federal government matching activities. The law requires federal agencies involved in matching activities to establish data integrity boards to oversee the activities.

1990 Tim Berners-Lee invents the World Wide Web at the European Particle Physics Laboratory in Switzerland. The first Web experiments go live in 1991 on the Swiss computer server info.cern.ch.

1990 In July, the Electronic Frontier Foundation is formed by Mitch Kapor, John Perry Barlow, and John Gilmore. Initial funding comes from Kapor and Steve Wozniak, cofounder of Apple Computers.

1991 Congress passes the Telephone Consumer Protection Act of 1991 to limit the use of automatic dialing systems, artificial or prerecorded voice messages, text messages received by cell phones, and unsolicited advertisements sent by fax machines. The Federal Communications Commission is given regulatory authority.

1992 The Privacy Rights Clearinghouse, a nonprofit consumer organization that offers consumers information about privacy and that undertakes consumer advocacy, is founded in San Diego, California, by Beth Givens.

1992 Newcastle, United Kingdom, becomes one of the first cities in England to install citywide closed-circuit television that integrates wirelessly to the local police station.

1993 Mosaic, the first Web browser to achieve widespread use is released in February by the National Center for Supercomputing Applications at the University of Illinois at Urbana-Champaign.

1993 The Clinton administration issues Presidential Decision Directive 5 on Public Encryption Management. The proposal for key escrow for encryption codes and for use of the Clipper chip sparks tremendous controversy and public debate, but it is never embraced by industry.

1994 Mark Rotenberg founds the Electronic Privacy Information Center in Washington, D.C.

1994 Reacting in part to the death of a television actress who was stalked and killed by a fan who found her address from a public record at the California Department of Motor Vehicles, Congress enacts the Drivers Privacy Protection Act, a law to regulate the disclosure of motor vehicle records by state motor vehicle agencies.

1994 Congress enacts the Communications Assistance for Law Enforcement Act to enhance the ability of law

1994 (*cont.*) enforcement and intelligence agencies to conduct electronic surveillance by requiring that telecommunications carriers and manufacturers of telecommunications equipment modify and design their equipment, facilities, and services to ensure that they have surveillance capabilities that will allow federal agencies to monitor digital telephone networks in real time. The act is controversial, especially among Internet activists.

1995 After five years of work and controversy, the European Union (EU) adopts Data Privacy Directive EU 95/46/EC. The directive seeks to harmonize different data protection regimes among member states and requires member states to adopt national laws that meet minimum standards. The goal is to protect individual privacy and to support the free flow of personal information across national borders. The directive immediately becomes the most important international influence on privacy laws of other countries.

1995 Beth Givens of the Privacy Rights Clearinghouse publishes an early report spotlighting identity theft as a growing threat to consumer privacy and providing advice to consumers who want to protect themselves.

1996 Congress passes the Telecommunications Act of 1996 and includes for the first time restrictions on the use and disclosure of customer proprietary network information by telephone carriers.

1996 Congress includes a privacy requirement in the Health Insurance Portability and Accountability Act of 1996. Privacy is seen as an essential counterpart to the act's administrative simplification provisions that seek to standardize and increase the use of electronic health care transactions. The law authorizes the Department of Health and Human Services to issue a health privacy rule if Congress fails to act within three years.

1997 Major amendments to the Fair Credit Reporting Act take effect, requiring creditors and others that furnish information to credit reporting agencies to ensure the accuracy of the information they supply. In addition, credit bureaus must provide greater rights to consumers who dispute information in their credit files.

1998 Congress passes the Children's Online Privacy Protection Act providing protections for personally identifiable online information about children under the age of 13. The law assigns the FTC to write regulations.

1998 The EU Data Privacy Directive goes into effect. The directive's limit on the export of personal data from EU member states to third countries that do not have "adequate" protections becomes the focus of much international attention.

1998 Congress passes the Identify Theft Assumption and Deterrence Act, a law that makes it a crime to transfer identification of another person with intent to violate the law. Many states also begin to pass statutes to address the growing problem of identity theft by providing consumers more rights, limiting disclosure of public records, and making prosecutions of criminals easier.

1999 Congress enacts the Gramm-Leach-Bliley Act, a major financial reform law that includes some privacy protections for consumers of financial institutions. The act requires financial institutions to provide privacy notices to customers and gives customers limited rights to opt out of the use and disclosure of their information.

1999 President Clinton appoints Ohio State University law professor Peter Swire as the first chief counselor for privacy in the Office of Budget and Management. The position continues to the end of the Clinton administration.

1999 In November, the FTC holds the first workshop on privacy and online profiling of consumers.

1999 In July, the Network Advertising Initiative is given the go-ahead by the FTC. It is the first self-regulatory program for online privacy and advertising. The term "opt-out cookie" is born, meaning a cookie placed on a user's computer that tells a specific website that the user does not want to be profiled.

2000 The FBI's Carnivore surveillance system comes to public attention and ignites significant public opposition from privacy and public interest groups concerned about online and telecommunications privacy. The FBI installed Carnivore on the computers of Internet service providers to monitor email communications and Web traffic. The FBI contends that its system obtains only information that it is authorized to receive. The Carnivore system is renamed by the FBI and eventually abandoned.

2000 The California legislature enacts a law creating the California Office of Privacy Protection. When established the following year, the office becomes one of the first formal governmental privacy offices in the United States.

2000 California Senator Liz Figueroa introduces Senate Bill 1607, a bill to require consumer reporting agencies and those who use credit scores in making loans to make credit scores to consumer. Prior to the bill's enactment, credit scores were considered secret and were not available to consumers directly. Credit scores promptly become well known to consumers.

2000 Canada's Personal Information Protection and Electronic Documents Act becomes law. Some of the provisions of the act, the first general purpose privacy law applicable to the private sector in Canada, were influenced by the requirements of the EU Data Protection Directive.

2000 DoubleClick, a prominent online ad network, suspends its controversial practice of matching online consumer Web browsing habits with home addresses and other offline personal information. The suspension follows protests by privacy groups and the announcement of an FTC investigation. The controversy arose after DoubleClick acquired the offline catalog information company Abacus in 1999.

2000 The United States and the EU establish a Safe Harbor Framework that allows U.S. companies to self-certify that they meeting the requirements of the framework. A European organization is permitted to export personal data to a U.S. company in the Safe Harbor without violating the data export limitations of the EU Data Protection Directive. Enforcement of the Safe Harbor is supposed to be provided by the FTC. The Safe Harbor Framework is eventually questioned over the degree to which companies in the Safe Harbor are actually in compliance.

2000 The online company Toysmart files for bankruptcy and proposes to sell its customer list despite a privacy policy that banned disclosure of customer names. The FTC intervenes and obtains a limit on the sale of the list. State attorneys general also intervene, seeking to fully enforce the no-sale promise. Eventually, the list is destroyed. The case highlights the possibility of enforcement of privacy policies and the threat that bankruptcy poses to those policies.

2000 The International Association of Privacy Professionals is founded as a global professional association for the privacy community. It eventually becomes the leading organization of its type for privacy professionals and offers a certification for privacy professionals.

2000 Real Networks's online music organizing and listening software is found to be scanning more than 13 million of its customers' hard drives and collecting users' musical preferences without the consent of users.

2001 President George W. Bush signs the Uniting and Strengthening America by Providing Appropriate Tools Required to Intercept and Obstruct Terrorism Act of 2001 into law October 26, 2001. This broad and complex law is a response to the terrorism events of September 11, 2001. The act dramatically increases the authority of U.S. law enforcement agencies to obtain data from telecommunications, the Internet, medical and financial records, and other data sources for both law enforcement and foreign intelligence purposes. The law includes an expansion of wiretapping authority, reduces the need for court orders to obtain personal records from third-party record keepers, and otherwise affects privacy protections previously available. The act is immediately controversial for many of its provisions.

2002 The EU adopts its Directive on Privacy and Electronic Communications. The directive is designed, among other things, to reduce spam and to control the use of cookies by Internet websites.

2002 The creator of the Melissa virus, which shut down Internet mail systems clogged with infected emails and caused tens of millions of dollars in damages, pleads guilty to both federal and state criminal charges resulting from his actions and is sentenced to up to 10 years in prison.

2002 The federal government begins the Total Information Awareness project, which is designed to merge information from government and commercial databases for use in identifying terrorists. The project becomes intensely controversial because of its scope and because of its sponsor, Admiral John Poindexter, former national security adviser to President Ronald Reagan. Congress defunds the program, but other similar programs continue under other names. Congress eventually enacts a data mining reporting law to bring more federal data mining activities to public scrutiny.

2002 California enacts the first data security breach legislation in the United States, requiring record keepers to disclose improper disclosures to data subjects. The legislation serves as a model for other states.

2002 In the Department of Homeland Security Act, Congress directs the department to designate a senior official to assume responsibility for privacy. The act includes the first U.S. statutory reference to Fair Information Practices. The creation of the department's privacy office encourages other federal agencies to create or enhance privacy offices.

2003 California enacts the California Online Privacy Protection Act. It is one of the first states to enact a law requiring certain businesses with websites to post a privacy policy.

2003 The health privacy rule issued by the Department of Health and Human Services under the authority of the Health Insurance Portability and Accountability Act takes effect for the first time in April. The rule establishes a floor of privacy protection that all health plans and nearly all health care providers must meet. Stronger state laws remain in effect.

2003 In June, the FTC begins operation of a National Do Not Call Registry in compliance with the Do-Not-Call Implementation Act of 2003. The start of the registry is briefly delayed by litigation brought by the telesales industry, but Congress quickly passes a law granting the FTC specific jurisdiction. Millions of Americans quickly sign up to be taken off telemarketing lists.

2003 The Controlling the Assault of Non-Solicited Pornography and Marketing Act of 2003 passes. The legislation includes a narrowly limited right of action for spam, and it preempts many state antispam laws. Both the FTC and the Federal Communications Commission are assigned enforcement responsibility for the act.

2003 Congress passes the Fair and Accurate Credit Transactions Act of 2003, a major amendment to the Fair Credit Reporting Act. Among other changes, the act allows consumers to obtain a free credit report every 12 months from each of the three nationwide consumer credit reporting companies. The act also addresses identify theft by giving consumers additional rights.

2004 The three national credit bureaus begin offering free annual credit reports to consumers. The program, operated at http://www.annualcreditreport.com, is the first time most consumers have the legal right to get credit reports each year free of charge.

2004 Executive Order 13335 is signed by President George W. Bush in April. The order establishes the position of the national health information technology coordinator within the Department of Health and Human Services. The executive order leads the first major official push toward electronic health care records and online distribution and sharing of those records.

2004 Google launches its Gmail email program. The email program allows Google to scan users' emails and integrate advertising in the emails on the basis of content. Thirty-one privacy and civil liberties organizations object to the program and ask for changes, Google ignores the campaign and goes forward without addressing the privacy issues raised by the groups.

2004 California and Utah enact the first laws regulating and prohibiting spyware. Among other things, the California law makes it illegal to transmit a computer virus, use a computer in a denial of service attack, or install computer software on a user's computer when the user declines an option. Utah's stronger law was enjoined by a judge.

2004 The Asian-Pacific Economic Cooperation ministers adopt the APEC Privacy Framework to promote

2004 (*cont.*) information privacy protection and the free flow of information in the Asia-Pacific region. The framework is seen as an attempt to create international privacy principles to compete with the EU.

2005 Congress changes the bankruptcy law to add a process designed to consider the privacy of individuals when a debtor had promised to limit the transfer of personal information through a privacy policy.

2005 In February, data broker ChoicePoint notifies about 35,000 Californians of a data breach that resulted from access to ChoicePoint records by criminals who used stolen identities to create businesses that allowed them access with the goal of engaging in identity theft. Only after other state attorneys general demand breach notification for their affected consumers does the company notify 111,000 consumers outside California. It was the first major notification made under the California data breach law. The incident makes apparent the difference in legal obligation between states that have breach notification laws and those that do not. The broad national attention to the breach encourages legislators in other states to propose and enact breach notification laws.

2005 The FTC brings an enforcement action against a credit bureau, Experian, for a website, freecreditreport.com, that misled consumers about its relationship with the annual free credit report program.

2005 The federal REAL ID Act of 2005 passes, establishing numerous requirements for state driver's licenses and ID cards. The act draws major opposition from privacy groups, consumer groups, and the states. Controversy erupts over the cost of the program, the unfunded mandate imposed on state motor vehicle departments, and the privacy consequences of an enhanced driver's license. Privacy concerns center on the prospect that REAL ID would create a de facto national ID card for U.S. citizens. Many states resist or refuse compliance with REAL ID.

2006 The term "medical identity theft" is coined in a World Privacy Forum report that describes and documents this crime for the first time. Medical identity theft occurs when someone uses an individual's name and sometimes other parts of their identity, such as insurance information, without the person's knowledge or consent to obtain medical services or goods or uses the person's identity information to make false claims for medical services or goods.

2006 Congress enacts the Telephone Records and Privacy Protection Act of 2006, making it a crime to engage in pretexting to buy, sell, or obtain personal phone records, except when conducted by law enforcement or intelligence agencies.

2006 The Department of Justice brings its first botnet case to trial. A botnet is an army of compromised computers used without the knowledge of their owners to launch destructive attacks, to send huge quantities of spam across the Internet, or to receive surreptitious installations of adware. The case results in a guilty plea and a sentence of nearly five years in prison.

2006 A series of new stories reveals that the international banking network Society for Worldwide Interbank Financial Telecommunication had been transferring customer data to U.S. law enforcement agencies contrary to privacy laws in the EU, resulting in a significant international privacy controversy.

2006 The Electronic Frontier Foundation sues AT&T for violating the Foreign Intelligence Surveillance Act because of AT&T's undisclosed wiretapping of U.S. customers for the National Security Administration. According to the lawsuit, the wiretapping was conducted without warrants and included terabytes of information on calls dating from 2001. In 2008, acting at the request of the Bush administration that conducted the wiretaps, Congress passes a law granting retroactive immunity to telecommunications companies for past violations

2006 (*cont.*) of the act, and the lawsuit is dismissed by the federal district court.

2006 The FTC brings an enforcement action against ChoicePoint, a data broker, because of its highly publicized data breach of consumers' information, and the FTC and ChoicePoint enter into a consent decree to resolve the complaint.

2007 Google announces that it has agreed to purchase the online advertising company DoubleClick for $3.1 billion.

2007 The FTC brings another enforcement action against credit bureau Experian for violating the consent decree in the 2005 case for misleading consumers.

2007 In July 2007, the United States and the EU reach an agreement over the exchange of passenger name records about air travelers. The agreement set the terms for exchanging passenger name records information between the countries. The agreement does not end the controversy over the disclosure of passenger name records to the United States.

2007 A two-day Berkeley meeting of U.S. privacy groups in October results in a Do Not Track proposal for online advertising. The idea is based on the successful Do Not Call Registry established for telemarketing calls. The groups submit the proposal to the FTC in October and discuss it at an FTC workshop on online behavioral advertising. This is the first proposal of a Do Not Track idea for websites.

2007 Facebook launches its Beacon program, an intrusive online ad program that raises immediate privacy concerns and problems. A large public outcry and grassroots campaign by Facebook users convinces Facebook to make the intrusive advertising program optional. The Beacon service is eventually closed entirely.

2007 Google Street View launches in the United States. Street View eventually expands worldwide. Initial controversies involve photos that reveal faces and vehicle license plate numbers, and Street View eventually suppresses these features. Street View remains highly controversial for years in many countries.

2007 Several Internet service providers in the United States, Canada, and the United Kingdom are found to be inspecting customer traffic for the purpose of making decisions about online advertising on the customer's computer. This practice, called deep packet inspection, became instantly controversial. Many Internet service providers dropped the practice under public pressure.

2008 The Department of Homeland Security issues its final regulations for the REAL ID plan, a law that seeks to enhance U.S. driver's licenses with biometric and other information. Numerous states continue to resist implementing the regulations, and the future of REAL ID remains in doubt.

2009 Civil society organizations publish the Madrid Declaration. The document reaffirms support for a global framework for privacy based on Fair Information Practices and calls for the establishment of a new international framework for privacy protection based on the rule of law. More than 100 leading privacy experts and 100 organizations worldwide sign the Madrid Declaration.

2010 In April, Germany announces publicly that Google Street View has been collecting information via WiFi, or wireless, networks. During the course of 2010, Google is investigated by numerous countries and U.S. states for its Street View activities that captured users' passwords, emails, and other information without notice or permission. The incident becomes known as the Google "Wi Spy" fiasco, and it results in congressional calls for action.

2010 The Supreme Court decides *City of Ontario v. Quon*, a case involving the privacy of text messages under the Stored Communications Act (a part of the Electronic Communications Privacy Act). In resolving the case, the Court observes that rapid changes in the dynamics of communication and information transmission are evident not just in the technology itself but also in what society accepts as proper behavior, and the Court cautions against making broad rulings prematurely.

2010 India launches its first biometric census of citizens over the age of 15. The census is to include photos and fingerprints, and plans are for the data to be linked to a national ID card.

2010 The National Institute of Standards and Technology publishes guidelines for privacy and security for the smart grid, an electricity network utilizing digital technology. A smart grid delivers electricity to consumers using two-way digital communications to control appliances at consumers' homes and has the potential to collect information on activities within a house that use electricity. The privacy implications of the smart grid become n a focus of attention by privacy groups.

2010 The Transportation Security Administration faces national public outcry over its use of electronic full-body scanners in airports. November 24 is designated as National Opt Out Day. Results of the opt out are uncertain, as the administration apparently did not use the controversial scanners in many locations.

2010 The FTC approves a consent agreement with an online data broker. The proposed settlement requires the data broker to honor its online privacy policy promising removal of consumer information from some online searches if a particular service was purchased and to make refunds to consumers who paid for the service.

2010 The international group of data protection commissioners admits the FTC into membership, the first time that any U.S. government agency achieves that status.

2010 The European Article 29 Data Protection Working Party formally criticizes Facebook for its privacy settings in May, leading to changes in privacy at Facebook. The Working Party also adopts a formal opinion that opt out is insufficient consent for behavioral advertising and said that opt in was the proper standard under the revised EU e-privacy standard.

2010 The FTC releases a preliminary staff report on online privacy that shows some support for the adoption of a Do Not Track list for online targeted ads. The Department of Commerce and the Internet Policy Task Force also issue a green paper on data privacy and the Internet.

2010 Minnesota passes one of the first state laws to require Internet service providers to keep certain customer data private and to get permission from subscribers before disclosing information about the subscribers' online surfing habits and Internet sites visited. Nevada passed a similar but less stringent law in 2009.

2010 Congress enacts the Social Security Number Protection Act of 2010, the latest in a long series of state and federal laws that seek to restrict the use and disclosure of Social Security numbers in government activities and in commerce. The new law prohibits federal, state, or local agencies from displaying a Social Security number on agency checks. The law takes effect in 2013.

2011 Reports that the Apple iPhone is maintaining location information in an undisclosed file on each iOS4 phone creates controversy, highlighting the sensitivity of location information on cell phones and other mobile devices that connect to the Internet.

5

Biographical Sketches

J. Howard Beales III

Howard Beales is associate professor of strategic management and public policy at George Washington University. His research interests include consumer protection regulatory issues, including privacy, law, and economics, and the regulation of advertising. He is an active scholar on these subjects. From 2001 through 2004, Dr. Beales served as the director of the Bureau of Consumer Protection at the Federal Trade Commission (FTC). He was appointed to the position by FTC Chairman Timothy Muris, who was an appointee of President George W. Bush. Beales previously worked at the FTC in various capacities as well as at the Office of Information and Regulatory Affairs in the Office of Management and Budget. He has a PhD in economics from the University of Chicago, which he earned in 1978. Notably, while serving as Consumer Protection Bureau director, Beales was involved with the implementation of the national Do Not Call Registry to stop unwanted telemarketing calls. The FTC opposed the creation of a Do Not Spam list. Beales was also involved with the development and implementation of the Fair and Accurate Credit Transactions Act of 2003. He worked to redirect the commission's approach to privacy to focus on consequences of information use and misuse. This position, with its focus on harms rather than on the rights of consumers, was controversial within the privacy advocacy community, although it was better received by the business community.

Jerry Berman

Jerry Berman is the founder and chairman of the Board of the Center for Democracy and Technology (CDT), an Internet public policy organization established in Washington, D.C., in December 1994. CDT has become a leading voice on democracy and civil liberties on the Internet, with a focus on privacy, free speech, Internet governance, and related matters. Berman served as CDT's original executive director. Prior to founding CDT, Berman was a director of the Electronic Frontier Foundation. From 1978 to 1988, he was chief legislative counsel at the American Civil Liberties Union (ACLU), where he started the ACLU Projects on Privacy and Information Technology. Berman is also president and chairman of the board of the Internet Education Foundation, a nonprofit based in Washington, D.C., supported by Internet companies and public interest groups to educate policymakers and the public about the commercial and democratic potential of the Internet. Berman also chairs the Advisory Committee to the Congressional Internet Caucus, a bipartisan group that seeks to increase congressional understanding of the Internet. Berman's work contributed significantly to privacy legislation, including the Foreign Intelligence Surveillance Act, the Electronic Communications Privacy Act of 1986, the cable television subscriber privacy statute, the Electronic Freedom of Information Act Amendments of 1996, and other laws affecting the Internet and telecommunications. However, his support for the Communications Assistance for Law Enforcement Act of 1994 created controversy within the privacy advocacy community. Berman has a law degree from the University of California, Berkeley. Berman has been effective throughout his career in bringing together companies, activists, trade associations, and other representing different points of view and finding consensus on legislative and policy matters.

Louis Brandeis

Louis Brandeis was a U.S. Supreme Court justice from 1916 to 1939. Along with Samuel Warren, Brandeis wrote "The Right to Privacy" in the *Harvard Law Review* in 1890, arguing that "existing law affords a principle which can properly be invoked to protect the privacy of the individual; and, if it does, what the nature and extent of such protection is." The article was inspired in part by the then new technology of "instant" (not formally posed) photography. The article's influence on the development of privacy law and scholarship is immense. In 1928, Brandeis dissented from the Supreme Court's decision in *Olmstead v. United States*, in which the Court declined to find a violation of the Fourth Amendment to the Constitution when federal government agents wiretapped an individual's telephone conversation without first obtaining a search warrant from a judge. Brandeis wrote that the Constitution protected "as against the Government, the right to be let alone—the most comprehensive of rights, and the right most valued by civilized men" and that constitutional protections must adapt to new technologies. Nearly 40 years later, the Supreme Court decided *Katz v. United States* (1967) and found that the Fourth Amendment did protect against government eavesdropping without a warrant. *Katz* overturned the ruling in *Olmstead* and adopted much of Brandeis's view of the Fourth Amendment. One measure of the importance of Brandeis to privacy is that his original *Harvard Law Review* article is perhaps the most cited law journal article ever written.

Julie Brill

Julie Brill has a long and distinguished career in public service oriented toward consumer protection. Many of her activities have had a substantial privacy focus, often coinciding with online and other technology issues. She has had a significant impact on data breach notification regulation as well as health privacy issues and issues relating to the Fair Credit Reporting Act. In 2010, Brill was appointed by President Barack Obama to be a commissioner at the Federal Trade Commission (FTC). Prior to that, she served as senior deputy attorney general and chief of consumer protection for the State of North Carolina, a post she held for one year. For the previous 20 years, Brill was the assistant attorney general of the Consumer Protection Division of the Vermont Attorney General's Office. While in Vermont, Brill was noted for her work on pharmaceutical privacy for consumers and physicians, among other issues. She also actively coordinated privacy matters with other the offices of other state attorneys general. She has received numerous awards for her consumer and privacy protection work, including a Brandeis award from Privacy International in 2001 and a Marvin award from the National Association of Attorneys General in 1995. Brill received her BA from Princeton University and holds a JD from New York University School of Law. She has been a lecturer in law at Columbia Law School. Privacy advocates expect that her appointment to the FTC will strengthen the agency's activities on privacy.

Jeff Chester

Jeff Chester is the executive director of the Center for Digital Democracy (http://www.democraticmedia.org), a nonprofit advocacy group based in Washington, D.C. Chester, a former social worker, is a notably effective advocate. His group is funded primarily by foundation grants and other nonindustry sources of funding. He is the author of *Digital Destiny: New Media and the Future of Democracy.* Chester formerly was cofounder of the Center for Media Education (CME). During his tenure at the CME, Chester's focus was on children's online privacy. His efforts were integral to passage of the landmark Children's Online Privacy Protection Act. Chester has also been extremely active in championing consumer's rights in the area of behaviorally targeted advertising online. His organization submitted a lengthy complaint to the Federal Trade Commission (FTC) about behaviorally targeted advertising. While the FTC never formally acted on the complaint, it nevertheless appears to have an influence because the FTC later had workshops on the subject, issued an updated set of policy guidelines, and generally showed rekindled interest in self-regulatory efforts by industry groups. Chester's efforts have also sparked congressional interest in legislation to give consumers more rights in the area of online advertising. Chester has played an important role in the privacy advocacy community by organizing and mobilizing groups on issues pertaining to online privacy and by publicizing hidden aspects of current online business practices affecting privacy.

Lorrie Faith Cranor

Lorrie Faith Cranor is associate professor of computer science and engineering and public policy at Carnegie Mellon University. She is also director of the CyLab Usable Privacy and Security Laboratory (CUPS) at Carnegie Mellon. She has a doctorate degree in engineering and policy from Washington University. Cranor led the team at the World Wide Web Consortium that developed the Platform for Privacy Preferences (P3P), a standard way for websites to communicate about their privacy practices. She wrote a book on P3P, *Web Privacy with P3P*, and she led the development of the Privacy Bird P3P user agent and the Privacy Finder P3P search engine. It is not clear, however, that P3P has been successful in the marketplace with consumers, and Cranor's later research highlighted some of the marketplace failures of P3P. Her other work addresses privacy decision making, supporting trust decisions (focused on antiphishing), user-controllable security and privacy (including location-sharing privacy and file access control in the home), and modeling "the human in the loop." Work at CUPS has focused on current privacy issues, including standardizing privacy notices using the nutrition label as a model, and studies of how people perceive online behavioral advertising. Cranor wrote numerous research papers on online privacy, phishing and semantic attacks, spam, electronic voting, anonymous publishing, and other matters. Along with other CUPS faculty, Cranor established Wombat Security Technologies to commercialize CUPS-developed antiphishing technology. She also serves on the board of directors of the Electronic Frontier Foundation. Cranor, her students, and other faculty at CUPS have made significant and innovative contributions to understanding of online privacy issues.

Mary Culnan

Mary J. Culnan is the Slade Professor of Management and Information Technology at Bentley University. She has a PhD from the University of California, Los Angeles. She also taught at Georgetown University; American University; the University of California, Berkeley; and the University of Virginia. Culnan's work has focused on, among other things, information privacy and marketing, including credit reporting, and her teaching interests include e-business and e-privacy. One of her most notable contributions was directing the Georgetown Internet Privacy Policy Survey in 1999, which served as a major input to the Federal

Trade Commission's (FTC's) July 1999 report to Congress, *Self-Regulation and Online Privacy: A Report to Congress*. The 1999 FTC report assessed the progress made in self-regulation to protect consumers' online privacy. That report, the Culnan study, and other FTC and congressional activities pressured Internet companies to post better and more balanced privacy policies on websites. Culnan also served as a commissioner on the President's Commission on Critical Infrastructure Protection, served on the FTC Advisory Committee on Access and Security, and is currently a member of the Government Accountability Office's Executive Committee on Information Management and Technology. She has testified before Congress on information privacy matters numerous times, published scholarly papers on privacy, and otherwise participated in privacy policy activities. Culnan has been one of the few business professors to demonstrate a longstanding interest in privacy and in online privacy.

Simon Davies

Simon Davies is a privacy advocate and researcher now based in London. He was an early advocate for privacy, having spearheaded the opposition to the Australia Card, a 1985 proposal for a national identification card for Australian citizens and resident foreigners. Davies founded the watchdog organization Privacy International in 1990 just as the privacy movement began in earnest. He later moved to London. Privacy International is a human rights group that functions as a watchdog on surveillance and privacy invasions by governments and corporations.

As a director of Privacy International, Davies has worked in emerging areas of privacy, such as electronic visual surveillance, identity systems, border security, encryption policy, and biometrics. He is well known for his populist privacy campaigns as well as for Privacy International's annual Big Brother Awards, which spotlight bad privacy actors around the world. Davies is a recipient of the Electronic Frontier Foundation's Pioneer Award for his contribution to online freedom, and in 2007 he was made a fellow of the British Computer Society. Davies has been a visiting fellow in law at both the University of Greenwich and the University of Essex and is currently a visiting senior fellow within the Department of Management of the London School of Economics. Davies frequently collaborates with the U.S.-based Electronic Privacy

Information Center in his work. Davies's activities as privacy advocate and consultant have been controversial at times.

David Flaherty

David Flaherty is a Canadian and an important figure in international data protection. Trained as a historian at McGill University and Columbia University (MA and PhD), he taught in several American colleges and was a professor of history and law at the University of Western Ontario from 1972 to 1999. Flaherty convened one of the first international conferences on data protection in 1984 in Bellagio, Italy, that brought together academics, scholars, and regulators. In 1989, he wrote the first book-length academic study of international data protection covering the development and implementation of privacy policy, *Protecting Privacy in Surveillance Societies: The Federal Republic of Germany, Sweden, France, Canada, and the United States*. Flaherty has been an author, activist, and authority on data protection in Canada, Europe, the United States, and elsewhere. He later became a privacy commissioner, serving as the first information and privacy commissioner for the province of British Columbia (1993–1999). Following his years as commissioner, Flaherty became a privacy and information policy consultant in Victoria, British Columbia. He is also an emeritus professor at the University of Western Ontario and a member of the External Advisory Committee to the Privacy Commissioner of Canada. As both an academic and a provincial commissioner, Flaherty has been a regular and influential participant in international data protection circles and in government transparency issues for several decades.

Michael Geist

Michael Geist is a law professor at the University of Ottawa and holds the university's Canada Research Chair in Internet and E-Commerce Law. Geist has degrees from law schools in Canada, the United Kingdom, and the United States. His areas of expertise include Internet law, copyright, privacy, technology law, and telecommunications, and he has written numerous scholarly articles, books, and reports on these subjects. His many activities include serving as editor in chief of the *Canadian Privacy Law Review*, being a member of the Privacy Commissioner of Canada's Expert Advisory Board, publishing widely syndicated columns on technology law issues, and running a blog on Internet and intellectual property law issues. When a controversy arose in British Columbia over the outsourcing of data processing to the United States, much of the focus was on the effect of the USA PATRIOT Act on the ability of law enforcement to obtain records on Canadians held in the United States. Geist coauthored an extensive report that showed that the authority of U.S. law enforcement agencies extended far beyond the PATRIOT Act and that there was other legal authority to compel disclosure of personal information held in the United States and even, in some circumstances, held in other countries. Geist is a participant and activist in Canadian privacy and online matters.

John Gilmore

John Gilmore is a computer expert and philanthropist with substantial interests in civil liberties and privacy, among other issues. Gilmore was an early employee of Sun Microsystems, and he founded or contributed to other important early computer organizations, companies, and software. He is important in privacy because of his influence in founding and supporting organizations that work on privacy issues as well as promoting digital civil liberties. Most recently, Gilmore has brought a great deal of attention to privacy rights associated with travel and with individual identification documents through a series of lawsuits against the Transportation Security Administration. Gilmore founded a group called the Identity Project, which focuses on this issue. Famously, Gilmore also cofounded the *Electronic Frontier Foundation* (EFF) (with Mitch Kapor, John Perry Barlow, and Steve Wozniak). He is still on EFF's board of directors. He also founded the *Cypherpunks* (with Eric Hughes and Tim May). The Cypherpunks in their prime were an informal group dedicated to public education and dissemination of encryption (also known as cryptography, the science and art of secret writing). He also founded the "*alt*" newsgroups on the Usenet in the early days of the Internet (with Brian Reid and Gordon Moffett). Gilmore is perhaps the archetype of the early, successful, active Internet entrepreneur who has used his resources to further privacy.

Beth Givens

Beth Givens is founder and director of the Privacy Rights Clearinghouse, established in 1992. Givens is best known as a consumer-focused privacy advocate and as the person who "discovered" identity theft and brought it to public attention for the first time in the early 1990s. Partly through her efforts, some of the first identity theft consumer protection laws were enacted. Givens produced numerous privacy fact sheets series as an author and/or editor. She is author of *The Privacy Rights Handbook: How to Take Control of Your Personal Information*, and she is coauthor of *Privacy Piracy: A Guide to Protecting Yourself from Identity Theft* (1999). She contributed a chapter on consumer and privacy rights to the 2006 book *RFID: Applications, Security and Privacy*. Givens and the Privacy Rights Clearinghouse also advocate for the interests of consumers in public policy proceedings at the state and federal levels (the California legislature, U.S. Congress, and federal and state regulatory agencies). Givens also participated in numerous task forces and commissions that addressed cutting-edge privacy issues, including California Real ID Act Privacy and Security Work Group, California Radio Frequency ID Advisory Committee, California Office of Privacy Protection Advisory Committee, California Secretary of State Voter Privacy Task Force, TRUSTe Wireless Advisory Committee, U.S. Decennial Census Advisory Committee, Justice Management Institute Advisory Committee on Electronic Access to Court Records, California Task Force on Criminal Records Identity Theft, California Legislature's Joint Task Force on Personal Information and Privacy, and the California Judicial Council's Subcommittee on Privacy and Access. Prior to her work as a consumer advocate, she was a librarian specializing in library network development and resource sharing. It is difficult to adequately describe her contributions by a recitation of her biographical accomplishments because they do not convey the broad impact Givens has had on privacy in the United States and abroad.

Susan Grant

Susan Grant is the director of consumer protection at the Consumer Federation of America (CFA), a large national nonprofit association that serves as an umbrella group for hundreds of consumer organizations across the United States. In her role at CFA, Grant has worked on a number of key online privacy issues, including online safety and security, in addition to her work on deceptive marketing, fraud, and general consumer protection. Grant also is a U.S. liaison for the Trans Atlantic Consumer Dialog (TACD) Information Society working group, which is a forum for U.S. and European Union (EU) consumer organizations that seek consensus consumer policy recommendations to promote consumer interests in EU and U.S. policymaking. At the TACD, she facilitates documents and meetings regarding privacy in the United States and in Europe. Grant was also instrumental in the creation of a TACD position paper on social networking and consumers as well as other white papers on aspects of online privacy. Grant is a regular participant in privacy advocacy meetings and in hearings and other congressional and government events. She began her career in the Consumer Protection Division of the Northwestern Massachusetts District Attorney's Office and formerly worked for the National Consumers League. Grant has been instrumental in bringing together the privacy and consumer protection advocacy communities.

Jim Harper

Jim Harper is the director of information policy studies at the Cato Institute in Washington, D.C. He is best known for his libertarian approach to privacy and for his work on privacy and government. He has been a regular speaker on privacy and participant in Washington, D.C., privacy activities; for example, he has testified at Federal Trade Commission privacy roundtables. His work has focused largely on identity issues and on government activities that affect privacy. Harper has served as a member of the Department of Homeland Security's Data Privacy and Integrity Advisory Committee. Harper has written a book dealing with identity fraud and identity theft, *Identity Crisis: How Identification Is Overused and Misunderstood*. Harper also maintains an online federal spending resource, *WashingtonWatch.com*, a high-traffic website. He holds a JD from the University of California, Hastings, College of Law.

Evan Hendricks

Evan Hendricks has been editor/publisher and founder of *Privacy Times*, a privacy newsletter based in the Washington, D.C., area. The newsletter has been published since 1981 covering privacy, online privacy, and freedom-of-information activities in the United States and around the world. Hendricks has also been part of most major privacy advocacy campaigns dating back to the 1980s. He has a particular expertise in financial privacy issues, including the Fair Credit Reporting Act, Gramm-Leach Bliley, and the USA PATRIOT Act. He wrote a definitive book about credit scoring and credit reports, *Credit Scores and Credit Reports: How the System Really Works, What You Can Do*. Hendricks has testified numerous times on privacy matters before Congress and the Federal Trade Commission. He has been qualified as an expert witness in Fair Credit Reporting Act and identity theft cases. Hendricks has a BA from Columbia College, Columbia University, and a background in journalism.

Chris Hoofnagle

Chris Jay Hoofnagle is director of the Berkeley Center for Law and Technology's information privacy programs and senior fellow to the Samuelson Law, Technology, and Public Policy Clinic. He is an expert in information privacy law. Hoofnagle is well known for his early work in shedding light on corporate practices affecting the privacy of personal information. While working at the Electronic Privacy Information Center, Hoofnagle focused on regulation of telemarketing, financial services privacy, and credit reporting, and he became an effective advocate for privacy through amicus briefs, complaints to the Federal Trade Commission, and otherwise. At the Berkeley Center, Hoofnagle has developed and published several influential public opinion polls. The polls, which are often conducted in collaboration with other academics and institutions, explore consumers' understanding of privacy and test notions of consumer autonomy underlying existing self-regulatory privacy rules. For example, one of Hoofnagle's surveys examined how youth view privacy and found that privacy is of interest to all age-groups, not just adults. Prior to joining Berkeley Law, Hoofnagle was a nonresidential fellow with Stanford Law School's Center for Internet and Society. Hoofnagle co-chairs (with George Washington Law School Professor Daniel Solove) the annual Privacy Law Scholars Conference, which brings together academics and others working on privacy policy matters and which has become an important event in the privacy community.

Masao Horibe

Dr. Masao Horibe is emeritus professor at Hitotsubashi University in Tokyo. His contributions to privacy scholarship have been influential in Japan and throughout Asia and have been recognized around the world. Dr. Horibe wrote a number of key, early books in Japan on privacy and freedom of information issues, including *Contemporary Privacy* (1980), *The Information Age and the Law* (1983), *Privacy in an Advanced Information Society* (1988), and *A Comparative Study of Disclosure of Information and Privacy* (1996). He has been integral in drafting and shaping Japanese privacy law for more than 30 years. He served as a chairperson of the Working Party on Personal Data Protection of the Information Technology Strategy Headquarters (1999–2000) headed by the prime minister and as a member of the Prime Minister's Working Party on Electronic Commerce at the Advanced Information and Telecommunications Society Promotion Headquarters. Since 1996, he has been a vice chairperson of the Organization for Economic Cooperation and Development Working Party on Information Security and Privacy. He was also the principal Diet (Parliament) expert during drafting of the Personal Information Protection Act adopted in 2003. Horibe is recognized as one of the most senior and most preeminent global experts on privacy and data protection in Japan, Asia, and elsewhere.

Jane Horvath

Jane Horvath is Google's senior privacy counsel, responsible for ensuring compliance with privacy laws and developing best practices for protecting the privacy of users. Prior to joining Google, Horvath served as the first chief privacy and civil liberties officer (CPCLO) in the Department of Justice, where she participated in department policymaking. She was appointed to the Justice Department position in 2006 by Attorney General Alberto R. Gonzales. The CPCLO worked with other government boards and agencies to, among other things, address terrorist watch list redress issues. While at the Justice Department, she also was a member of the High Level Contact Group and leader of the U.S. delegation of experts tasked with exploring common ground between the European Union's Third Pillar data protection principles and U.S. privacy laws. She also served as assistant general counsel at America Online (AOL), where she helped draft AOL's first privacy policies. Horvath is also a member of the board of directors of the International Association of Privacy Professionals, a global association of privacy and security professionals. She has a law degree from the University of Virginia. Horvath is an example of a lawyer whose career has routinely involved privacy issues from a corporate or governmental perspective.

Peter Hustinx

Peter J. Hustinx is a citizen of the Netherlands, with law degrees from both the Netherlands and the United States. He was president of the Dutch Data Protection Authority (College bescherming persoonsgegevens) from 1991 to 2004, having been reappointed to the authority twice. From 1996 until 2000, he served as chairman of the Article 29 Working Party, a group established under the European Union (EU) Data Protection Directive to give opinions on the level of protection within the EU and in third countries and to provide advice to the European Commission on matters pertaining to the processing of personal data. Hustinx helped to make the Article 29 Working Party an influential organization in Europe. In January 2004, he was appointed by the European Parliament and the European Council to serve as the first European Data Protection Supervisor (EDPS), where he is responsible for advising EU institutions on proposals for legislation and other new developments that have an impact on the protection of personal data. He was appointed to a second term of five years. Hustinx has been an active and influential participant in EU data protection legislation, studies, and conferences. He has contributed to the EU's directive on privacy and electronic communications (e-privacy), cloud computing, data retention, law enforcement, and many other current privacy matters. As a member of the EU Data Protection Directive's Article 29 Working Party, the EDPS actively contributed to work on data protection and search engines and on issues pertaining to other new technologies. The annual report of the EDPS is a useful resource for data protection activities and controversies within the EU. Hustinx has been a long-standing, well-respected, and active figure in EU privacy matters.

Nuala O'Connor Kelly

Nuala O'Connor Kelly is the chief privacy leader of General Electric, a position she has held since 2005. Prior to that, she was the first chief privacy officer of the Department of Homeland Security (DHS), an appointment made by Secretary Tom Ridge in 2003. In this capacity, she was the first person to serve in a statutorily created privacy office. The office's functions included oversight of the Privacy Act of 1974, compliance with the Freedom of Information Act, and completion of privacy impact assessments on new department programs as required by the E-Government Act of 2002. Prior to her service at DHS, she served as chief privacy officer for the Department of Commerce and as that department's chief counsel for technology and as deputy director of the Office of Policy and Strategic Planning. Earlier, O'Connor Kelly served as vice president of data protection and chief privacy officer for emerging technologies for the online media services company DoubleClick. O'Connor Kelly was responsible for the creation of privacy and data protection policies and procedures for the company and for its clients and partners. Her service at DoubleClick coincided with significant public controversy about the privacy consequences of DoubleClick's operations. She has a law degree from the Georgetown University Law Center. O'Conner Kelly is generally credited with giving the DHS Privacy Office a good foundation for its activities and for trying to give privacy sufficient visibility in a department whose activities affect online and offline privacy.

Orin S. Kerr

Orin S. Kerr is a professor of law at the George Washington University Law School. His expertise includes computer crime law and Internet surveillance. He worked earlier in the Computer

Crime and Intellectual Property Section of the Department of Justice's Criminal Division. Kerr was a law clerk for Justice Anthony M. Kennedy of the Supreme Court, and he has a law degree from Harvard Law School. His scholarly contributions have included electronic communications, computer crime, cyberlaw, wiretapping, electronic evidence, privacy, Internet law, the Electronic Communications Privacy Act, and the USA PATRIOT Act. His work has been regularly cited in judicial opinions. He is also a regular contributor to the Volokh Conspiracy blog, whose focus includes Internet privacy law. He has written extensively, including a 2004 article in the *George Washington Law Review* titled "A User's Guide to the Stored Communications Act, and a Legislator's Guide to Amending It." Kerr is one of the most influential academic voices on Fourth Amendment jurisprudence.

Patrick Leahy

Patrick Leahy is a Democratic senator from Vermont, having served in the Senate since 1974. Leahy is widely recognized as one of the leading privacy advocates in the Congress. A longtime member of the Senate Judiciary and Chairman of the Committee, in recent years Leahy has spoken out, held hearings, and sponsored legislation on many privacy issues. Leahy was the original sponsor of the Senate version of the Electronic Communications Privacy Act of 1986 and has been outspoken about the law and its shortcomings. When President Ronald Reagan nominated Robert Bork to be a justice of the Supreme Court in 1987, Leahy responded to the disclosure of Bork's video rental records and sponsored a bill to protect the confidentiality of the records. The Video Privacy Protection Act resulted. Leahy has also sponsored legislation on health privacy, security breach notification, and data. He spoke out about the potential risks that radio-frequency identification tagging may pose to privacy and civil liberties. Leahy was a primary author of the controversial USA PATRIOT Act, but he later objected to its reauthorization and held hearings on abuses of the government's authority to conduct searches and use national security letters. Leahy has also been a longtime proponent of openness in government legislation and the principal congressional sponsor of several Freedom of Information Act amendments seeking to recognize the effect of new technology on information disclosure by federal agencies.

Jon Leibowitz

Jon Leibowitz is the chairman of the Federal Trade Commission (FTC). He was appointed as a commissioner of the FTC by President George W. Bush in 2004 and was designated to serve as chairman by President Barack Obama in 2009. Previously, Leibowitz was the Democratic chief counsel and staff director for the Senate Antitrust Subcommittee from 1997 to 2000. He also served as chief counsel and staff director for the Senate Subcommittee on Terrorism and Technology from 1995 to 1996 and the Senate Subcommittee on Juvenile Justice from 1991 to 1994. In addition, he served as chief counsel to Senator Herb Kohl from 1989 to 2000. Leibowitz also worked for the Motion Picture Association of America. He has a law degree from New York University School of Law. Leibowitz has shown strong interest in online privacy issues while serving on the commission. For example, in a concurring statement to a staff report, *Self-Regulatory Principles for Online Behavioral Advertising*, issued just before he became chairman, Leibowitz signaled that the commission's previous willingness to accept self-regulation to balance marketing and data collection practices with the privacy interest of consumers may have gone as far as it is likely to go. He warned that a "day of reckoning" may be fast approaching for the online advertising industry. He also called for better understanding of how companies use offline and online consumer data to build detailed consumer profiles and of the uses of online tracking data for other purposes beyond behavioral advertising.

Takato Natsui

Takato Natsui is professor at Meiji University Faculty of Law and Graduate School of Law in Tokyo as well as a practicing lawyer at the Hayabusa Asuka Law Office in Tokyo. He has been active in technology and law topics relating to privacy and security in Japan. Notably, he has done a great deal of writing on cybercrime and information security. Most recently, Mr. Natsui has done pioneering thinking on cloud computing and cybersecurity. He was one of the first to raise questions about the intersection of cloud computing and issues such as bankruptcy and the potential for data transfers and other mischief. His areas of focus include cyberlaw (data protection, network contents, electronic commerce, and cybercrimes) and information security. Previously, he was a judge in the Tokyo District Court. He graduated from National Yamagata University (economics, 1978) and from the Legal Training and Research Institute (1983). Professor Natsui's work in privacy is a good example of how privacy expertise and scholarship is developing in Asia and other Pacific Rim countries.

Jules Polonetsky

Jules Polonetsky is co-chair and director of the Future of Privacy Forum, a think tank based in Washington, D.C., that seeks to advance responsible data practices. The forum began in 2008, and it has become an active participant and convener in privacy policy activities. Previously, Polonetsky was chief privacy officer and senior vice president for consumer advocacy for America Online (AOL). Prior to that, he was vice president for integrity assurance at AOL, where he was responsible for consumer protection and risk management issues. Polonetsky also served as chief privacy officer and special counsel for DoubleClick. From 1998 to 2000, he was the New York City's consumer affairs commissioner for Mayor Rudolph Giuliani. Polonetsky had an earlier career as an elected politician, serving as a member of the New York State Assembly from 1994 to 1997. He has served on the boards of privacy and consumer protection organizations including TRUSTe, the International Association of Privacy Professionals, the Privacy Committee of the Direct Marketing Association, the Children's Advertising Review Unit of the Council of Better Business Bureaus, and the Network Advertising Initiative. He has a law degree from New York University. He has been active in public policy activities about privacy and has testified before congressional committees and the Federal Trade Commission with an industry perspective. Polonetsky is widely recognized for his active and honest participation in privacy debates and his business perspective.

Marc Rotenberg

Marc Rotenberg is founder and executive director of the Electronic Privacy Information Center (EPIC) in Washington, D.C. He also teaches information privacy law at Georgetown

University Law Center and frequently testifies before Congress on many issues, including access to information, encryption policy, consumer protection, computer security, and communications privacy. He testified before the 9-11 Commission on "Security and Liberty: Protecting Privacy, Preventing Terrorism." He has served on several national and international advisory panels, including the expert panels on Cryptography Policy and Computer Security for the Organisation for Economic Cooperation and Development, the Legal Experts on Cyberspace Law for UNESCO, and the Countering Spam program of the International Telecommunication Union. He is the editor of *Privacy and Human Rights* and *The Privacy Law Sourcebook* and coeditor (with Daniel J. Solove and Paul Schwartz) of *Information Privacy Law,* a casebook for law schools. He is a graduate of Harvard College and Stanford Law School. He served as counsel to Senator Patrick J. Leahy on the Senate Judiciary Committee. He is a fellow of the American Bar Foundation and the recipient of several awards, including the World Technology Award in Law. Rotenberg is one of the best-known privacy advocates in the United States and around the world, and EPIC is recognized as one of the premier privacy advocacy organizations.

Rebecca Schaeffer

Rebecca Schaeffer was an American actress on a popular sitcom named *My Sister Sam* who inadvertently had an impact on privacy in the United States through the circumstances of her death. Schaeffer was stalked and subsequently murdered in 1989 by a fan who paid a detective agency $250 to obtain her personal information from the California Division of Motor Vehicles (DMV). The fan used the DMV information to find and visit Schaeffer's personal home, where he murdered her. Schaeffer's death prompted the passage of some of the first antistalking laws in California and in the United States. Following Schaeffer's murder, California changed its law to limit the public disclosure of DMV information. Later, Congress enacted the Driver's Privacy Protection Act, a law that established a nationwide floor of privacy protection for DMV records in all 50 states. The passage of these driver privacy laws is illustrative of the importance of "horror stories" in generating enough support for privacy legislation.

Spiros Simitis

Spiros Simitis was the first data protection commissioner in the world. When the German state of Hesse enacted the first general purpose data protection law in response to concerns about the implications of automated data processing, Simitis was appointed as its data protection commissioner. He served in the post from 1975 to 1991. He was chairman of the Council of Europe's Experts Committee on data protection from 1982 to 1986. He has served as a consultant to the European Commission in matters of data protection. Simitis is also professor of labor and civil Law, computer science, and law at the Johann Wolfgang Goethe University, Frankfurt am Main, and director of the Research Centre for Data Protection at the university. He has also been a visiting professor at the Yale Law School and the University of Paris. Simitis served as consultant of the International Labour Office for the drafting of a regulation concerning the processing of employee data during 1994 and 1995. More recently, he was chairman of the German National Ethics Council from 2001 to 2005. Simitis has been an important and influential voice for privacy in European debates over data protection matters dating back to before the development and enactment of the 1977 German Federal Data Protection Act 1997 and the 1995 European Union Directive on Data Protection. He has written extensively on data protection matters as well. Simitis has been one of the most influential participants in European Union privacy activities and debates, especially in the first two decades.

Richard M. Smith

Richard M. Smith is the former chief technology officer for the Privacy Foundation at the Denver University School of Law. He has made significant contributions in the area of technology and privacy. He is well known for finding and publicizing security and privacy flaws in technical systems such as Microsoft's Word documents, RealNetworks, and Tivo, among others. One set of issues that Smith publicized to great effect dealt specifically with the effect on online privacy of Web bugs, cookies, and other methods of online tracking. After leaving the Privacy Foundation,

Smith formed Boston Software forensics and has worked as an Internet consultant for the past 10 years. His clients include government agencies, corporations, law firms, and nonprofits. Most recently, Smith was asked by the Federal Trade Commission to testify and assist in the technical aspects of its Privacy Roundtable series. Smith has been active in the computer security area for more than 15 years. Prior to working at the Privacy Foundation, Smith was a cofounder and former chief executive officer of Phar Lap Software, a software tools company. Thanks to Smith's efforts, numerous security flaws have been found and fixed, and Internet privacy issues have received much public attention. Richard M. Smith is one of the archetypal technical privacy experts.

Robert Ellis Smith

Robert Ellis Smith is the publisher of *Privacy Journal*, a longstanding privacy magazine that has been continuously published since 1974. He is a journalist, a lawyer, an author of several books on privacy, and a privacy advocate. His privacy activities and publications cover the Internet, credit reporting, medical records, computer security, unwanted telephone calls, electronic surveillance, access to an individual's own records, the impact of European and Canadian practices on the United States, biometric identification systems, the common law of privacy, the constitutional right to privacy, and much more. Smith is the author of the notable privacy book *Ben Franklin's Web Site: Privacy and Curiosity from Plymouth Rock to the Internet*, which offers a historical look at privacy in the United States. His first book, *Privacy: How to Protect What's Left of It*, was nominated for the National Book Award in 1980. Smith also publishes a compilation of federal and state laws on privacy and a directory of privacy professionals. A graduate of Harvard College and Georgetown University Law Center, Smith was a daily news reporter, weekly newspaper editor, and then assistant director of civil rights in the Department of Health and Human Services before starting *Privacy Journal* in 1974. He has taught at Harvard, Brown University, Emerson College, and the University of Maryland. Smith may have been a privacy advocate longer than anyone else in the United States.

Christopher Soghoian

Christopher Soghoian is a technology-focused privacy and security researcher based in Washington, D.C. Soghoian's work largely focuses on online privacy issues. He has consistently brought technical privacy issues into broader public debate, and he rapidly became a significant voice in that debate, with his writings and activities broadly cited by others.

His work addresses consumer interests in privacy as well as issues such as government surveillance of Internet and telecommunications activities. He is a Graduate Fellow at the Center for Applied Cybersecurity Research, and a Ph.D. Candidate in the School of Informatics and Computing at Indiana University. His Ph.D dissertation is on the role that companies play in either resisting or facilitating surveillance of their customers.

Soghoian has famously used the Freedom of Information Act and other investigative techniques to shed light on the substantial US government surveillance of Internet communications and mobile telephones. Soghoian's work in this area has been influential, and has been cited the 9th Circuit Court of Appeals, among others. He worked as the first in-house technologist at the Federal Trade Commission (FTC)'s Division of Privacy and Identity Protection. Prior to his year at the FTC, he created a web browser add-on for Firefox called the Targeted Advertising Cookie Opt-Out ("TACO") that was downloaded more than 700,000 times in its first year before he sold it to Abine, Inc.

Soghoian has also worked at or interned with the Berkman Center for Internet & Society at Harvard University, the American Civil Liberties Union (ACLU) of Northern California, NTT DoCoMo Euro Labs, Google, Apple and IBM Research Zurich.

Tim Sparapani

Tim Sparapani is the director of public policy at Facebook, where he is responsible for developing and implementing the company's interaction with the federal, state, and local governments and with opinion makers and policymakers. Prior to joining Facebook, Sparapani was senior legislative counsel at the American Civil Liberties Union (ACLU), where his work focused on privacy matters and where he was an important and effective member of the broad privacy advocacy community. He represented the ACLU before Congress, the executive branch, and the media. Prior to his work at the ACLU, Sparapani worked at the law firm of Dickstein Shapiro. Sparapani has a bachelor's degree from Georgetown University and a JD from the University of Michigan Law School. Sparapani is one of several privacy professionals who moved from the public interest advocacy community to a company or government agency that was the target of attention and criticism for their privacy activities. His service at Facebook coincided with intense consumer and media attention to Facebook's privacy policies, which have changed considerably during that period.

Latanya Sweeney

Latanya Sweeney is Distinguished Career Professor at the Carnegie Mellon University, School of Computer Science, Institute for Software Research, and a visiting professor at Harvard University in 2011. She is also the founder and director of the Laboratory for International Data Privacy at the School of Computer Science, Carnegie Mellon University. She is a computer scientist with an interest in statistics and public policy. She was recently appointed to the Privacy and Security Seat of the Department of Health and Human Services Federal Health Information Technology Policy Committee, the group responsible for advising the Office of the National Coordinator on policy for the national health information infrastructure. Her work has included research on data anonymity, privacy technology, reidentification, and data linkage, often with a focus on creating technologies and related policies with provable guarantees of privacy protection while allowing society to collect and share person-specific information for beneficial purposes. She regularly works on current issues including surveillance, genetics, patient privacy under the federal Health Insurance Portability and Accountability Act, face recognition, and privacy for the homeless. Her documentation of the ability to identify particular individuals from information that does not include names, numbers, addresses, or other individual identifiers has had a major influence on public policy debates over the availability of supposedly deidentified data. Sweeney is a prolific author and inventor. She holds a patent on an algorithm or process that anonymizes data by ensuring that each entity in the data is indistinguishable from at least a specific number of other such entities in the data (k-Anonymity). Sweeney's research has significantly changed understanding of identification policy and made it much more difficult for policymakers to assume that any data are securely deidentified.

Lee Tien

Lee Tien is a senior staff attorney with the Electronic Frontier Foundation (EEF), specializing in free speech law, including intersections with intellectual property law and privacy law. He is well known in the privacy community for his work on privacy litigation; Freedom of Information Act (FOIA) expertise; knowledge of the Electronic Communications Privacy Act (ECPA); health care privacy, particularly as it relates to technology; and other technology-intensive issues, including biometrics. Tien litigated the EFF's high-profile case against AT&T after the company was found to be intercepting communications as part of a federal law enforcement effort. Tien has also been influential on health privacy guidelines and policies in California through his extensive work on a state-level board creating guidelines on privacy for electronic health information exchanges. Before joining EFF, Lee was a solo practitioner specializing in FOIA litigation. Tien has published articles on children's sexuality and information technology, anonymity, surveillance, and the First Amendment status of publishing computer software. He received an undergraduate degree in psychology from Stanford University, where he was active in journalism at the *Stanford Daily*. After working as a news reporter at the *Tacoma News Tribune* for a year, he went to law school at Boalt Hall, University of California, Berkeley. Tien's privacy work in the area of the ECPA and the FOIA has helped to shape legal thinking in these areas and is of considerable importance.

David C. Vladeck

David C. Vladeck became the director of the Bureau of Consumer Protection of the Federal Trade Commission (FTC) at the beginning of the Obama administration. His tenure at the FTC coincided with the FTC's series of workshops that sought to shed light on what privacy frameworks should guide privacy at the FTC going forward. Vladeck, in his speeches, criticized the "harm-based" FTC model of privacy protection, saying famously that privacy harms can also be dignitary harms. In his role at the FTC, Vladeck had an impact on the FTC's policies regarding online privacy, especially of behaviorally based advertising. Immediately prior to his government service, he was professor of law, codirector of the Institute for Public Representation at Georgetown University Law Center, and director of the Center on Health Regulation and Governance of the O'Neill Institute for National and Global Health Law. He was formerly director of the Public Citizen Litigation Group, where he was involved with a broad range of public interest litigation, including First Amendment, health and safety, civil rights, class actions, and open government cases. He has argued cases before the Supreme Court, state courts of last resort, and federal courts of appeal. Vladeck's statements and work at the FTC signaled a significant change in perspective from the bureau during the Bush administration.

Willis H. Ware

Willis H. Ware is a senior computer scientist on the corporate research staff at the RAND Corporation with a PhD in electrical engineering. Ware chaired and was a member of numerous advisory panels to government agencies and task forces for the National Research Council at the National Academy of Sciences. Perhaps his most important contribution to privacy came when he chaired the Secretary of the Department of Health, Education, and Welfare's (now the Department of Health and Human Services) Special Advisory Committee on Automated Personal Data Systems. The committee proposed the first formulation of Fair Information Practices, which became a worldwide set of principles for information privacy applicable just as well to online and offline environments. Many national privacy laws and international privacy instruments are based on Fair Information Practices. The Advisory Committee also proposed legislation that later became the Privacy Act of 1974, the first privacy law based on Fair Information Practices. The Privacy Act of 1974 applies to federal agencies. Ware also served on the Privacy Protection Study Commission, a federal advisory committee established in

1975. Ware was appointed to the commission by President Gerald Ford and served as its vice chairman. The commission's 1977 report *Personal Privacy in an Information Society* had limited influence. Ware is a fellow of the Institute of Electrical and Electronics Engineers and a member of the National Academy of Engineering. Ware's authorship of the first formulation of Fair Information Practices made him a major influence on the worldwide development of privacy policy that continues in the online environment.

Daniel J. Weitzner

Daniel J. Weitzner joined the Obama administration as associate administrator for the Office of Policy Analysis and Development in the National Telecommunications and Information Administration at the Department of Commerce. Weitzner is playing a role in the department's Internet Policy Task Force's comprehensive review of the nexus between privacy policy and innovation in the Internet economy. Previously, Weitzner was principal research scientist as well as the founder and director of the Decentralized Information Group of the Massachusetts Institute of Technology's (MIT's) Computer Science and Artificial Intelligence Laboratory. Weitzner teaches Internet public policy at MIT. He was also technology and society policy director for the World Wide Web Consortium, an international community where member organizations, a full-time staff, and the public work together to develop Web standards. Weitzner was a cofounder of the Center for Democracy and Technology, an Internet civil liberties organization, and he served as its deputy director. Weitzner has a degree in law from Buffalo Law School. He has served on several National Academy of Sciences study panels, including the Committee on Technical and Privacy Dimensions of Information for Terrorism Prevention and Other National Goals and the Committee on Authentication Technologies and Their Privacy Implications. In addition, Weitzner has been regularly involved in public policy activities, including testimony before Congress and several federal regulatory bodies. He has written and contributed to books and scholarly articles about privacy, Internet, and other issues. He participated in the development of the Platform for Privacy Preferences. Weitzner is a major Internet and privacy policy thinker who has played a leading role in a variety of organizations.

Philip R. Zimmermann

Philip R. Zimmermann became well known in the early days of the Internet for his creation of Pretty Good Privacy (PGP), an email encryption software package. Originally intended to be a human rights tool that would allow encrypted communications, PGP was published as freeware on the Internet in 1991 and became a widely used email encryption program. Because of government export restrictions on cryptographic software, Zimmermann became the target of a lengthy criminal investigation for making PGP available worldwide. That investigation made Zimmermann a famous and heroic figure in Internet circles. The government eventually dropped its case in 1996, and Zimmermann started a company that offered security for communications. Zimmermann is a special adviser to PGP Corporation, the company that ultimately acquired his original company. Previously to his work on PGP, Zimmerman was a software engineer specializing in cryptography and data security, data communications, and real-time embedded systems. Zimmermann has a degree in computer science. He served on the Roundtable on Scientific Communication and National Security, a collaborative project of the National Research Council and the Center for Strategic and International Studies. He also served on the board of directors for Computer Professionals for Social Responsibility and currently serves on the advisory boards for Santa Clara University's Department of Computer Engineering and for several private companies. Zimmerman's work on PGP ultimately played an important role in forcing a change in encryption policy during the Clinton administration.

6

Data and Documents

Council of Europe Convention for the Protection of Human Rights and Fundamental Freedoms (9150)

The European Convention for the Protection of Human Rights and Fundamental Freedoms is an international convention that defines a wide range of civil and political rights and provides a means for the enforcement of those rights. Article 8 defines privacy as a human right using broad and nonspecific language.

http://conventions.coe.int/Treaty/en/Treaties/Html/005.htm

Article 8—Right to respect for private and family life

1. Everyone has the right to respect for his private and family life, his home and his correspondence.
2. There shall be no interference by a public authority with the exercise of this right except such as is in accordance with the law and is necessary in a democratic society in the interests of national security, public safety or the economic well-being of the country, for the prevention of disorder or crime, for the protection of health or morals, or for the protection of the rights and freedoms of others.

Organisation for Economic Cooperation and Development (OECD) 1980 Privacy Guidelines

The 1980 OECD Privacy Guidelines have been the most influential international statement of the policy principles that form the basis for information privacy. The Council of Europe issued a similar statement about privacy around the same time in its Convention on Privacy. Most national privacy laws implement the fair information practices described in the OECD Privacy Guidelines.

Organisation for Economic Cooperation and Development, Recommendation of the Council concerning Guidelines Governing the Protection of Privacy and Transborder Flows of Personal Data (23 September 1980—C[80]58/Final)

http://webdomino1.oecd.org/horizontal/oecdacts.nsf/Display/4449EB897F8F4566C1257297005F724B?OpenDocument

PART TWO: BASIC PRINCIPLES OF NATIONAL APPLICATION

Collection Limitation Principle

7. There should be limits to the collection of personal data and any such data should be obtained by lawful and fair means and, where appropriate, with the knowledge or consent of the data subject.

Data Quality Principle

8. Personal data should be relevant to the purposes for which they are to be used, and, to the extent necessary for those purposes, should be accurate, complete and kept up-to-date.

Purpose Specification Principle

9. The purposes for which personal data are collected should be specified not later than at the time of data collection and the subsequent use limited to the fulfilment of those purposes or such others as are not incompatible with those purposes and as are specified on each occasion of change of purpose.

Use Limitation Principle

10. Personal data should not be disclosed, made available or otherwise used for purposes other than those specified in accordance with Paragraph 9 except:

(a) with the consent of the data subject; or
(b) by the authority of law.

Security Safeguards Principle
11. Personal data should be protected by reasonable security safeguards against such risks as loss or unauthorised access, destruction, use, modification or disclosure of data.

Openness Principle
12. There should be a general policy of openness about developments, practices and policies with respect to personal data. Means should be readily available of establishing the existence and nature of personal data, and the main purposes of their use, as well as the identity and usual residence of the data controller.

Individual Participation Principle
13. An individual should have the right:

(a) to obtain from a data controller, or otherwise, confirmation of whether or not the data controller has data relating to him;
(b) to have communicated to him, data relating to him;
 (i) within a reasonable time;
 (ii) at a charge, if any, that is not excessive;
 (iii) in a reasonable manner; and
 (iv) in a form that is readily intelligible to him;
(c) to be given reasons if a request made under sub-paragraphs a) and b) is denied, and to be able to challenge such denial; and
(d) to challenge data relating to him and, if the challenge is successful, to have the data erased, rectified, completed or amended.

Accountability Principle
14. A data controller should be accountable for complying with measures which give effect to the principles stated above.

Warren and Brandeis, *The Right to Privacy,* Harvard Law Review 1890

The Warren and Brandeis law journal article from 1890 sought to establish the need for and nature of a legally enforceable right to privacy. Nearly all academic discussions of privacy cite and discuss privacy as described by Warren and Brandeis. A host of scholarship on all sides of the right of privacy exists. Reproduced here are the first few paragraphs of the article that address "recent inventions and business methods" that create the need for a new privacy right.

Samuel D. Warren and Louis D. Brandeis. *The Right to Privacy* 4 Harvard Law Review (1890) (footnotes omitted)

That the individual shall have full protection in person and in property is a principle as old as the common law; but it has been found necessary from time to time to define anew the exact nature and extent of such protection. Political, social, and economic changes entail the recognition of new rights, and the common law, in its eternal youth, grows to meet the new demands of society. Thus, in very early times, the law gave a remedy only for physical interference with life and property, for trespasses vi et armis. Then the "right to life" served only to protect the subject from battery in its various forms; liberty meant freedom from actual restraint; and the right to property secured to the individual his lands and his cattle. Later, there came a recognition of man's spiritual nature, of his feelings and his intellect. Gradually the scope of these legal rights broadened; and now the right to life has come to mean the right to enjoy life,—the right to be let alone; the right to liberty secures the exercise of extensive civil privileges; and the term "property" has grown to comprise every form of possession—intangible, as well as tangible.

Thus, with the recognition of the legal value of sensations, the protection against actual bodily injury was extended to prohibit mere attempts to do such injury; that is, the putting another in fear of such injury. From the action of battery grew that of assault. Much later there came a qualified protection of the individual against offensive noises and odors, against dust and smoke, and excessive vibration. The law of nuisance was developed. So regard for human emotions soon extended the scope of personal immunity beyond the body of the individual. His reputation, the standing among his fellow-men, was considered, and the law of slander and libel arose. Man's family relations became a part of the legal conception of his life, and the alienation of a wife's affections was held remediable. Occasionally the law halted, as in its refusal to recognize the intrusion by seduction upon the honor of the family. But even here the demands of society were met. A mean fiction, the action per quod servitium amisit, was resorted to, and by allowing damages for injury to the parents' feelings, an adequate remedy was ordinarily afforded. Similar to the expansion of the right to life was the growth of the legal conception of property. From corporeal property arose the incorporeal rights issuing out of it; and then there opened the wide realm of intangible property, in the products and processes of the mind, as works of literature and art, goodwill, trade secrets, and trademarks.

This development of the law was inevitable. The intense intellectual and emotional life, and the heightening of sensations which came with the advance of civilization, made it clear to men that only a part of the pain, pleasure, and profit of life lay in physical things. Thoughts, emotions, and sensations demanded legal recognition, and the beautiful capacity for growth which characterizes the common law enabled the judges to afford the requisite protection, without the interposition of the legislature.

Recent inventions and business methods call attention to the next step which must be taken for the protection of the person, and for securing to the individual what Judge Cooley calls the right "to be let alone" Instantaneous photographs and newspaper enterprise have invaded the sacred precincts of private and domestic life; and numerous mechanical devices threaten to make good the prediction that "what is whispered in the closet shall be proclaimed from the house-tops." For years there has been a feeling that the law must afford some remedy for the unauthorized circulation of portraits of private persons; and the evil of invasion of privacy by the newspapers, long keenly felt, has been but recently discussed by an able writer. The alleged facts of a somewhat notorious case brought before an inferior tribunal in New York a few months ago, directly involved the consideration of the right of circulating portraits; and the question whether our law will recognize and protect the right to privacy in this and in other respects must soon come before our courts for consideration.

Of the desirability—indeed of the necessity—of some such protection, there can, it is believed, be no doubt. The press is overstepping in every direction the obvious bounds of propriety and of decency. Gossip is no longer the resource of the idle and of the vicious, but has become a trade, which is pursued with industry as well as effrontery. To satisfy a prurient taste the details of sexual relations are spread broadcast in the columns of the daily papers. To occupy the indolent, column upon column is filled with idle gossip, which can only be procured by intrusion upon the domestic circle. The intensity and complexity of life, attendant upon advancing civilization, have rendered necessary some retreat from the world, and man, under the refining influence of culture, has become more sensitive to publicity, so that solitude and privacy have become more essential to the individual; but modern enterprise and invention have, through invasions upon his privacy, subjected him to mental pain and distress, far greater than could be inflicted by mere bodily injury. Nor is the harm wrought by such invasions confined to the suffering of those who may be the subjects of journalistic or other enterprise. In this, as in other branches of commerce, the supply creates the demand. Each crop of unseemly gossip, thus harvested, becomes the seed of more, and, in direct proportion to its circulation, results in the lowering of social standards and of morality. Even gossip apparently harmless, when widely and persistently circulated, is potent for evil. It both belittles and perverts. It belittles by inverting the relative importance of things, thus dwarfing the thoughts and aspirations of a people. When personal gossip attains the dignity of print, and crowds the space available for matters of real interest to the community, what wonder that the ignorant and thoughtless mistake its relative importance. Easy of comprehension, appealing to that weak side of human nature which is never wholly cast down by the misfortunes and frailties of our neighbors, no one can be surprised that it usurps the place of interest in brains capable of other things. Triviality destroys at once robustness of thought and delicacy of feeling. No enthusiasm can flourish, no generous impulse can survive under its blighting influence.

Olmstead v. United States

In this 1928 decision, the Supreme Court refused to extend the protections of the Fourth Amendment's rules against unreasonable searcher and seizures to the wiretapping of telephones. Justice Brandeis's famous dissent contains a strong echo of his 1890 Harvard Law Review *article, and that dissent became the law of the land after the Court overruled Olmstead in* Katz v. United States.

277 U.S. 438 (1928)

Excerpts from the Syllabus of the Majority Opinion

1. Use in evidence in a criminal trial in a federal court of an incriminating telephone conversation voluntarily conducted by the accused and secretly overheard from a tapped wire by a government officer does not compel the accused to be a witness against himself in violation of the Fifth Amendment.
2. Evidence of a conspiracy to violate the Prohibition Act was obtained by government officers by secretly tapping the lines of a telephone company connected with the chief office and some of the residences of the conspirators, and thus clandestinely overhearing and recording their telephonic conversations concerning the conspiracy and in aid of its execution. The tapping connections were made in the basement of a large office building and on public streets, and no trespass was committed upon any property of the defendants. Held, that the obtaining of the evidence and its use at the trial did not violate the Fourth Amendment.
3. The principle of liberal construction applied to the Amendment to effect its purpose in the interest of liberty will not justify enlarging it beyond the possible practical meaning of "persons, houses, papers, and effects," or so applying "searches and seizures" as to forbid hearing or sight.
4. The policy of protecting the secrecy of telephone messages by making them, when intercepted, inadmissible as evidence in federal criminal trials may be adopted by Congress through legislation, but it is not for the courts to adopt it by attributing an enlarged and unusual meaning to the Fourth Amendment.

Excerpts from Justice Louis Brandeis's Dissenting Opinion (footnotes and citations omitted):

> When the Fourth and Fifth Amendments were adopted, "the form that evil had theretofore taken" had been necessarily simple. Force and violence were then the only means known to man by which a Government could directly effect self-incrimination. It could compel the individual to testify—a compulsion effected, if need be, by torture. It could secure possession of his papers and other articles incident to his private life—a seizure effected, if need be, by breaking and entry. Protection against such invasion of "the sanctities of a man's home and the privacies of life" was provided in the Fourth and Fifth Amendments by specific language. Boyd v. United States, ***. But "time works changes, brings into existence new conditions and purposes." Subtler and more far-reaching means of invading privacy have become available to the Government. Discovery and invention have made it possible for the Government, by means far more effective than stretching upon the rack, to obtain disclosure in court of what is whispered in the closet.
>
> Moreover, "in the application of a constitution, our contemplation cannot be only of what has, been but of what may be." The progress of science in furnishing the Government with means of espionage is not likely to stop with wiretapping. Ways may someday be developed by which the Government, without removing papers from secret drawers, can reproduce them in court, and by which it will be enabled to expose to a jury the most intimate occurrences of the home. Advances in the psychic and related sciences may bring means of exploring unexpressed beliefs, thoughts and emotions. "That places the liberty of every man in the hands of every petty officer" was said by James Otis of much lesser intrusions than these. To Lord Camden, a far slighter intrusion seemed "subversive of all the comforts of society." Can it be that the Constitution affords no protection against such invasions of individual security?
>
> A sufficient answer is found in Boyd v. United States, ***, a case that will be remembered as long as civil liberty lives in the United States. This Court there reviewed the history that lay behind the Fourth and Fifth Amendments. We said with reference to Lord Camden's judgment in Entick v. Carrington, ***:

"The principles laid down in this opinion affect the very essence of constitutional liberty and security. They reach farther than the concrete form of the case there before the court, with its adventitious circumstances; they apply to all invasions on the part of the Government and its employes of the sanctities of a man's home and the privacies of life. It is not the breaking of his doors, and the rummaging of his drawers, that constitutes the essence of the offence; but it is the invasion of his indefeasible right of personal security, personal liberty and private property, where that right has never been forfeited by his conviction of some public offence—it is the invasion of this sacred right which underlies and constitutes the essence of Lord Camden's judgment. Breaking into a house and opening boxes and drawers are circumstances of aggravation; but any forcible and compulsory extortion of a man's own testimony or of his private papers to be used as evidence of a crime or to forfeit his goods is within the condemnation of that judgment. In this regard, the Fourth and Fifth Amendments run almost into each other."

In Ex parte Jackson, ***, it was held that a sealed letter entrusted to the mail is protected by the Amendments. The mail is a public service furnished by the Government. The telephone is a public service furnished by its authority. There is, in essence, no difference between the sealed letter and the private telephone message. As Judge Rudkin said below:

"True, the one is visible, the other invisible; the one is tangible, the other intangible; the one is sealed, and the other unsealed, but these are distinctions without a difference."

The evil incident to invasion of the privacy of the telephone is far greater than that involved in tampering with the mails. Whenever a telephone line is tapped, the privacy of the persons at both ends of the line is invaded and all conversations between them upon any subject, and, although proper, confidential and privileged, may be overheard. Moreover, the tapping of one man's telephone line involves the tapping of the telephone of every other person whom he may call or who may call him. As a means of espionage, writs of assistance and general warrants are but puny instruments of tyranny and oppression when compared with wiretapping.

Katz v. United States

The issuance of this decision by the Supreme Court overturning Olmstead and holding that wiretapping was subject to the Fourth Amendment lead directly to the passage of Title III of the Omnibus Crime Control and Safe Streets Act of 1968, 18 U.S.C. §§ 2510-20. This law established the rules for obtaining judicial warrants for law enforcement wiretapping. Harlan's concurrence proposed a "reasonable expectation of privacy" test that, essentially, became the most important holding of the case and that has continued to have influence far beyond wiretapping.

389 U.S. 347 (1967).

From the Majority Opinion

We decline to adopt this formulation of the issues. In the first place, the correct solution of Fourth Amendment problems is not necessarily promoted by incantation of the phrase "constitutionally protected area." Secondly, the Fourth Amendment cannot be translated into a general constitutional "right to privacy." That Amendment protects individual privacy against certain kinds of governmental intrusion, but its protections go further, and often have nothing to do with privacy at all. Other provisions of the Constitution protect personal privacy from other forms of governmental invasion. But the protection of a person's general right to privacy—his right to be let alone by other people—is, like the protection of his property and of his very life, left largely to the law of the individual States.

Because of the misleading way the issues have been formulated, the parties have attached great significance to the characterization of the telephone booth from which the petitioner placed his calls. The petitioner has strenuously argued that the booth was a "constitutionally protected area." The Government has maintained with equal vigor that it was not. But this effort to decide whether or not a given "area," viewed in the abstract, is "constitutionally protected" deflects attention from the problem presented by this case. For the Fourth Amendment protects people, not places. What a person knowingly exposes to the public, even in his own home or office, is not a subject of Fourth Amendment protection. See Lewis v. United States, ***; United States v. Lee, ***. But what he seeks to preserve as private, even in an area accessible to the public, may be constitutionally protected.

* * *

> We conclude that the underpinnings of Olmstead and Goldman have been so eroded by our subsequent decisions that the "trespass" doctrine there enunciated can no longer be regarded as controlling. The Government's activities in electronically listening to and recording the petitioner's words violated the privacy upon which he justifiably relied while using the telephone booth, and thus constituted a "search and seizure" within the meaning of the Fourth Amendment. The fact that the electronic device employed to achieve that end did not happen to penetrate the wall of the booth can have no constitutional significance.

Concurring Opinion of Justice Harlan

> As the Court's opinion states, "the Fourth Amendment protects people, not places." The question, however, is what protection it affords to those people. Generally, as here, the answer to that question requires reference to a "place." My understanding of the rule that has emerged from prior decisions is that there is a twofold requirement, first that a person have exhibited an actual (subjective) expectation of privacy and, second, that the expectation be one that society is prepared to recognize as "reasonable." Thus, a man's home is, for most purposes, a place where he expects privacy, but objects, activities, or statements that he exposes to the "plain view" of outsiders are not "protected," because no intention to keep them to himself has been exhibited. On the other hand, conversations in the open would not be protected against being overheard, for the expectation of privacy under the circumstances would be unreasonable.

Electronic Communications Privacy Act

Title I amends the Wiretap Act, a criminal statute that seeks (1) to protect the privacy of wire and oral communications and (2) to set out the circumstances and conditions under which the interception of wire and oral communications may be authorized. Title II of the Electronic Communications Privacy Act is the Stored Communications Act, which protects email and similar electronic communications and protects data transfers between businesses and customers. Major sections of Title II are set out here.

18 U.S.C. § 2701. Unlawful access to stored communications

(a) Offense.—Except as provided in subsection (c) of this section whoever—

(1) intentionally accesses without authorization a facility through which an electronic communication service is provided; or

(2) intentionally exceeds an authorization to access that facility;

and thereby obtains, alters, or prevents authorized access to a wire or electronic communication while it is in electronic storage in such system shall be punished as provided in subsection (b) of this section.

(b) Punishment.—The punishment for an offense under subsection (a) of this section is—

(1) if the offense is committed for purposes of commercial advantage, malicious destruction or damage, or private commercial gain, or in furtherance of any criminal or tortious act in violation of the Constitution or laws of the United States or any State—

(A) a fine under this title or imprisonment for not more than 5 years, or both, in the case of a first offense under this subparagraph; and

(B) a fine under this title or imprisonment for not more than 10 years, or both, for any subsequent offense under this subparagraph; and

(2) in any other case—

(A) a fine under this title or imprisonment for not more than 1 year or both, in the case of a first offense under this paragraph; and

(B) a fine under this title or imprisonment for not more than 5 years, or both, in the case of an offense under this subparagraph that occurs after a conviction of another offense under this section.

(c) Exceptions.—Subsection (a) of this section does not apply with respect to conduct authorized—

(1) by the person or entity providing a wire or electronic communications service;

(2) by a user of that service with respect to a communication of or intended for that user; or

(3) in section 2703, 2704 or 2518 of this title.

18 U.S.C. § 2702. Voluntary disclosure of customer communications or records

(a) Prohibitions.—Except as provided in subsection (b) or (c)—

(1) a person or entity providing an electronic commu nication service to the public shall not knowingly divulge to any person or entity the contents of a communication while in electronic storage by that service; and

(2) a person or entity providing remote computing service to the public shall not knowingly divulge to any person or entity the contents of any communication which is carried or maintained on that service—

(A) on behalf of, and received by means of electronic transmission from (or created by means of computer processing of communications received by means of electronic transmission from), a subscriber or customer of such service;

(B) solely for the purpose of providing storage or computer processing services to such subscriber or customer, if the provider is not authorized to access the contents of any such communications for purposes of providing any services other than storage or computer processing; and

(3) a provider of remote computing service or electronic communication service to the public shall not knowingly divulge a record or other information pertaining to a subscriber to or customer of such service (not including the contents of communications covered by paragraph (1) or (2)) to any governmental entity.

(b) Exceptions for disclosure of communications.—A provider described in subsection (a) may divulge the contents of a communication—

(1) to an addressee or intended recipient of such communication or an agent of such addressee or intended recipient;

(2) as otherwise authorized in section 2517, 2511 (2)(a), or 2703 of this title;

(3) with the lawful consent of the originator or an addressee or intended recipient of such communication, or the subscriber in the case of remote computing service;

(4) to a person employed or authorized or whose facilities are used to forward such communication to its destination;

(5) as may be necessarily incident to the rendition of the service or to the protection of the rights or property of the provider of that service;
(6) to the National Center for Missing and Exploited Children, in connection with a report submitted thereto under section 2258A;
(7) to a law enforcement agency—
  (A) if the contents—
    (i) were inadvertently obtained by the service provider; and
    (ii) appear to pertain to the commission of a crime; or
  (B) [Repealed. Pub. L. 108–21, title V, § 508(b)(1)(A), Apr. 30, 2003, 117 Stat. 684]
(8) to a governmental entity, if the provider, in good faith, believes that an emergency involving danger of death or serious physical injury to any person requires disclosure without delay of communications relating to the emergency.

(c) Exceptions for Disclosure of Customer Records.—A provider described in subsection (a) may divulge a record or other information pertaining to a subscriber to or customer of such service (not including the contents of communications covered by subsection (a)(1) or (a)(2))—
(1) as otherwise authorized in section 2703;
(2) with the lawful consent of the customer or subscriber;
(3) as may be necessarily incident to the rendition of the service or to the protection of the rights or property of the provider of that service;
(4) to a governmental entity, if the provider, in good faith, believes that an emergency involving danger of death or serious physical injury to any person requires disclosure without delay of information relating to the emergency;
(5) to the National Center for Missing and Exploited Children, in connection with a report submitted thereto under section 2258A; or
(6) to any person other than a governmental entity.

(d) Reporting of Emergency Disclosures.—On an annual basis, the Attorney General shall submit to the Committee on the Judiciary of the House of Representatives and the Committee on the Judiciary of the Senate a report containing—

(1) the number of accounts from which the Department of Justice has received voluntary disclosures under subsection (b)(8); and

(2) a summary of the basis for disclosure in those instances where—

  (A) voluntary disclosures under subsection (b)(8) were made to the Department of Justice; and

  (B) the investigation pertaining to those disclosures was closed without the filing of criminal charges.

18 U.S.C. § § 2703. Required disclosure of customer communications or records

(a) Contents of Wire or Electronic Communications in Electronic Storage.—A governmental entity may require the disclosure by a provider of electronic communication service of the contents of a wire or electronic communication, that is in electronic storage in an electronic communications system for one hundred and eighty days or less, only pursuant to a warrant issued using the procedures described in the Federal Rules of Criminal Procedure by a court with jurisdiction over the offense under investigation or equivalent State warrant. A governmental entity may require the disclosure by a provider of electronic communications services of the contents of a wire or electronic communication that has been in electronic storage in an electronic communications system for more than one hundred and eighty days by the means available under subsection (b) of this section.

(b) Contents of Wire or Electronic Communications in a Remote Computing Service.—

  (1) A governmental entity may require a provider of remote computing service to disclose the contents of any wire or electronic communication to which this paragraph is made applicable by paragraph (2) of this subsection—

    (A) without required notice to the subscriber or customer, if the governmental entity obtains a warrant issued using the procedures described in the Federal Rules of Criminal Procedure by a court with jurisdiction over the offense under investigation or equivalent State warrant; or

    (B) with prior notice from the governmental entity to the subscriber or customer if the governmental entity—

(i) uses an administrative subpoena authorized by a Federal or State statute or a Federal or State grand jury or trial subpoena; or

(ii) obtains a court order for such disclosure under subsection (d) of this section; except that delayed notice may be given pursuant to section 2705 of this title.

(2) Paragraph (1) is applicable with respect to any wire or electronic communication that is held or maintained on that service—

(A) on behalf of, and received by means of electronic transmission from (or created by means of computer processing of communications received by means of electronic transmission from), a subscriber or customer of such remote computing service; and

(B) solely for the purpose of providing storage or computer processing services to such subscriber or customer, if the provider is not authorized to access the contents of any such communications for purposes of providing any services other than storage or computer processing.

(c) Records Concerning Electronic Communication Service or Remote Computing Service.—

(1) A governmental entity may require a provider of electronic communication service or remote computing service to disclose a record or other information pertaining to a subscriber to or customer of such service (not including the contents of communications) only when the governmental entity—

(A) obtains a warrant issued using the procedures described in the Federal Rules of Criminal Procedure by a court with jurisdiction over the offense under investigation or equivalent State warrant;

(B) obtains a court order for such disclosure under subsection (d) of this section;

(C) has the consent of the subscriber or customer to such disclosure;

(D) submits a formal written request relevant to a law enforcement investigation concerning telemarketing fraud for the name, address, and place of business of a subscriber or customer of such provider, which subscriber or customer is engaged in telemarketing (as such term is defined in section 2325 of this title); or

(E) seeks information under paragraph (2).

(2) A provider of electronic communication service or remote computing service shall disclose to a governmental entity the—

(A) name;

(B) address;

(C) local and long distance telephone connection records, or records of session times and durations;

(D) length of service (including start date) and types of service utilized;

(E) telephone or instrument number or other subscriber number or identity, including any temporarily assigned network address; and

(F) means and source of payment for such service (including any credit card or bank account number), of a subscriber to or customer of such service when the governmental entity uses an administrative subpoena authorized by a Federal or State statute or a Federal or State grand jury or trial subpoena or any means available under paragraph (1).

(3) A governmental entity receiving records or information under this subsection is not required to provide notice to a subscriber or customer.

(d) Requirements for Court Order.—A court order for disclosure under subsection (b) or (c) may be issued by any court that is a court of competent jurisdiction and shall issue only if the governmental entity offers specific and articulable facts showing that there are reasonable grounds to believe that the contents of a wire or electronic communication, or the records or other information sought, are relevant and material to an ongoing criminal investigation. In the case of a State governmental authority, such a court order shall not issue if prohibited by the law of such State. A court issuing an order pursuant to this section, on a motion made promptly by the service provider, may quash or modify such order, if the information or records requested are unusually voluminous in nature or compliance with such order otherwise would cause an undue burden on such provider.

(e) No Cause of Action Against a Provider Disclosing Information Under This Chapter.—No cause of action shall lie in any court against any provider of wire or electronic communication service, its officers, employees, agents, or other specified persons for providing information, facilities, or assistance in accordance with the terms of a court order, warrant, subpoena, statutory authorization, or certification under this chapter.

(f) Requirement To Preserve Evidence.—

(1) In general.—A provider of wire or electronic communication services or a remote computing service, upon the request of a governmental entity, shall take all necessary steps to preserve records and other evidence in its possession pending the issuance of a court order or other process.

(2) Period of retention.—Records referred to in paragraph (1) shall be retained for a period of 90 days, which shall be extended for an additional 90-day period upon a renewed request by the governmental entity.

(g) Presence of Officer Not Required.—Notwithstanding section 3105 of this title, the presence of an officer shall not be required for service or execution of a search warrant issued in accordance with this chapter requiring disclosure by a provider of electronic communications service or remote computing service of the contents of communications or records or other information pertaining to a subscriber to or customer of such service.

18 U.S.C. § 2711. Definitions for chapter

As used in this chapter—

(1) the terms defined in section 2510 of this title have, respectively, the definitions given such terms in that section;

(2) the term "remote computing service" means the provision to the public of computer storage or processing services by means of an electronic communications system;

(3) the term "court of competent jurisdiction" has the meaning assigned by section 3127, and includes any Federal court within that definition, without geographic limitation; and

(4) the term "governmental entity" means a department or agency of the United States or any State or political subdivision thereof.

Children's Online Privacy Protection Act

The Children's Online Privacy Protection Act of 1998 was one of the first U.S. laws to regulate websites. Regulations implementing the law were issued by the Federal Trade Commission. Major provisions of the law are set out here.

15 U.S.C. § § 6501. Definitions
In this chapter:

(1) Child

The term "child" means an individual under the age of 13.

(2) Operator

The term "operator"—

(A) means any person who operates a website located on the Internet or an online service and who collects or maintains personal information from or about the users of or visitors to such website or online service, or on whose behalf such information is collected or maintained, where such website or online service is operated for commercial purposes, including any person offering products or services for sale through that website or online service, involving commerce—

(i) among the several States or with 1 or more foreign nations;

(ii) in any territory of the United States or in the District of Columbia, or between any such territory and—

(I) another such territory; or

(II) any State or foreign nation; or

(iii) between the District of Columbia and any State, territory, or foreign nation; but

(B) does not include any nonprofit entity that would otherwise be exempt from coverage under section 45 of this title.

(3) Commission

The term "Commission" means the Federal Trade Commission.

(4) Disclosure

The term "disclosure" means, with respect to personal information—

(A) the release of personal information collected from a child in identifiable form by an operator for any purpose, except where such information is provided to a person other than the operator who provides support for the internal operations of the website and does not disclose or use that information for any other purpose; and

(B) making personal information collected from a child by a website or online service directed to children or with actual knowledge that such information was collected from a child, publicly available in identifiable form, by any means including by a public posting, through the Internet, or through—

(i) a home page of a website;
(ii) a pen pal service;
(iii) an electronic mail service;
(iv) a message board; or
(v) a chat room.

(5) Federal agency

The term "Federal agency" means an agency, as that term is defined in section 551 (1) of title 5.

(6) Internet

The term "Internet" means collectively the myriad of computer and telecommunications facilities, including equipment and operating software, which comprise the interconnected world-wide network of networks that employ the Transmission Control Protocol/Internet Protocol, or any predecessor or successor protocols to such protocol, to communicate information of all kinds by wire or radio.

(7) Parent

The term "parent" includes a legal guardian.

(8) Personal information

The term "personal information" means individually identifiable information about an individual collected online, including—

(A) a first and last name;
(B) a home or other physical address including street name and name of a city or town;
(C) an e-mail address;
(D) a telephone number;
(E) a Social Security number;
(F) any other identifier that the Commission determines permits the physical or online contacting of a specific individual; or
(G) information concerning the child or the parents of that child that the website collects online from the child and combines with an identifier described in this paragraph.

(9) Verifiable parental consent

The term "verifiable parental consent" means any reasonable effort (taking into consideration available technology), including a request for authorization for future collection, use, and disclosure described in the notice, to ensure that a parent of a child receives notice of the operator's personal information collection, use, and disclosure practices, and authorizes the collection, use, and disclosure, as applicable, of personal information and the subsequent use of that information before that information is collected from that child.

(10) Website or online service directed to children

(A) In general

The term "website or online service directed to children" means—

(i) a commercial website or online service that is targeted to children; or

(ii) that portion of a commercial website or online service that is targeted to children.

(B) Limitation

A commercial website or online service, or a portion of a commercial website or online service, shall not be deemed directed to children solely for referring or linking to a commercial website or online service directed to children by using information location tools, including a directory, index, reference, pointer, or hypertext link.

(11) Person

The term "person" means any individual, partnership, corporation, trust, estate, cooperative, association, or other entity.

(12) Online contact information

The term "online contact information" means an e-mail address or another substantially similar identifier that permits direct contact with a person online.

15 U.S.C. § 6502. Regulation of unfair and deceptive acts and practices in connection with collection and use of personal information from and about children on the Internet

(a) Acts prohibited

(1) In general

It is unlawful for an operator of a website or online service directed to children, or any operator that has actual knowledge that it is collecting personal information from a child, to collect personal information from a child in a manner that violates the regulations prescribed under subsection (b) of this section.

(2) Disclosure to parent protected

Notwithstanding paragraph (1), neither an operator of such a website or online service nor the operator's agent shall be held to be liable under any Federal or State law for any disclosure made in good faith and following reasonable procedures in responding to a request for disclosure of personal information under subsection (b)(1)(B)(iii) of this section to the parent of a child.

(b) Regulations

(1) In general

Not later than 1 year after October 21, 1998, the Commission shall promulgate under section 553 of title 5 regulations that—

(A) require the operator of any website or online service directed to children that collects personal information from children or the operator of a website or online service that has actual knowledge that it is collecting personal information from a child—

(i) to provide notice on the website of what information is collected from children by the operator, how the operator uses such information, and the operator's disclosure practices for such information; and

(ii) to obtain verifiable parental consent for the collection, use, or disclosure of personal information from children;

(B) require the operator to provide, upon request of a parent under this subparagraph whose child has provided personal information to that website or online service, upon proper identification of that parent, to such parent—

(i) a description of the specific types of personal information collected from the child by that operator;

(ii) the opportunity at any time to refuse to permit the operator's further use or maintenance in retrievable form, or future online collection, of personal information from that child; and

(iii) notwithstanding any other provision of law, a means that is reasonable under the circumstances for the parent to obtain any personal information collected from that child;

(C) prohibit conditioning a child's participation in a game, the offering of a prize, or another activity on the child disclosing more personal information than is reasonably necessary to participate in such activity; and

(D) require the operator of such a website or online service to establish and maintain reasonable procedures to protect the confidentiality, security, and integrity of personal information collected from children.

(2) When consent not required

The regulations shall provide that verifiable parental consent under paragraph (1)(A)(ii) is not required in the case of—

(A) online contact information collected from a child that is used only to respond directly on a one-time basis to a specific request from the child and is not used to recontact the child and is not maintained in retrievable form by the operator;

(B) a request for the name or online contact information of a parent or child that is used for the sole purpose of obtaining parental consent or providing notice under this section and where such information is not maintained in retrievable form by the operator if parental consent is not obtained after a reasonable time;

(C) online contact information collected from a child that is used only to respond more than once directly to a specific request from the child and is not used to recontact the child beyond the scope of that request—

(i) if, before any additional response after the initial response to the child, the operator uses reasonable efforts to provide a parent notice of the online contact information collected from the child, the purposes for which it is to be used, and an opportunity for the parent to request that the operator make no further use of the information and that it not be maintained in retrievable form; or

(ii) without notice to the parent in such circumstances as the Commission may determine are appropriate, taking into consideration the benefits to the child of access to information and services, and risks to the security and privacy of the child, in regulations promulgated under this subsection;

(D) the name of the child and online contact information (to the extent reasonably necessary to protect the safety of a child participant on the site)—

(i) used only for the purpose of protecting such safety;

(ii) not used to recontact the child or for any other purpose; and

(iii) not disclosed on the site,

if the operator uses reasonable efforts to provide a parent notice of the name and online contact information collected from the child, the purposes for which it is to be used, and an opportunity for the parent to request that the operator make no further use of the information and that it not be maintained in retrievable form; or

(E) the collection, use, or dissemination of such information by the operator of such a website or online service necessary—

(i) to protect the security or integrity of its website;

(ii) to take precautions against liability;

(iii) to respond to judicial process; or

(iv) to the extent permitted under other provisions of law, to provide information to law enforcement agencies or for an investigation on a matter related to public safety.

(3) Termination of service

The regulations shall permit the operator of a website or an online service to terminate service provided to a child whose parent has refused, under the regulations prescribed under paragraph (1)(B)(ii), to permit the operator's further use or maintenance in retrievable form, or future online collection, of personal information from that child.

(c) Enforcement

Subject to sections 6503 and 6505 of this title, a violation of a regulation prescribed under subsection (a) of this section shall be treated as a violation of a rule defining an unfair or deceptive act or practice prescribed under section 57a (a)(1)(B) of this title.

(d) Inconsistent State law

No State or local government may impose any liability for commercial activities or actions by operators in interstate or foreign commerce in connection with an activity or action described in this chapter that is inconsistent with the treatment of those activities or actions under this section.

Controlling the Assault of Non-Solicited Pornography and Marketing Act of 2003

This act, the CAN-SPAM Act, was an attempt by Congress to regulate the sending of commercial electronic mail. Importantly, the law mostly preempted state laws that sought to give most recipients of spam a judicial remedy. The congressional findings and policy are set out there.

15 U.S.C. § 7701. Congressional findings and policy

(a) Findings

The Congress finds the following:

(1) Electronic mail has become an extremely important and popular means of communication, relied on by millions of Americans on a daily basis for personal and commercial purposes. Its low cost and global reach make it extremely convenient and efficient, and offer unique opportunities for the development and growth of frictionless commerce.

(2) The convenience and efficiency of electronic mail are threatened by the extremely rapid growth in the volume of unsolicited commercial electronic mail. Unsolicited commercial electronic mail is currently estimated to account for over half of all electronic mail traffic, up from an estimated 7 percent in 2001, and the volume continues to rise. Most of these messages are fraudulent or deceptive in one or more respects.

(3) The receipt of unsolicited commercial electronic mail may result in costs to recipients who cannot refuse to accept such mail and who incur costs for the storage of such mail, or for the time spent accessing, reviewing, and discarding such mail, or for both.

(4) The receipt of a large number of unwanted messages also decreases the convenience of electronic mail and creates a risk that wanted electronic mail messages, both

commercial and noncommercial, will be lost, overlooked, or discarded amidst the larger volume of unwanted messages, thus reducing the reliability and usefulness of electronic mail to the recipient.

(5) Some commercial electronic mail contains material that many recipients may consider vulgar or pornographic in nature.

(6) The growth in unsolicited commercial electronic mail imposes significant monetary costs on providers of Internet access services, businesses, and educational and nonprofit institutions that carry and receive such mail, as there is a finite volume of mail that such providers, businesses, and institutions can handle without further investment in infrastructure.

(7) Many senders of unsolicited commercial electronic mail purposefully disguise the source of such mail.

(8) Many senders of unsolicited commercial electronic mail purposefully include misleading information in the messages' subject lines in order to induce the recipients to view the messages.

(9) While some senders of commercial electronic mail messages provide simple and reliable ways for recipients to reject (or "opt-out" of) receipt of commercial electronic mail from such senders in the future, other senders provide no such "opt-out" mechanism, or refuse to honor the requests of recipients not to receive electronic mail from such senders in the future, or both.

(10) Many senders of bulk unsolicited commercial electronic mail use computer programs to gather large numbers of electronic mail addresses on an automated basis from Internet websites or online services where users must post their addresses in order to make full use of the website or service.

(11) Many States have enacted legislation intended to regulate or reduce unsolicited commercial electronic mail, but these statutes impose different standards and requirements. As a result, they do not appear to have been successful in addressing the problems associated with unsolicited commercial electronic mail, in part because, since an electronic mail address does not specify a geographic location, it can be extremely difficult for law-abiding businesses to know with which of these disparate statutes they are required to comply.

(12) The problems associated with the rapid growth and abuse of unsolicited commercial electronic mail cannot

be solved by Federal legislation alone. The development and adoption of technological approaches and the pursuit of cooperative efforts with other countries will be necessary as well.

(b) Congressional determination of public policy

On the basis of the findings in subsection (a), the Congress determines that—

(1) there is a substantial government interest in regulation of commercial electronic mail on a nationwide basis;
(2) senders of commercial electronic mail should not mislead recipients as to the source or content of such mail; and
(3) recipients of commercial electronic mail have a right to decline to receive additional commercial electronic mail from the same source.

World Privacy Forum, *Privacy in the Clouds: Risks to Privacy and Confidentiality from Cloud Computing*

Cloud computing involves third-party storage of information that might otherwise remain in the direct possession of consumers and businesses. Third-party storage of personal and other data raises greater legal concerns for the protection of the data against the government and other third parties. A 2009 report by a nonprofit public interest research and consumer education group set out the basic privacy issues. The report's findings are set out here.

http://www.worldprivacyforum.org/pdf/WPF_Cloud_Privacy_Report.pdf

This analysis of cloud computing finds the following:

- Cloud computing has significant implications for the privacy of personal information as well as for the confidentiality of business and governmental information. This document identifies multiple and complex privacy and confidentiality issues that may be of interest or concern to cloud computing participants. While storage of user data on remote servers is not a new activity, the current emphasis on and expansion of cloud computing warrants a more careful look at the privacy and confidentiality consequences.
- A user's privacy and confidentiality risks vary significantly with the terms of service and privacy policy established by the cloud provider. Those risks may be magnified when the cloud

provider has reserved the right to change its terms and policies at will. The secondary use of a cloud computing user's information by the cloud provider may violate laws under which the information was collected or are otherwise applicable to the original user. A cloud provider will also acquire transactional and relationship information that may itself be revealing or commercially valuable. For example, the sharing of information by two companies may signal a merger is under consideration. In some instances, only the provider's policy will limit use of that information. Many users are likely not aware of the details set out in the terms of service for cloud providers or of the consequences of sharing information with a cloud provider.

- For some types of information and some categories of cloud computing users, privacy and confidentiality rights, obligations, and status may change when a user discloses information to a cloud provider. Procedural or substantive barriers may prevent or limit the disclosure of some records to third parties, including cloud computing providers. For example, health record privacy laws may require a formal agreement before any sharing of records is lawful. Other privacy laws may flatly prohibit personal information sharing by some corporate or institutional users. Professional secrecy obligations, such as those imposed on lawyers, may not allow the sharing of client information. Sharing information with a cloud provider may undermine legally recognized evidentiary privileges. Records management and disposal laws may limit the ability of a government agency to use cloud computing for official records.
- Disclosure and remote storage may have adverse consequences for the legal status of or protections for personal or business information. For example, a trade secret shared with a cloud provider may lose some of its legal protections. When a person stores information with a third party (including a cloud computing provider), the information may have fewer or weaker privacy protections than when the information remains only in the possession of the person. Government agencies and private litigants may be able to obtain information from a third party more easily than from the original owner or creator of the content. A cloud provider might even be compelled to scan or search user records to look for fugitives, missing children, copyright violations, and other information of interest to government or private parties. Remote storage may additionally undermine security or audit requirements.
- The location of information in the cloud may have significant effects on the privacy and confidentiality protections of

information and on the privacy obligations of those who process or store the information. Any information stored in the cloud eventually ends up on a physical machine owned by a particular company or person located in a specific country. That stored information may be subject to the laws of the country where the physical machine is located. For example, personal information that ends up maintained by a cloud provider in a European Union Member State could be subject permanently to European Union privacy laws.

- Information in the cloud may have more than one legal location at the same time, with differing legal consequences. A cloud provider may, without notice to a user, move the user's information from jurisdiction to jurisdiction, from provider to provider, or from machine to machine. The legal location of information placed in a cloud could be one or more places of business of the cloud provider, the location of the computer on which the information is stored, the location of a communication that transmits the information from user to provider and from provider to user, a location where the user has communicated or could communicate with the provider, and possibly other locations.
- Laws could oblige a cloud provider to examine user records for evidence of criminal activity and other matters. Some jurisdictions in the United States require computer technicians to report to police or prosecutors evidence of child pornography that they find when repairing or otherwise servicing computers. To the extent that cloud computing places a diverse collection of user and business information in a single location, it may be tempting for governments to ask or require cloud providers to report on particular types of criminal or offensive behavior or to monitor activities of particular types of users (e.g., convicted sex offenders). Other possibilities include searching for missing children and for music or software copyright violations.
- Legal uncertainties make it difficult to assess the status of information in the cloud as well as the privacy and confidentiality protections available to users. The law badly trails technology, and the application of old law to new technology can be unpredictable. For example, current laws that protect electronic communications may or may not apply to cloud computing communications or they may apply differently to different aspects of cloud computing.
- Responses to the privacy and confidentiality risks of cloud computing include better policies and practices by cloud providers, changes to laws, and more vigilance by users. If the

cloud computing industry would adopt better and clearer policies and practices, users would be better able to assess the privacy and confidentiality risks they face. Users might avoid cloud computing for some classes of information and might be able to select a service that meets their privacy and confidentiality needs for other categories of information. For those risks that cannot be addressed by changes in policies and practices, changes in laws may be appropriate. Each user of a cloud provider should pay more—and indeed, close—attention to the consequences of using a cloud provider and, especially, to the provider's terms of service.

Federal Trade Commission Staff Report: Self-Regulatory Principles for Online Behavioral Advertising (2009)

Behavioral targeting of online consumers has been a controversial issue for some time, and the Federal Trade Commission has spent considerable time looking at the issue and the scope of industry self-regulatory efforts. A 2009 report summarized ongoing activities and the views of the commission staff. The executive summary of the report is set out here. Those interested in the subject should also read the concurring statements of Commissioner Harbour and Commissioner Leibowitz.

http://www.ftc.gov/os/2009/02/P085400behavadreport.pdf

Since the emergence of "e-commerce" in the mid-1990s, the online marketplace has continued to expand and evolve, creating new business models that allow greater interactivity between consumers and online companies. This expanding marketplace has provided many benefits to consumers, including free access to rich sources of information and the convenience of shopping for goods and services from home. At the same time, the ease with which companies can collect and combine information from consumers online has raised questions and concerns about consumer privacy.

Starting in 1995, the Federal Trade Commission ("FTC" or "Commission") has sought to understand the online marketplace and the privacy issues it raises for consumers. The Commission has hosted numerous public workshops and has issued public reports focusing on online data collection practices, industry self-regulatory efforts, and technological developments affecting consumer privacy. As part of this effort, the Commission has examined online behavioral advertising—the practice of tracking an individual's online activities in order to deliver advertising tailored to the individual's interests. In November 2007, the FTC held a two-day "Town Hall," which brought together numerous interested parties to discuss online behavioral advertising in a public forum.

Participants at the Town Hall discussed the potential benefits of the practice to consumers, including the free online content that online advertising generally supports, the personalized advertising that many consumers may value, and a potential reduction in unwanted advertising. They also discussed the privacy concerns that the practice raises, including the invisibility of the data collection to consumers; the shortcomings of current disclosures about the practice; the potential to develop and store detailed profiles about consumers; and the risk that data collected for behavioral advertising—including sensitive data regarding health, finances, or children—could fall into the wrong hands or be used for unanticipated purposes. Following the Town Hall, FTC staff released for public comment a set of proposed principles (the "Principles") designed to serve as the basis for industry self-regulatory efforts to address privacy concerns in this area.

In drafting the Principles, FTC staff drew upon its ongoing examination of behavioral advertising, as well as the public discussion at the Town Hall. Staff also attempted to balance the potential benefits of behavioral advertising against the privacy concerns. Specifically, the Principles provide for transparency and consumer control and reasonable security for consumer data. They also call for companies to obtain affirmative express consent from consumers before they use data in a manner that is materially different than promised at the time of collection and before they collect and use "sensitive" consumer data for behavioral advertising. In addition to proposing the Principles, staff also requested information concerning the use of tracking data for purposes unrelated to behavioral advertising.

Staff received sixty-three comments on the Principles from eighty-seven stakeholders, including individual companies, business groups, academics, consumer and privacy advocates, and individual consumers. Many commenters addressed the Principles' scope, an issue that cuts across each of the individual principles. In particular, commenters discussed whether the Principles should apply to practices involving information that is not personally identifiable and whether they should apply to "first party" and "contextual" behavioral advertising models. As discussed further in this Report, staff believes that the Principles should apply to data that could reasonably be associated with a particular consumer or computer or other device, regardless of whether the data is "personally identifiable" in the traditional sense. Indeed, in the context of online behavioral advertising, rapidly changing technologies and other factors have made the line between personally identifiable and non-personally identifiable information increasingly unclear. Moreover, this approach is consistent with existing self-regulatory efforts in this area.

Staff agrees with some of the commenters, however, that the Principles' scope could be more narrowly focused in two important respects. First, it appears that "first party" behavioral advertising—behavioral advertising by and at a single website—is more likely to be consistent with consumer expectations, and less likely to lead to consumer harm, than other forms of behavioral advertising. Second, staff believes that contextual advertising—advertising based on a consumer's current visit to a single web page or a single search query that involves no retention of data about the consumer's online activities beyond that necessary for the immediate delivery of an ad or search result—is likely to be less invasive than other forms of behavioral advertising. Accordingly, staff believes that the Principles need not cover these practices. Staff notes, however, that some of the Principles are based on existing Commission law and policy. Therefore, regardless of the scope of the Principles, companies must still comply with existing legal obligations to provide reasonable security for consumer data. Further, companies must adhere to the promises they make regarding how they collect, use, store, and disclose data, and cannot make unilateral, "material changes" to such promises without consumers' consent.

In addition to addressing the Principles' overall scope, numerous commenters discussed the individual principles. In particular, commenters discussed whether and how to provide transparency and consumer choice for online behavioral advertising. They also raised issues related to the material change principle and questioned how to define "sensitive" data and the appropriate protections for such data. Relatively few of the commenters answered staff's request for additional information on other uses for tracking data. This Report discusses the main points addressed in the comments, provides further guidance regarding the scope and application of the Principles, and sets forth revised Principles. It also discusses recent initiatives by industry, consumer groups, and others to address the consumer privacy concerns raised by online behavioral advertising.

This Report constitutes the next step in an ongoing process to examine behavioral advertising that involves the FTC, industry, consumer and privacy organizations, and individual consumers. Although the comments have helped to frame the policy issues and inform public understanding of online behavioral advertising, the practices continue to evolve and significant work remains. Some companies and industry groups have begun to develop new privacy policies and self-regulatory approaches, but more needs to be done to educate consumers about online behavioral advertising and provide effective protections for consumers' privacy. Staff, therefore, will continue to examine this marketplace and take actions to protect consumers as appropriate.

California Online Privacy Protection Act

California is one of the first states to pass a law specific to online privacy policies. The law stipulates that certain types of commercial websites must have a privacy policy and that the privacy policy must contain certain information and have certain characteristics. Several privacy groups used this law to force Google, based in California, to link directly to its privacy policy from its home page, which is one of the requirements of the law.

http://www.leginfo.ca.gov/cgi-bin/displaycode?section=bpc&group=22001-23000&file=22575-22579

BUSINESS AND PROFESSIONS CODE

SECTION 22575-22579

22575.

(a) An operator of a commercial Web site or online service that collects personally identifiable information through the Internet about individual consumers residing in California who use or visit its commercial Web site or online service shall conspicuously post its privacy policy on its Web site, or in the case of an operator of an online service, make that policy available in accordance with paragraph (5) of subdivision (b) of Section 22577. An operator shall be in violation of this subdivision only if the operator fails to post its policy within 30 days after being notified of noncompliance.

(b) The privacy policy required by subdivision (a) shall do all of the following:

(1) Identify the categories of personally identifiable information that the operator collects through the Web site or online service about individual consumers who use or visit its commercial Web site or online service and the categories of third-party persons or entities with whom the operator may share that personally identifiable information.

(2) If the operator maintains a process for an individual consumer who uses or visits its commercial Web site or online service to review and request changes to any of his or her personally identifiable information that is collected through the Web site or online service, provide a description of that process.

(3) Describe the process by which the operator notifies consumers who use or visit its commercial Web site or online service of material changes to the operator's privacy policy for that Web site or online service.

(4) Identify its effective date.

22576. An operator of a commercial Web site or online service that collects personally identifiable information through the Web site or online service from individual consumers who use or visit the commercial Web site or online service and who reside in California shall be in violation of this section if the operator fails to comply with the provisions of Section 22575 or with the provisions of its posted privacy policy in either of the following ways:

(a) Knowingly and willfully.
(b) Negligently and materially.

22577. For the purposes of this chapter, the following definitions apply:

(a) The term "personally identifiable information" means individually identifiable information about an individual consumer collected online by the operator from that individual and maintained by the operator in an accessible form, including any of the following:
    (1) A first and last name.
    (2) A home or other physical address, including street name and name of a city or town.
    (3) An e-mail address.
    (4) A telephone number.
    (5) A social security number.
    (6) Any other identifier that permits the physical or online contacting of a specific individual.
    (7) Information concerning a user that the Web site or online service collects online from the user and maintains in personally identifiable form in combination with an identifier described in this subdivision.
(b) The term "conspicuously post" with respect to a privacy policy shall include posting the privacy policy through any of the following:
    (1) A Web page on which the actual privacy policy is posted if the Web page is the homepage or first significant page after entering the Web site.
    (2) An icon that hyperlinks to a Web page on which the actual privacy policy is posted, if the icon is located on the homepage or the first significant page after entering the Web site, and if the icon contains the word "privacy." The icon shall also use a color that contrasts with the background color of the Web page or is otherwise distinguishable.

(3) A text link that hyperlinks to a Web page on which the actual privacy policy is posted, if the text link is located on the homepage or first significant page after entering the Web site, and if the text link does one of the following:
   (A) Includes the word "privacy."
   (B) Is written in capital letters equal to or greater in size than the surrounding text.
   (C) Is written in larger type than the surrounding text, or in contrasting type, font, or color to the surrounding text of the same size, or set off from the surrounding text of the same size by symbols or other marks that call attention to the language.
(4) Any other functional hyperlink that is so displayed that a reasonable person would notice it.
(5) In the case of an online service, any other reasonably accessible means of making the privacy policy available for consumers of the online service.

(c) The term "operator" means any person or entity that owns a Web site located on the Internet or an online service that collects and maintains personally identifiable information from a consumer residing in California who uses or visits the Web site or online service if the Web site or online service is operated for commercial purposes. It does not include any third party that operates, hosts, or manages, but does not own, a Web site or online service on the owner's behalf or by processing information on behalf of the owner.
(d) The term "consumer" means any individual who seeks or acquires, by purchase or lease, any goods, services, money, or credit for personal, family, or household purposes.

22578. It is the intent of the Legislature that this chapter is a matter of statewide concern. This chapter supersedes and preempts all rules, regulations, codes, ordinances, and other laws adopted by a city, county, city and county, municipality, or local agency regarding the posting of a privacy policy on an Internet Web site.

22579. This chapter shall become operative on July 1, 2004.

California Office of Privacy Protection

Created by a state law enacted in 2000, the California Office of Privacy Protection is the first statutory state-level privacy office in the United States. The Office of Privacy Protection's mission is to protect the privacy of individuals' personal information in a manner consistent with the California constitution by identifying consumer problems in the privacy area and facilitating the development of Fair Information Practices.

http://www.leginfo.ca.gov/cgi-bin/displaycode?section=gov&group=11001-12000&file=11549-11549.6

GOVERNMENT CODE

SECTION 11549-11549.6

11549.

(a) There is in state government, in the State and Consumer Services Agency, the Office of Information Security and Privacy Protection. The purpose of the office is to ensure the confidentiality, integrity, and availability of state systems and applications, and to promote and protect consumer privacy to ensure the trust of the residents of this state.
(b) The office shall be under the direction of an executive officer, who shall be appointed by, and serve at the pleasure of, the Governor. The executive officer shall report to the Secretary of State and Consumer Services, and shall lead the office in carrying out its mission.
(c) The duties of the office, under the direction of the executive officer, shall include, but are not limited to, all of the following:
    (1) Provide direction for information security and privacy to state government agencies, departments, and offices, pursuant to Section 11549.3.
    (2) Administer constituent programs and the Office of Privacy Protection pursuant to Section 11549.5.

11549.1. As used in this chapter, the following terms have the following meanings:

(a) "Executive officer" means the executive officer of the Office of Information Security and Privacy Protection.
(b) "Office" means the Office of Information Security and Privacy Protection.
(c) "Program" means an information security program established pursuant to Section 11549.3.

11549.2.

(a) Employees assigned to the security unit of the Office of Technology Review, Oversight, and Security within the Department of Finance, and the employees of the Office of Privacy Protection within the Department of Consumer Affairs are transferred to the office, within the State and Consumer Services Agency.

(b) The status, position, and rights of an employee transferred pursuant to this section shall not be affected by the transfer.

11549.3.

(a) The executive officer shall establish an information security program. The program responsibilities include, but are not limited to, all of the following:
   (1) The creation, updating, and publishing of information security and privacy policies, standards, and procedures for state agencies in the State Administrative Manual.
   (2) The creation, issuance, and maintenance of policies, standards, and procedures directing state agencies to effectively manage security and risk for all of the following:
      (A) Information technology, which includes, but is not limited to, all electronic technology systems and services, automated information handling, system design and analysis, conversion of data, computer programming, information storage and retrieval, telecommunications, requisite system controls, simulation, electronic commerce, and all related interactions between people and machines.
      (B) Information that is identified as mission critical, confidential, sensitive, or personal, as defined and published by the office.
   (3) The creation, issuance, and maintenance of policies, standards, and procedures directing state agencies for the collection, tracking, and reporting of information regarding security and privacy incidents.
   (4) The creation, issuance, and maintenance of policies, standards, and procedures directing state agencies in the development, maintenance, testing, and filing of each agency's operational recovery plan.
   (5) Coordination of the activities of agency information security officers, for purposes of integrating statewide security initiatives and ensuring compliance with information security and privacy policies and standards.
   (6) Promotion and enhancement of the state agencies' risk management and privacy programs through education, awareness, collaboration, and consultation.
   (7) Representing the state before the federal government, other state agencies, local government entities, and private industry on issues that have statewide impact on information security and privacy.

(b)

(1) Every state agency, department, and office shall comply with the information security and privacy policies, standards, and procedures issued pursuant to this chapter by the Office of Information Security and Privacy Protection.
(2) Every state agency, department, and office shall comply with filing requirements and incident notification by providing timely information and reports as required by policy or directives of the office.
(3) The office may conduct, or require to be conducted, independent security assessments of any state agency, department, or office, the cost of which shall be funded by the state agency, department, or office being assessed.
(4) The office may require an audit of information security to ensure program compliance, the cost of which shall be funded by the state agency, department, or office being audited.
(5) The office shall report to the office of the State Chief Information Officer any state agency found to be noncompliant with information security program requirements.

11549.4. The office shall consult with the State Chief Information Officer, the Office of Emergency Services, the Director of General Services, the Director of Finance, and any other relevant agencies concerning policies, standards, and procedures related to information security and privacy.

11549.5.

(a) There is hereby created in the office, the Office of Privacy Protection. The purpose of the Office of Privacy Protection shall be to protect the privacy of individuals' personal information in a manner consistent with the California Constitution by identifying consumer problems in the privacy area and facilitating the development of fair information practices in adherence with the Information Practices Act of 1977 (Chapter 1 (commencing with Section 1798) of Title 1.8 of Part 4 of Division 3 of the Civil Code).
(b) The Office of Privacy Protection shall inform the public of potential options for protecting the privacy of, and avoiding the misuse of, personal information.
(c) The Office of Privacy Protection shall make recommendations to organizations for privacy policies and practices that promote and protect the interests of the consumers of this state.

(d) The Office of Privacy Protection may promote voluntary and mutually agreed upon nonbinding arbitration and mediation of privacy-related disputes where appropriate.

(e) The Office of Privacy Protection shall do all of the following:

   (1) Receive complaints from individuals concerning a person obtaining, compiling, maintaining, using, disclosing, or disposing of personal information in a manner that may be potentially unlawful or violate a stated privacy policy relating to that individual, and provide advice, information, and referral, where available.

   (2) Provide information to consumers on effective ways of handling complaints that involve violations of privacy-related laws, including identity theft and identity fraud. If appropriate local, state, or federal agencies are available to assist consumers with those complaints, the office shall refer those complaints to those agencies.

   (3) Develop information and educational programs and materials to foster public understanding and recognition of the purposes of this article.

   (4) Investigate and assist in the prosecution of identity theft and other privacy-related crimes, and, as necessary, coordinate with local, state, and federal law enforcement agencies in the investigation of similar crimes.

   (5) Assist and coordinate in the training of local, state, and federal law enforcement agencies regarding identity theft and other privacy-related crimes, as appropriate.

   (6) The authority of the Office of Privacy Protection to adopt regulations under this article shall be limited exclusively to those regulations necessary and appropriate to implement subdivisions (b), (c), (d), and (e).

11549.6. This chapter shall not apply to the State Compensation Insurance Fund, the Legislature, or the Legislative Data Center in the Legislative Counsel Bureau.

7

Directory of Organizations

American Civil Liberties Union
Website: http://www.aclu.org

The American Civil Liberties Union (ACLU) is a membership organization that works to defend and preserve individual rights and liberties protected by the U.S. Constitution and laws of the United States. The ACLU headquarters are in New York City, but it has also offices in Washington, D.C., and local affiliates in every state. Some ACLU state affiliates, particularly the ACLU of Northern California, have been very active on privacy matters. The focus of the organization is on First Amendment rights, equal protection against unlawful discrimination, due process (fair treatment regarding loss of property or liberty), and right of privacy (freedom from unwarranted intrusion). There can be conflicts between some of these concerns. For example, the right to free speech and the right to privacy can clash at times. Founded in 1920, the ACLU has been, from time to time during its history, the subject of significant political controversy. The ACLU's technology and liberty project (http://www.aclu.org/technology-and-liberty) focuses on Internet privacy matters, surveillance workplace privacy, medical privacy, and similar issues at the cutting edge of civil liberties and technology. The ACLU has been an effective advocate in legislative debates in Washington and elsewhere around the country.

Association for Computing Machinery
Website: http://www.acm.org

The Association for Computing Machinery (ACM) is the world's largest educational and scientific computing society. ACM hosts a variety of special interest groups (SIGs) that are subgroups of the organization. One of these SIGs is noteworthy for its work in online privacy, the Special Interest Group on Computing and Society (SIGCAS). This SIG addresses the social and ethical consequences of widespread computer usage. SIGCAS's main goals are to raise awareness about the impacts that technology has on society and to support and advance the efforts of those who are involved in this area of work. SIGCAS's primary focal areas include computer ethics, promoting access to computer technology, security, and privacy, among other issues. Notably, SIGCAS now hosts the Computers, Freedom, and Privacy Conference (http://www.consumersinternational.org).

Berkeley Center for Law and Technology's Information Privacy Program
Website: http://www.law.berkeley.edu/bclt.htm

The Berkeley Center for Law and Technology maintains a busy, varied, and influential research program in the area of privacy. Often, online privacy is a central aspect of the center's research. One of the key projects of the Berkeley Center for Law and Technology is its Consumer Privacy Project, which has published numerous studies providing baselines of consumer opinion and expectations in the area of online privacy. Research from the center and its students has made a seminal contribution to understanding contemporary consumer notions of online privacy. The director of Berkeley's Information Privacy Programs, Chris Hoofnagle, also cohosts (along with Professor Daniel Solove) an annual Privacy Law Scholar's Conference, an important gathering of the nation's top legal scholars. At the conference, privacy scholars submit papers in progress for discussion prior to publication. Many of the papers presented at this conference have gone on to become important contributions to the privacy literature, including online privacy. The conference alternates annually between the Berkeley Center for Law and George Washington University in Washington, D.C.

BEUC: The European Consumers' Organization
Website: http://www.beuc.org

BEUC (Bureau Européen des Unions de Consommateurs), the European Consumers' Organisation, has a significant membership of more than 40 well-respected, independent national consumer organizations from 31 European countries (the European Union [EU], the European Economic Area, and applicant countries). BEUC acts as a sort of "embassy" for these organizations in Brussels, Belgium, with its primary mission being to represent its members and defend the interests of all Europe's consumers. BEUC, as a large consumer umbrella group, has diverse interests beyond privacy. For example, BEUC works on food safety and quality issues. However, online privacy is an integral aspect of its work, and BEUC has been an important force in the EU working toward online privacy rights for EU consumers. One of the BEUC's core missions is to "give consumers a secure digital environment, including effective control over their personal data and privacy." BEUC's policies favor strict, binding rules on new digital practices. The group is interested in creating good default settings for consumers through "security-by-design" settings for digital products. BEUC receives funding from the EU as well as its members. Founded in 1962, BEUC has a staff of approximately three dozen individuals.

California Office of Privacy Protection
Website: http://www.privacy.ca.gov

The California Office of Privacy Protection is the leading example of a state-level privacy supervisory office at the state level in the United States. Created by statute in 2000, the office opened its doors in 2001. It was the first state-level privacy office created in the United States. Headed from the beginning by Joanne McNabb, the California Office of Privacy Protection has as its mission to identify consumer problems in the areas of privacy and security and to encourage the development of fair information practices. Areas the office has worked actively on include identity theft, security freeze (or credit freeze), online privacy, cybersafety for children, privacy notices, and the creation of numerous guides for business and consumers (http://www.privacy.ca.gov/consumer_information_sheet.htm). In the area of online privacy, the office has created materials for consumers regarding hacking and privacy policies. The online privacy page is an important resource for many aspects of online privacy. (http://www.privacy.ca.gov/online.htm). The office has also held a number of informational conferences dealing with aspects of privacy, including online privacy. Most recently, the office has been involved in a long-term effort to create guidelines for the privacy and security of networked electronic healthcare records in the state of California.

Canadian Internet Policy and Public Interest Clinic
Website: http://www.cippic.ca/en

The Canadian Internet Policy and Public Interest Clinic (CIPPIC) is located at the University of Ottawa, Faculty of Law. It began in 2003 with grants from an Amazon.com cy pres fund and from the Ontario Research Network for Electronic Commerce. Subsequently, Dr. Robert Glushko and Professor Pamela Samuelson provided additional funds. CIPPIC provides training for students, but its broader importance comes from its work on technology policy and its service to underrepresented organizations and individuals on public policy debates on technology law issues. The clinic's mandate includes intellectual property, consumer protection in electronic commerce, domain name governance, personal information protection, and privacy. Influential CIPPIC reports include *Digital Rights Management and Consumer Privacy: An Assessment of DRM Applications under Canadian Privacy Law* and *On the Data Trail: How Detailed Information about You Gets into the Hands of Organizations with Whom You Have No Relationship.* CIPPIC also actively files complaints with Canada's federal Office of the Privacy Commissioner, including an influential 2008 complaint about Facebook's violations of Canada's privacy laws. This was one of the early complaints about Facebook's privacy policies, and the complaint eventually led to an official report of findings from the Canadian Privacy Commissioner (http://www.priv.gc.ca/cf-dc/2009/2009_008_0716_e.cfm) and better policies in Canada and elsewhere. A 2004 CIPPIC complaint about Abika.com and National Locator Services resulted in a court battle over the powers of the Office of the Privacy Commissioner that greatly expanded the powers of the office.

Cato Institute
Website: http://www.cato.org/privacy-issues

The Cato Institute is a large, politically oriented nonprofit think tank based in Washington, D.C, and dedicated to the principles of individual liberty, limited government, free markets and peace. Cato was founded in 1977 and is funded by individual donations, foundations, corporations, and the sale of its publications. One of its research areas is privacy, and within this, Cato explores some topics related to online privacy such as spyware. While much of its research has been on national identification systems, employment verification systems, and electronic surveillance, some of Cato's more recent research has focused on online privacy. This research has included papers on data breaches, the online privacy of publishers, congressional testimony on consumer privacy online, and work on how the Electronic Communications Privacy Act could be updated. Cato staff regularly participates in Washington, D.C., privacy community activities.

Center for Digital Democracy
Website: http://www.democraticmedia.org

The Center for Digital Democracy (CDD) is a Washington, D.C.–based nonprofit consumer advocacy group. Jeffrey Chester, a well-known consumer advocate who at one time worked with Ralph Nader, founded CDD. CDD is best known for its groundbreaking work bringing the Children's Online Privacy Protection Act into law. It is also known for its energetic work in the area of online advertising, particularly advertising that is targeted to individuals. In 2007, CDD filed a petition with the Federal Trade Commission (FTC) regarding consumer privacy issues related to online advertising. The CDD asked the FTC to investigate the online advertising industry. Following the CDD request, the FTC held a hearing about the issue and later released new principles and a significant report that invigorated public debate and discussion of the topic among lawmakers. The CDD additionally filed a complaint on mobile phone advertising with the FTC as well as complaints about online pharmaceutical marketing. The group remains very active, providing leadership to other organizations in areas of online privacy relating to advertising and marketing.

Center for Democracy and Technology
Website: http://www.cdt.org

The Center for Democracy and Technology (CDT) is a Washington, D.C.–based nonprofit public interest organization founded in 1994 by Jerry Berman, who was formerly with the American Civil Liberties Union and the Electronic Frontier Foundation. The CDT focuses on law, technology, and policy matters related to the Internet, telecommunications, and privacy. Beginning in 2008, CDT became one of the few privacy or consumer organizations working actively on health privacy matters, and it is heavily involved in activities relating to the developing health information technology infrastructure. Unlike most other public interest groups working on these issues, CDT invites companies and trade associations, as well as other public interest groups, to participate in its consensus building activities. The CDT is sometimes controversial among privacy advocates, in part because a significant part of its funding comes from the companies that participate in its activities. The CDT also receives foundation support and has been an effective lobbyist on Capitol Hill and elsewhere in Washington. It has also been active on international issues, including Internet governance.

Computers, Freedom and Privacy Conference
Website: http://www.cfp.org

The Computers, Freedom and Privacy Conference (CFP) is considered to be a key privacy conference, and it is known primarily for bringing together Internet activists, academics, privacy advocates, government, legal experts, and technical experts. The conference has been held annually in an American or Canadian city since 1991. The current conference sponsor is the Association for Computing Machinery. The original conference sponsor was Computer Professionals for Social Responsibility. CFP has been noteworthy, especially in early years, for bringing together a wide range of leading experts in privacy from many fields for discussion and confrontation on current controversies and legislation. Participants include technologists, legal experts, academics, government agencies, and business representatives. International participation from privacy experts outside the United States has increased in recent years. Conference-sponsored Birds-of-a-Feather sessions are sometimes a starting mechanism for collaborative activity on key technical or policy issues. The CFP remains an important conference or privacy matters and provides a forum for airing substantive online privacy tools, techniques, and issues.

Computer Professionals for Social Responsibility
Website: http://cpsr.org

Computer Professionals for Social Responsibility (CPSR) is a global organization promoting the responsible use of computer technology. Founded in 1981, CPSR educates policymakers and the public on a wide range of issues including but not limited to privacy. CPSR has incubated numerous projects, but by far its most notable incubation project in the area of privacy has been the Electronic Privacy Information Center, which went on to become a critically important independent privacy organization. Other notable incubation efforts include the Civil Society Project and the Computers, Freedom, and Privacy Conference, which is ongoing and now run by the Association for Computing Machinery. Originally founded by U.S. computer scientists, CPSR now has members in 26 countries on six continents. The CPSR is involved in various Internet governance issues, including participation in the World Summit on the Information Society process and the Internet Corporation for Assigned Names and Numbers. CPSR has awarded three privacy and civil liberties experts the Norbert Wiener Award for outstanding contributions for social responsibility in computing technology. The organization created a set of electronic privacy principles that are enshrined in a set of guidelines in the CPSR Cyberspace Privacy Paper approved by the CPSR board and published in 1996.

Computer Science and Telecommunications Board
Website: http://sites.nationalacademies.org/cstb

The Computer Science and Telecommunications Board (CTSB), part of the National Research Council at the National Academy of Sciences in Washington, D.C., provides advice to Congress, federal agencies, and others on technical and public policy aspects of information technology. Projects are often sponsored by federal agencies, but the work is performed independently of CTSB sponsors. Additional support comes from corporations and foundations. Projects utilize CTSB staff, highly qualified subject matter experts, and balanced committees of respected outsiders that oversee each project. CTSB has a positive reputation for the quality of its work and its nonpartisanship, and Congress sometimes asks for reports on specific controversial topics and uses the reports as background or guidance for legislation. Recent reports include *Toward a Safer and More Secure Cyberspace, Information Technology Research, Innovation, and E-Government, Embedded, Everywhere: A Research Agenda for Networked Systems of Embedded Computers, Engaging Privacy and Information Technology in a Digital Age, Who Goes There? Authentication through the Lens of Privacy, Engaging Privacy and Information Technology in a Digital Age,* and *Technology, Policy, Law, and Ethics regarding U.S. Acquisition and Use of Cyberattack Capabilities.*

Consumer Action
Website: http://www.consumer-action.org

Consumer Action is a large, well-established, and well-funded national nonprofit consumer education and advocacy organization. Founded in 1971, the group has offices in San Francisco, California, and Washington, D.C. The group focuses on financial literacy and consumer protection. It also works on issues related to online privacy and electronic health care. Consumer Action is best known for its significant contribution to consumer financial protection via informational publications in numerous languages, including Chinese, English, Korean, Spanish, Vietnamese, and others. A key publication is the *Consumer Action Consumer Services Guide*, a directory of consumer resources. In 2006, the group launched its Housing Information Project. This program assists consumers with information on home ownership, including tips on how to avoid foreclosure and general advice about the housing and mortgage markets. Consumer Action's Managing Money project (http://www.managing-money.org) is a financial literacy clearinghouse. Consumer Action also has an Insurance Education Project and a Privacy Information Project. Consumer Action's Privacy Information Project focuses on personal privacy and why it is important to be careful about who has access to your personal information. Consumer Action has been actively involved in discussions of the Do Not Track proposal and other online privacy initiatives.

Consumer Federation of America
Website: http://www.consumerfed.org

The Consumer Federation of America (CFA) is a national umbrella organization for U.S.-based nonprofit consumer groups. The CFA has made important contributions to the online privacy debate and has been deeply involved in most policy discussions on the topic in recent years, including frequently testifying before congressional committees considering online privacy legislation. The CFA was founded in 1968 and now boasts approximately 300 consumer groups as members. The members include about 100 state and local advocacy and education groups, several dozen national advocacy and education groups, about 100 consumer cooperative groups (mainly credit unions and rural electric cooperatives), public power groups, and state and local consumer protection agencies. The CFA functions as a research, advocacy, education, and policy organization. While it is active in many areas of consumer interest, CFA maintains a significant focus on privacy through its consumer privacy project. In the past several years, CFA's well-known director of research Mark Cooper contributed important ideas and consumer perspectives to the policy discussions about market failure of self-regulation in the privacy space. The CFA's consumer protection director, Susan Grant, has been an active participant in privacy community work on online digital privacy rights and Do Not Track legislation. CFA is also active in the Trans Atlantic Consumer Dialogue (TACD).

Consumers International
Website: http://www.consumersinternational.org

Consumer's International (CI), founded in 1960, is a large membership organization based in the United Kingdom. The group has over 220 member organizations is 115 countries. Its interests include sustainable development, climate change, assisting consumer-focused organizations, and online privacy, among many others. In the area of online privacy, CI actively participates in debates in the European Union EU regarding online social networking, search privacy, mobile privacy, and privacy in advertising. CI has published a number of influential papers on online privacy, including papers comparing online privacy across countries. CI is a key member of the Trans Atlantic Consumer Dialogue.

Consumer Watchdog
Website: http://www.consumerwatchdog.org

Consumer Watchdog is a Los Angeles–based nonprofit organization formerly known as the Foundation for Consumer and Taxpayer Rights. It works on consumer issues such as health care, insurance, and online privacy. Some of Consumer Watchdog's most notable contributions to online privacy have come from its Inside Google Project. This project is focused on urging Google to increase its privacy for its users, based on the notion that as an industry leader Google will influence the rest of the online industry by establishing a high standard that others will be pressured to adopt. The desired result will be to give consumers control over their online lives. Consumer Watchdog's effectiveness may be measured in part by a complaint that Google made to one of the group's funders about its work. Consumer Watchdog is funded primarily by foundations and individual donations.

Council for Responsible Genetics
Website: http://www.councilforresponsiblegenetics.org

The Council for Responsible Genetics (CRG) is a small nonprofit focused on genetic privacy and is based in Cambridge, Massachusetts. CRG was founded in 1983 and is funded largely by grants. Its mission and focus are primarily on non-online aspects of privacy, such as genetic regulations. However, some of CRG's work has involved online privacy, particularly in the area of online purveyors of direct-to-consumer genetic testing. In this area, the CRG has been active in seeking to influence legislation and publicize the issues surrounding genetic tests sold online. The CRG publishes a newsletter, *GeneWatch*, that highlights these issues. The group has been active in monitoring compliance with the 2008 Genetic Information Nondiscrimination Act, a federal law that highlighted the importance of genetics in health care, insurance, employment, and elsewhere.

Cylab Usable Privacy and Security Laboratory at Carnegie Mellon University
Website: http://cups.cs.cmu.edu

Founded in 2004, the Carnegie Mellon University Usable Privacy and Security Laboratory (CUPS) brought together many Carnegie

Mellon University high-powered researchers working on projects related to understanding and improving the usability of privacy and security software and systems. People associated with CUPS include Lorrie Cranor, who is the director; economist Alessandro Acquisiti; and many others. Areas of concentration include privacy decision making (focusing on understanding how individuals make privacy-related decisions and developing a "nutrition label" for privacy), user-controllable security and privacy (developing new user interfaces to allow users to understand and manage security and privacy policies), usable access control with smart phones (creating universal and secure access-control software for cell phones), usable cybertrust indicators (designing systems to minimize human security functions and reducing the need for security warnings that people tend to ignore), and the economics of privacy. CUPS also involved in and supports the Platform for Privacy Preferences (P3P), a machine-readable language that allows a website to describe its privacy practices in formal terms that a user's browser can understand. The goal is to match privacy practices with users' privacy requirements. P3P is complicated, has been criticized by some privacy advocates, and has not been a success in the marketplace and with users. Even CUPS recognizes—and has done work showing—that P3P has had limited success in the online marketplace. The work of CUPS is characteristically creative and has been influential in driving privacy debates and in shaping the design of privacy tools for websites and browsers. CUPS is one of the premier organizations of its type.

Department of Commerce
Website: http://www.commerce.gov

The Department of Commerce is a cabinet-level department with a mission of promoting job creation and improved living standards by promoting economic growth, technological competitiveness, and sustainable development. Some of the department's activities affect privacy, although those activities have been intermittent over the past 30 years. In the late 1970s and early 1980, the department played a role in privacy policy and in international privacy negotiations. Later, following the adopting of the European Union (EU) Data Protection Directive in 1995, the department worked with the European Commission to create a safe harbor framework. The goal of the framework is to allow for the export from Europe of personal information to U.S. businesses that voluntarily and publicly endorse a privacy code. The EU agreed to accept the privacy code as meeting the adequacy standard of the directive. The department's operation of the safe harbor framework has been repeatedly questioned because many participants have not complied with the requirements. The department has also been instrumental in the development of the Asia-Pacific Economic Cooperation 2004 Privacy Framework, an attempt to create an international privacy regime as an alternative to the EU. In 2010, the Obama administration designated the Department of Commerce as co-chair of a newly established Subcommittee on Privacy and Internet Policy. Shortly thereafter, the department issued a green paper with policy recommendations aimed at promoting consumer privacy online while ensuring that the Internet remains a platform that spurs innovation, job creation, and economic growth. This paper and the department's role in setting administration policy for the Internet may be important in future online privacy policies, regulations, and legislation.

Department of Homeland Security Privacy Office
Website: http://www.dhs.gov/xabout/structure/editorial_0510.shtm

The Department of Homeland Security (DHS) operates the first federal privacy office established by statute. The 2002 statute that created the DHS mandated the establishment of the DHS Privacy Office. The office's functions include ensuring that the use of technologies sustain and do not erode privacy protections relating to the use, collection, and disclosure of personal information; ensuring that personal information is handled in full compliance with Fair Information Practices as set out in the Privacy Act of 1974; evaluating legislative and regulatory proposals on privacy; conducting a privacy impact assessment of department activities; coordinating with the department's officer for civil rights and civil liberties; and preparing an annual report to Congress. The reference to Fair Information Practices in the DHS statute was the first in U.S. law. The office also handles Freedom of Information Act requests for the entire department. The DHS Privacy Office has been influential within the department, has been controversial outside for what it has done and not done, and has represented the United States in dealings with data protection supervisory authorities of other countries. While the department does not regulate online activities, the Privacy Office has been active in following President Obama directions to harness new technology tools to engage the public. The DHS Privacy Office has been reviewing privacy issues raised by the government's use of social media, including contributing to government-wide efforts to develop policy.

Direct Marketing Association
Website: http://www.the-dma.org/index.php

The Direct Marketing Association (DMA) is a global trade association with both business and nonprofit members who use direct marketing tools and techniques. The DMA, which represents over 3,000 members, including half of the Fortune 100 companies, establishes industry standards for marketing activities. The DMA also provides a third-party dispute resolution mechanism for handling privacy complaints under the Safe Harbor Framework negotiated by the European Commission and the Department of Commerce, although it is not clear if the DMA has actually handled any complaints. The DMA has been a sponsor of and advocate for some self-regulatory efforts for privacy. It encourages its members to adopt privacy policies and manages a mail preference service that gives consumers some control over the amount of advertising mail they receive. It also operates an electronic mail preference service. The effectiveness of both of these services has been questioned. A DMA-sponsored telephone preference service was abandoned after Congress mandated that the Federal Trade Commission create a national Do Not Call list for the same purpose. The DMA is an active lobbyist in Washington, D.C., and in the states. Its efforts against mail fraud are often welcomed by consumer groups, but DMA positions on privacy are frequently at odds with privacy advocates.

Electronic Frontier Foundation
Website: http://www.eff.org

The Electronic Frontier Foundation (EFF) is a large nonprofit digital civil liberties organization based in San Francisco, California. Founded in 1990, EFF is primarily a donor-funded organization. It has made extremely significant contributions to online privacy both legally and technically. EFF houses a unique group of experts that can litigate online and digital privacy cases in court, provide technical expertise to the privacy community and others, and create privacy enhancing technologies for consumers to use. The EFF has undertaken critical litigation in the area of online privacy. Some past cases include Freedom of Information Act litigation, including a suit seeking government policies on the monitoring of social networking websites. Other privacy suits include *Washak v. United States* (seizure of email) *US v. Maynard* (GPS systems), *Hersh v. Chen* (bloggers privacy rights), *City of Ontario v. Quon* (texting privacy), *Internet Archive v. Mukasey* (unconstitutional National Security Letter served on the Internet Archive), and, famously, the EFF case against the U.S. government over the interception by the National Security Agency of data about AT&T's customers. Technical privacy issues that EFF has tackled include creating and maintaining the TOR (originally an acronym for the onion router project) tool set that protects Web browsing privacy and offers electronic mail confidentiality as well as a variety of other tools to protect online privacy, such as a security tool to protect against Firesheep hacks. Much of EFF's work in technical privacy tips and tools can be found online through its Surveillance Self-Defense Project at https://ssd.eff.org.

Electronic Privacy Information Center
Website: http://epic.org

The Electronic Privacy Information Center (EPIC) is a Washington, D.C.–based public interest research organization founded established in 1994 by Marc Rotenberg, David Banisar, and David Sobel as a project of the Fund for Constitutional Government and Computer Professionals for Social Responsibility. EPIC became an independent nonprofit organization in 2000. EPIC works on emerging civil liberties issues, privacy, First Amendment, and constitutional matters, with a heavy emphasis on the Internet and technology issues. In its early years, EPIC concentrated on government surveillance and cryptography issues, opposing the Clipper Chip (a Clinton administration–sponsored chip set for encrypting telecommunications) and the 1994 Communications Assistance for Law Enforcement Act (CALEA). EPIC's fight against the Clipper Chip was successful, but CALEA became law. EPIC undertakes research, maintains a popular website, publishes newsletters and books, and engages in litigation, including filing amicus curiae briefs in many cases. It is active internationally on privacy and Internet governance issues. EPIC also runs the Privacy Coalition, a loosely organized group of privacy advocates and others with an interest in privacy and related issues. EPIC also is an effective participant in freedom-of-information legal and policy matters and on First Amendment issues. EPIC routinely publishes books containing basic sources and other materials on privacy and freedom-of-information topics. It now publishes *Litigation under Federal Open Government Laws*, an important resource for those interested in the Freedom of Information or the Privacy Act of 1974. EPIC is funded by foundations and individuals.

European Union Article 29 Working Group
Website: http://ec.europa.eu/justice_home/fsj/privacy/workinggroup/index_en.htm

The Article 29 Working Party was established pursuant to the terms of Articles 29 and 30 of the European Union (EU) Directive 95/46/EC of October 24, 1995, on the protection of individuals with regard to the processing of personal data and on the free movement of such data (the EU Data Protection Directive). Members of the Working Party are the supervisory authorities of EU member states plus representatives of the EU Commission. The goals of the Working Party are to provide expert opinions, promote the uniform application of EU data protection principles in all member states, advise the commission on the processing of personal data, and make recommendations to the public and EU institutions on privacy. The Working Party has become an important institution both in Europe and elsewhere because of the quality and range of its activities, its influential membership, and the central importance of the EU Data Protection Directive in international privacy affairs. It produces opinions and other documents on relevant privacy topics, including the adequacy of privacy protection in third countries. Some of its work addresses innovative privacy topics affecting online privacy, including social networking, electronic commerce, search engines, and the concept of personal data. Its documents are a worldwide resource for anyone analyzing privacy issues, but the analyses are especially useful in interpreting how the EU Data Protection Directive applies to new technologies and applications.

Federal Communications Commission
Website: http://www.fcc.gov

The Federal Communications Commission (FCC) is an independent regulatory agency in the United States established by the Communications Act of 1934. The commission generally regulates use of the radio spectrum (including radio and television broadcasting), interstate telecommunications (wire, satellite, and cable), and international communications that originate or terminate in the United States. Its members are appointed by the president, confirmed by the Senate, and serve a fixed term. Privacy is not a primary focus of the FCC. However, because of the importance of wired and wireless communications to online privacy, the FCC remains an important player and sometime regulator. Specific commission activities affecting online privacy include rule-making and enforcement authority for the Communications Assistance for Law Enforcement Act, for customer proprietary network information pursuant to the Telecommunications Act of 1996, and for the sending of unwanted commercial electronic mail messages to wireless devices pursuant to the Controlling the Assault of Non-Solicited Pornography and Marketing (CAN-SPAM) Act. In the case of the CAN-SPAM Act, the FCC shares jurisdiction with the Federal Trade Commission. The FCC's general investigatory and enforcement powers also involve the commission in privacy controversies, including the legality of Google's Street View and review of allegations that U.S. telecommunications carriers broke the law by aiding the National Security Agency to wiretapping telecommunications customers. Other broader issues that fall under the FCC's areas of responsibility that have specific implications for online privacy include Net neutrality, location tracking rules for wireless communication devices, and standards for telecommunications devices. The FCC's importance and potentially broad regulatory authority led a number of privacy groups and interested academics to file in 2010, in response to the FCC's National Broadband Plan, a comment urging the commission to adopt Fair Information Practices as part of that plan to provide an impetus to the development of comprehensive privacy legislation.

Federal Trade Commission
Website: http://ftc.gov/privacy

The Federal Trade Commission (FTC) is an independent regulatory agency in the United States with many functions relating to consumer protection, including privacy. Its members are appointed by the president, confirmed by the Senate, and serve a fixed term. The agency's jurisdiction over privacy is broad in some respects, deep where it has been assigned a specific legislative role, and absent altogether in other areas (e.g., most government and nonprofit activities). The FTC has specific regulatory authority, including the authority to issue regulations, over privacy laws such as the Fair Credit Reporting Act, the Children's Online Privacy Protection Act, and the Controlling the Assault of Non-Solicited Pornography and Marketing Act of 2003. The FTC shares jurisdiction with other federal agencies over the Gramm-Leach-Bliley Act, a law regulating banks and other financial institutions. The FTC also has general authority over unfair or deceptive trade acts or practices in interstate commerce. However, the FTC's authority to issue general regulations on unfair or deceptive activities is significantly constrained, and the agency often proceeds by bringing specific actions against companies that engage in inappropriate practices that harm consumers. These actions have the effect of illustrating the views of the FTC regarding the boundaries between proper and improper business operations. Traditionally, a majority of the commission's members are from the political party of the president, and the FTC's actions often reflect the general political philosophy of the White House. The FTC's interest in privacy has waxed and waned over the years, but the commission has been more consistently active since the early 1990s. The FTC's work sometimes directly influences congressional activities. Pressure from the agency helped convince more commercial websites to adopt privacy policies in the early 1990s. The FTC also has at times encouraged the use of self-regulation as a method of establishing and overseeing privacy standards for commercial activities. The effectiveness of privacy self-regulation and of the FTC's oversight of self-regulation has been controversial. Data protection authorities in Europe and elsewhere did not recognize the FTC as the equivalent of a privacy supervisory authority partly because of the FTC's limited privacy portfolio and authority. However, the FTC was accepted as a full member at the International Data Protection

Commissioners Conference in 2011. Some of the FTC's rule-making authority for laws affecting privacy is being transferred to the Consumer Financial Protection Bureau established at the Federal Reserve under the Dodd-Frank Wall Street Reform and Consumer Protection Act. The FTC will retain enforcement authority and will continue to have general authority to prevent unfair or deceptive acts or practices affecting commerce. Much of the FTC's online privacy work falls under that general authority rather than under specific statutory authority.

Identity Theft Resource Center
Website: http://www.idtheftcenter.org

The Identity Theft Resource Center (ITRC) is one of the few privacy-focused organizations that offers primarily direct assistance to consumers. The group assists victims of identity theft via a well-staffed hotline. The ITRC also acts as the official consumer identity theft "help center" for some businesses. The ITRC receives its funding from industry and foundations and is not notably active in the legislative arena. The ITRC tracks identity theft trends through its work with victims and publishes regular reports about these trends. These reports have become an important source of benchmarks for the crime of identity theft. Began as a subgroup of the Privacy Rights Clearinghouse run by Beth Givens, the ITRC later split off, and it now operates under its own charter. The group is based in San Diego, California.

International Association of Privacy Professionals
Website: https://www.privacyassociation.org

The International Association of Privacy Professionals (IAPP), founded in 2000, is a 7,000-member international organization of individuals who work in some capacity as privacy professionals. Chief privacy officers, compliance officers, privacy attorneys, and privacy-focused nonprofit organizations are among the members, with the bulk of the membership being chief privacy officers of large and midsize corporations. Some academics are members, as are some federal government privacy professionals. The director of members of the IAPP reads as a virtual "who's who" of privacy. The group is based in Maine and has a large support staff that publishes numerous newsletters, Web publications, books, and legislative analyses. IAPP holds conferences all over the world, and its events have become popular annual meeting spots for privacy experts. The IAPP also offers a privacy certification that has gained some credibility and wide acceptance.

Liberty Coalition
Website: http://www.libertycoalition.net

The Liberty Coalition, based in Washington, D.C., has been a vigorous and active organization with a full roster of high-profile members, such as the American Civil Liberties Union, Amnesty International, Common Cause, and the Electronic Frontier Foundation, among several dozens other groups. The coalition works on many issues, one of which is privacy. The group states that its primary focus is on working on issues related to restrictions on privacy, autonomy, and liberty, including the USA PATRIOT Act, national identification cards, REAL ID, and government privacy. Notably, the coalition has also collaborated with privacy-focused groups, such as Patient Privacy Rights and others, in specific privacy-focused campaigns, the most notable of which is the Medical Privacy Coalition, a subproject of the Liberty Coalition. The medical privacy coalition has been active in calling attention to the issue of breaches of medical information as well as other privacy breaches that include disclosures of Social Security numbers.

Massachusetts Institute of Technology Media Lab
Website: http://www.media.mit.edu

The Massachusetts Institute of Technology (MIT) Media Lab is a research laboratory focused on exploring the impact of emerging technologies on everyday life. The group works across traditional disciplines, utilizing designers, engineers, artists, and scientists working collaboratively in many different areas. The Media Lab's projects have encompassed online privacy in innovative ways. Past projects include Personal Video Layers for Privacy, Configurable Dynamic Privacy for Pervasive Sensor Networks, Location Sharing in Large Indoor Environments, Connected Strangers: Manipulating Social Perceptions to Study Trust, and many others. While Media Lab projects tend to be more theoretical, some of its studies have had an influence on national debates; for example, the Social Perceptions study exposed troubling aspects of a lack of online privacy in connection with social networks.

National Workrights Institute
Website: http://www.workrights.org

The National Workrights Institute (NWI) was founded in 2000 as an organization devoted to human rights in the workplace. The NWI observes that of the seven workplace rights called for by the Universal Declaration of Human Rights and International Covenant of Economic, Social and Cultural Rights, none receives adequate protection under U.S. law. One of the NWI's core issues is privacy, which focuses on employer monitoring of employee behavior and communications. It believes that monitoring should be disclosed to employees and should generally not extend beyond the workplace. The NWI is concerned that online and other forms of monitoring have been made easier, less expensive, and less transparent by evolving technology. The NWI has been actively developing guidelines for the responsible use of identity management, including biometrics.

Network Advertising Initiative
Website: http://www.networkadvertising.org

The Network Advertising Initiative (NAI) is a membership supported group of online advertisers such as Google, Microsoft, Yahoo!, and others. The group was formed in 1999 as a part of a formal proposal to the Federal Trade Commission (FTC) to provide a self-regulatory framework for online advertising privacy. In a rare move, the FTC initially applauded the creation of the NAI and its self-regulatory framework. However, the NAI became controversial for periods of low membership (at one point there were only two members) and for a lack of meaningful enforcement of its principles and requirements. More recently, increased discussions about the ineffectiveness of self-regulation in the area of privacy and online advertising and about the possibility of new regulatory or legislative requirements revived the NAI, resulting in new activity and membership. The threat that new rules might be imposed made the NAI more active in promoting a new self-regulatory program and in revising its principles to reflect ongoing developments in online advertising and behavioral targeting. The original NAI agreement introduced the "opt-out cookie." An opt-out cookie is a cookie that tells an online advertiser to not track the computer containing the cookie for certain types of advertising. The actual value of the opt-out cookie in allowing consumers to protect their own privacy interests continues to be hotly contested.

Office of the Privacy Commissioner of Canada
Website: http://www.priv.gc.ca

The Office of the Privacy Commissioner (OPC) of Canada is an independent privacy office that reports to Parliament (and not to the prime minister). The OPC oversees compliance with both the Privacy Act, which covers the personal information-handling practices of Canada's federal government, and the Personal Information Protection and Electronic Documents Act (PIPEDA), Canada's private sector privacy law. The position of Canadian privacy commissioner was first created by the Canadian Parliament in 1977 as part of the Canadian Human Rights Act. The office itself was established by law in 1983. Additional functions and authorities were assigned to OPC in PIPEDA. The privacy commissioner holds office for a seven-year term. Since 2003, Jennifer Stoddart has held the office, and she was appointed to a second term in 2010. The OPC has some authority to investigate complaints, issue reports with recommendations to the federal government and to the private sector, bring cases in Canadian federal courts, and conduct independent audits of compliance with Canadian privacy laws. The OPC is structured with seven main branches, which are in the areas of investigations, audits, research and education, communications, human resources, corporate services, and legal and parliamentary affairs. The OPC has been criticized by some for lack of aggressiveness, although the commissioner's inability to issue binding orders, limited discretion to initiate complaints, and limits on the disclosure of information about investigations may be to blame in part. The office functions more on an ombudsman model.

Patient Privacy Rights
Website: http://patientprivacyrights.org

Patient Privacy Rights is a Texas-based nonprofit organization that focuses on health care privacy, including the privacy of traditional health records and of newer types of health records, such as personal health records. The group is an active voice on health care legislation at the national level and in some key states. The group is notable for its coalition of privacy and health care groups that share its interest in health care privacy issues. It conducts letter-writing campaigns, writes regulatory comments, sits on various health care privacy committees, and issues white papers as well. The group focuses much of its efforts on the federal health privacy rules issued under the Health Insurance Portability and Accountability Act. Patient Privacy Rights was founded by Deborah C. Peel, MD, in 2004 in Austin, Texas.

Privacy and Civil Liberties Board
Website: None currently. Bush administration website: http://georgewbush-whitehouse.archives.gov/privacyboard

The Privacy and Civil Liberties Oversight Board was created by the Intelligence Reform and Terrorism Prevention Act of 2004 in response to the recommendations contained in the report of the National Commission on Terrorist Attacks upon the United States (9/11 Commission). The board's mission is to review the privacy and civil liberties issues raised by the government's national security policies and programs. The board was originally housed within the Executive Office of the President. Board members were appointed by the president and confirmed by the Senate. The first meeting of the board was in March 2006. Little more than a year later, the only Democratic member of the board resigned over its lack of access to agencies and records and its lack of independence from the White House. This and other criticism of the board led to a change in the 2007 Implementing Recommendations of the 9/11 Commission Act. The new law moved the board out of the Executive Office of the President so that it has a degree of independence. The new law also gave the board subpoena power and established fixed, staggered terms for its bipartisan membership of five people. In 2008, President George W. Bush nominated three Republican and, later, one Democratic member to the board, but the Senate never acted on the nominations. It was not until late in his second year in office that President Barack Obama nominated members to the board. The board is viewed by some as a potentially important institution in striking a balance between the need to protect privacy rights and civil liberties in government national security policies and programs. However, the persistent failure of the board to have members and to function makes it a theoretical player at best. The board should not be confused with the Department of Justice Privacy and Civil Liberties Board, an organization internal to the Department of Justice.

Privacy International
Website: http://www.privacyinternational.org/index.shtml

Privacy International (PI) is a London-based independent nonprofit organization chartered in the United Kingdom. It was founded in 1990 by Simon Davies, who remains as PI's director. PI describes its mission as campaigning across the world to protect people against intrusion by governments and corporations that seek to erode privacy. PI actively opposes increased levels of surveillance in Britain and elsewhere. It also promotes government openness and transparency. PI is difficult to characterize, claiming to be a "chameleon-like group" that is a "troublemaker and think-tank, campaigner and researcher." It undertakes activities in many countries around the world. Funding comes primarily from foundations, academic establishments, and nongovernment organizations. Although nearly 20 years old, PI has a small staff, although it does have affiliates in other countries. Some contend that its work, while highly diverse topically and geographically, seems to lack a clear focus. In recent years, PI has attempted to work more closely with industry to develop meaningful safeguards for privacy, and these activities have raised questions about conflicts on PI's role as both advocates and consultants.

Privacy Rights Clearinghouse
Website: http://www.privacyrights.org

The Privacy Rights Clearinghouse (PRC) is a nonprofit organization founded in 1992 by Beth Givens. It is located in San Diego, California, and operates as an independent program of the Utility Consumers' Action Network, a nonprofit membership organization that advocates for consumers' interests in telecommunications, energy, and the Internet. The PRC's mission is upholding the right to privacy and protecting consumers against identity theft and other privacy crimes. Unusual for a privacy organization, the PRC's mission includes providing advice and assistance directly to consumers. Its services include a consumer hotline for reporting privacy abuses and requesting information on ways to protect privacy. The PRC also maintains more than 30 fact sheets (some in Spanish) on privacy topics, including many related to online privacy issues and to telecommunications. Another unusual PRC service is connecting journalists and policymakers with victims of privacy abuses who are willing to tell their stories. A victim with a compelling story is often essential to attract attention and enact privacy legislation. Despite a small staff and funding constraints, the PRC provides a wide array of consumer services and also is an active and influential lobbyist in the California legislature. The PRC's funding sources normally include foundations and cy pres funds from settlements of consumer lawsuits.

Stanford Law School, Center for Internet and Society
Website: http://cyberlaw.stanford.edu

The Stanford Law School's Center for Internet and Society (CIS) is home to innovative online privacy research through its Consumer Privacy Project. Through this project, CIS conducts early research in the area of Facebook third-party applications. CIS scholars have also become important participants in the ongoing debate about the technology and policy of an online Do Not Track mechanism. One of the CIS technology scholars, Arvind Narayanan, (http://cyberlaw.stanford.edu/node/6573), conceptualized the Do Not Track technology in a new way, influencing the technical implementation of Do Not Track in Web browsers. The CIS vision of how Do Not Track technology can work online also influenced policy and legislative discussions of how to protect consumers from online tracking of their Web behaviors.

Trans Atlantic Consumer Dialogue
Website: http://www.tacd.org

The Trans Atlantic Consumer Dialogue (TACD) is a forum of U.S. and European Union (EU) consumer organizations. The member organizations include privacy organizations in the United States and the EU, and one of the working groups of the TACD focuses on the informational privacy of consumers (Information Society Working Group). The TACD holds regular meetings in Europe and in the United States to develop and agree on joint consumer policy recommendations to the U.S. government and to the EU. The TACD's issues include but are not limited to privacy. For example, some 2010 recommendations included documents on social networking privacy and on food safety. Established in September 1998, the TACD holds a formal position in the EU policymaking fabric with a mission to provide input to political negotiations and agreements and to explore ways to strengthen the EU and U.S. consumer view at the international level. The TACD is also a member of the advisory group to the Trans Atlantic Economic Council. Membership in the TACD is limited to consumer-focused groups that are nonprofit and noncommercial. Members in the United States include the Electronic Privacy Information Center, the World Privacy Forum, the Consumer Federation of America, the Electronic Frontier Foundation, the Privacy Rights Clearinghouse, the Center for Digital Democracy, and others.

ThePrivacyPlace.org
Website: http://theprivacyplace.org

Annie Antón, professor in the Department of Computer Science at the College of Engineering at North Carolina State University (NCSU), is the founder and director of ThePrivacyPlace.org, an interdisciplinary research group of students and faculty in NCSU's computer science and business management departments as well as the Georgia Tech College of Computing, the Purdue University Department of Computer Science, and the University of Lugano Department of Communication Sciences. The research group develops technologies and tools to help ensure that privacy policies are aligned with the software systems that they govern, particularly Web-based and e-commerce systems in which the security of personal and private information is vulnerable. The group has received funding from the National Science Foundation. Theprivacyplace.org materials are of high caliber. In 2009, the group released a longitudinal technical report by Dr. Annie I. Antón, Dr. Julia B. Earp, and Jessica D. Young detailing the evolution of Internet users' privacy concerns since 2002. The report created an important baseline for online privacy values. ThePrivacyPlace.org undertakes collaborative efforts with policy-oriented academics; for example, the organization worked with Peter Swire, a law professor at Ohio State University, to coauthor comments to the Federal Trade Commission about online behavioral advertising. The comments focused on technology-based solutions.

Verbraucherzentrale Bundesverband (Federation of German Consumer Organizations)
Website: https://www.vzbv.de/start/index.php?page=english

The Federation of German Consumer Organizations (Verbraucherzentrale Bundesverband [VZBW]) is a large, well-staffed nonprofit organization that functions as an umbrella organization for 42 German consumer associations. The group is based in Berlin, Germany, and has a staff of more than 100. It was formed in 2000 as a result of the merger of three federal consumer organizations. Funding came from the Federal Ministry of Consumer Affairs, Nutrition, and Agriculture, along with additional income from the proceeds of publications, membership fees, and project funds. The VZBW acts as a lobbying group and also litigates and provides professional training for member organizations. It works both regionally in Germany and across the European Union (EU). It also provides consumer advice regionally via 16 consumer centers of the German states (Verbraucherzentralen). The group is especially active in online privacy issues, particularly related to social networking privacy. The VZBW has brought a number of actions against Facebook and aggressively seeks to increase privacy protections online in the EU.

Worldwide Web Consortium
Website: http://www.w3.org

The World Wide Web Consortium is an international standards-setting body comprised of a diverse array of member organizations, a full-time staff, and members of the public. The W3C sets standards for various layers of the Web. For example, the group sets technical specifications for how Web pages are displayed. It also establishes standards for various Web applications, such as how interactive television, mobile phones, and cars interact with the Web. The standards and draft standards are accessible via the group's website, and they are actively maintained and updated. Many of the standards have direct bearing on how privacy is facilitated (or not) on the Web and other platforms. The group worked actively on the Platform for Privacy Preferences as well as on Mozilla (a Web browser) privacy enhancement technology standards. The group has more than 300 members, many of which are large multinational companies, such as Google, IBM, Nokia, and other companies with Internet components. Academic organizations are also members, including the University of Edinburgh, the American University, and Beijing University. W3C is an extremely important organization for the Internet.

World Privacy Forum
Website: http://worldprivacyforum.org

The World Privacy Forum (WPF) is a small, nonprofit, nonpartisan public interest research group based in San Diego, California. The organization conducts in-depth research, analysis, and consumer education in the area of privacy. The WPF was founded in 2003 and is funded primarily by foundations. Among the WPF's influential reports was a 2006 report on medical identity theft. This report was the first to bring public and policy attention to the previously unknown crimes and activities that constitute medical identity theft. The WPF publishes consumer education materials on medical identity theft and other health privacy matters, including a consumer guide the federal Health Insurance Portability and Accountability Act. The executive director of the board was appointed to the California Privacy and Security Advisory Board, which is tasked with finding ways to protect patient privacy and security in the electronic health care sector. Other WPF areas of specialty include online job search privacy, behavioral targeting and advertising on the Internet, and privacy and other issues relating to cloud computing. The WPF is active in public policy forums, commenting on proposed federal regulations and testifying at congressional and Federal Trade Commission hearings and workshops. The WPF convened an international privacy and security conference in Japan in 2008, and in 2011 initiated privacy research projects in India.

8

Resources

Books

Fiction

Orwell, George. *1984*. New York: Signet Books, 1990.

George Orwell's dystopian novel—featuring a governmental Big Brother undertaking constant surveillance of citizens—was so successful and insightful that, more than 60 years later, the phrase "Big Brother" remains a universal shorthand for privacy invasion. "Orwellian" as a general term has come to mean a totalitarian privacy-invasive system or act. This book, which pre-dates the online world by decades, contributed important philosophical ideas to many campaigns of dissent against privacy intrusions regardless of technology. Privacy groups around the world give Big Brother Awards to government agencies and others whose actions undermine privacy values.

Kafka, Franz. *The Trial*. Oxford: Oxford World Classics, 2009.

Kafka's novel from 1925 tells the story of Joseph K., who is arrested and prosecuted by a remote, inaccessible authority and whose crime is never disclosed in the course of the book. K.'s attempts to learn more about the charges and the applicable procedures fail, and he is executed in the end without explanation. Kafka's treatment of unknown charges and secret procedures has become a metaphor for contemporary privacy, where secret records compiled by unknown companies can affect or control an individual's online experience and offline opportunities. An important modern privacy scholar, law professor Daniel Solove, named Kafka's *The Trial* as the privacy metaphor that works effectively in a digital environment because so much can happen without explanation or notice to the individual.

Nonfiction

Agre, Philip E., and Marc Rotenberg, eds. *Technology and Privacy: The New Landscape*. Cambridge, MA: MIT Press, 1997.

This collection of essays offers a broad and diverse framework for considering privacy issues in an era of rapidly changing technology. The essay authors are internationally recognized experts from half a dozen different countries. Chapters address privacy in the context of computing and communications, global data protection policies, privacy-enhancing technologies, the commoditization of privacy, controlling surveillance, privacy law, evolution of data protection in Europe, cryptography, and interactivity. The book provides insights into the origins of debates about computers, networks, and privacy that remain useful today.

Ahearn, Frank, and Eileen Horan. *How to Disappear: The World's 1st Guide on How to Lower Your Profile and Reduce Your Digital Footprint*. New York: Lyons Press, 2010.

This book is coauthored by Frank Ahearn, a nationally known skip tracer who was hired to find deadbeats as well as former acquaintances of at least one U.S. president. The book contains much material relevant to online privacy. The chapters illustrate how digital footprints contained in electronic databases and online sources reveal details about an individual. Much of the information results from records of seemingly innocuous transactions conducted on the Web. Although this is strictly a how-to book, it contains useful information about the inner workings of online data sources and the consequences of data retention.

Alderman, Ellen, and Caroline Kennedy. *The Right to Privacy*. New York: Knopf, 1995.

This book focuses on the legal right to privacy as revealed by judicial decisions. The authors use a series of court cases to illustrate the scope of privacy rights and the conflicts that invariably develop with other important societal interests. The analysis goes far beyond the legal opinions and includes the real story behind the case law, with descriptions of the facts, the people, and the conflicts that produced the lawsuits in the first place. While online privacy cases are still relatively rare, the in-depth analysis of older cases offers an understanding of how lawsuits arise and what motivates people to invade and to sue to protect their privacy.

Battelle, John. *The Search: How Google and Its Rivals Rewrote the Rules of Business and Transformed Our Culture.* New York, NY: Portfolio, 2005.

John Battelle has written what remains the definitive book on Google's origins and Google's threat to privacy. Battelle obtained good access for interviews, and as a result his book shines with insider knowledge of Google's ins and outs. He also spent some time determining how to analyze Google in a broad societal context. Battelle argues that Google presents a privacy threat because of the nature of its size, scope, and reach combined with an informational dependence on search engines. He captured the nature of the Google privacy problem in a phrase describing Google's intimate knowledge of consumers as Google storing a "database of intentions." This book was written prior to Facebook's rise, and Battelle's analysis reflects this. It is nevertheless an important entry in the online privacy bookshelf.

Bennett, Colin. *Regulating Privacy.* Ithaca, NY: Cornell University Press, 1992.

Although this book pre-dates the modern online world, it provides essential insights into the international policy process that still operates today to make decisions about online privacy. Bennett takes a political scientist's approach to explaining how the same concerns arose in many countries about the effects of technology on the processing of personal information. Starting in the late 1960s, Fair Information Practices emerged as a common set or principles for addressing those concerns, and Bennett traces their spread. Fair Information Practices remain the most important international principles for privacy online and offline, and Bennett shows us why and how that happened.

Bennett, Colin. ***The Privacy Advocates.*** **Cambridge, MA: MIT Press, 2008.**

To write this book, Bennett, a Canadian political scientist, privacy scholar, and privacy advocate, interviewed privacy experts and advocates in the United States and elsewhere around the world. He seeks to describe privacy advocates, their organizations and operations, why they succeed or fail, and the future of the privacy movement. His insider's knowledge provided him with unparalleled access to many members of the privacy community. His analysis will be valuable to anyone who wants to conduct a privacy campaign, understand why a campaign succeeded or failed, or obtain insight into the people and the organizations that advocate for privacy. The book is recent enough that it includes examples of online privacy activities and campaigns and discusses activities of current online privacy activists.

Brin, David. ***The Transparent Society: Will Technology Force Us to Choose between Privacy and Freedom?*** **New York: Bantam, 1999.**

While Brin is better known as a science fiction writer, his nonfiction book on transparency has had a notable influence on debates about privacy in a networked society. *The Transparent Society* argues that if members of a society are being surveilled by law enforcement or other governmental entities, the best response for increased freedom and for achieving a more equitable balance of power is to allow for "watching the watchers," or surveilling back. For example, Brin suggests that police will show more respect for constitutional rights if cameras in the police station broadcast interactions with the public 24 hours a day. Some see Brin as antiprivacy, but Brin would counter that transparency and accountability are important values as well. The ever-increasing capabilities of new technology give this book continued relevance.

Cavoukian, Ann. ***Privacy by Design.*** **Ontario, Canada: Information and Privacy Commission of Ontario Canada, 2009.**

The author is one of the longest-serving privacy commissioners anywhere in the world, and her book promotes building privacy into information technology, business practices, and physical design. Cavoukian seeks to make privacy an original feature rather than an afterthought and to produce better and less expensive privacy outcomes. The notion of privacy by design is somewhat of a successor to privacy-enhancing technologies, a concept that received considerable attention in the 1990s but produced few noteworthy results.

Electronic Privacy Information Center. ***Privacy and Human Rights*****. Washington, D.C.: Electronic Privacy Information Center, 2006.**

This report by a leading U.S. privacy organization offers an overview of important privacy subjects as well as a review of the state of privacy in more than 75 countries. The international material was written with the assistance of hundreds of experts from around the world. It is a unique document and an excellent starting point for those who need to know the basic privacy laws in any particular country.

Groebner, Valentin. ***Who Are You? Identification, Deception, and Surveillance in Early Modern Europe*****. New York, NY: Zone Books, 2007.**

This book covers a period that predates the Internet by centuries, yet it still has relevance today. Groebner, a history professor in Switzerland, reviews identification issues in the thirteenth through seventeenth centuries. We wrestle today with these same problems on the Internet and elsewhere, and the history of this issue shows that there is nothing new under the sun when it comes to identifying individuals. Governments, law enforcement, banks, churches, and others all faced the same problems that we do today in determining who an individual is and what his authority is, but they did not have fingerprints, photographs, or administrative states to issue credentials. They used the facilities that they had, however imperfect the processes and the technologies. For example, artists were commissioned to engrave images of bankrupts, delinquents, and traitors. The parallels to today are consistently striking. Then, as now, we still ask, "Are we who we are, or are we who our *papers* say we are?"

Harper, Jim. ***Identity Crisis: How Identification Is Overused and Misunderstood*****. Washington, D.C.: Cato Institute, 2006.**

A member of the Washington, D.C., privacy community from his perch as director of information policy studies at the Cato Institute,

Harper tackles the problem of identification, a difficult and controversial issue for both the online and the offline world. The book offers a readable review of the basics of identification and the policy problems that better identification systems present. Harper's prescription is for multiple identification systems designed for different and narrow uses.

National Commission on Terrorist Attacks. ***The 9/11 Commission Report: Final Report of the National Commission on Terrorist Attacks upon the United States.*** **New York: Norton, 2004.**

The 9/11 Commission report was a major influence on policy and law in the years following the events of 9/11. Congress drew on the report to draft and enact laws affecting government surveillance, intelligence operations, and information networks. The commission's report remains a relevant privacy reference for this reason. For example, the report called for more secure identification of individuals and that recommendation inspired the REAL ID Act.

Nissenbaum, Helen. ***Privacy in Context: Technology, Policy, and the Integrity of Social Life.*** **Stanford, CA: Stanford Law Books, 2010.**

As a professor of media, culture, and communication and computer science at New York University, Nissenbaum brings a different perspective to the never-ending quest to understand what privacy means. Her main contribution is the recognition that context matters. People understand that different privacy norms apply in the workplace, in health care, in schools, and among family members. Nissenbaum argues that privacy violations occur when information sharing is inappropriate for a particular context. Nissenbaum's book also contains a useful review of the general academic literature on privacy and of the evolution of other theories about the meaning and importance of privacy.

O'Harrow, Robert. ***No Place to Hide.*** **New York: Free Press, 2005.**

The author was the leading reporter on privacy for several years for the *Washington Post*, and his stories had a significant effect on public awareness, company practices, and legislation. This book mostly covers the post-9/11 period when private database companies and governments worked together to use private dossiers about individuals to support the government's war on terrorism. Much of what O'Harrow wrote about has become much more common and familiar today, something that has made neither privacy advocates happy nor government efforts against terrorism necessarily more successful.

Parenti, Christian. ***The Soft Cage: Surveillance in America from Slavery to the War on Terror.*** **New York: Basic Books, 2004.**

Parenti's book details the technologies enabling surveillance through the years and decades. The book begins with the civil war era, detailing the technologies of cards and permits. As the chronology matures to the modern era, Parenti's research leads him to the newer surveillance technologies mediated through the Internet.

Regan, Priscilla M. ***Legislating Privacy: Technology, Social Values, and Public Policy.*** **Chapel Hill: University of North Carolina Press, 1995.**

This older book remains vital today for several reasons. Regan, a political scientist who also worked for the Congress, uses her Capitol Hill experience to tell stories behind the passage of several important privacy laws. These insights are essential for anyone who wants to understand how privacy problems receive enough public attention and activity to successfully drive new laws through the political process. One of the laws covered by the book is the Electronic Communications Privacy Act. The book also covers the 40-year legislative struggle that produced the first comprehensive federal wiretapping law in 1969. Regan also offers an original view of privacy as a value to society and not just a value to the individual, a perspective that continues to attract academic and other attention.

Shenk, David. ***The End of Patience.*** **Bloomington: Indiana University Press, 1999.**

Shenk is a longtime and astute observer of technology and its impact on people and culture. His first book on the topic, *Data Smog*, focuses on how too much information is too much of a good thing. In *The End of Patience*, Shenk, through a series of sharply honed essays, comments on how technology is simply not neutral. His discussions of ad creep, technological paparazzi, disclosure, personalized news, and technorealism contribute important thinking in the area of privacy and technology.

Solove, Daniel. ***The Digital Person.*** **New York: New York University Press, 2006.**

Law professor Daniel Solove offers an insightful look at what "digital dossiers" individuals leave online and what laws protect and do not protect privacy in this context. Among other topics, Solove explores the importance of metaphor in thinking about privacy and includes a discussion of both Kafka and Orwell.

Solove, Daniel. ***Understanding Privacy.*** **Cambridge, MA: Harvard University Press, 2008.**

Drawing in part on his writing in law journals, Solove explains why it is so hard to conceptualize the concept of privacy. He concludes that privacy is a plurality of different things without a singular essence. The book includes a detailed taxonomy of privacy that provides a more granular description of privacy violations than is traditionally found in American tort law. The taxonomy is a major contribution to analyzing what privacy really means in the law.

Schwartz, Paul M., and Daniel J. Solove. ***Information Privacy, Statutes and Regulations 2010–2011.*****New York, NY: Aspen Publishers, 2009.**

This reference brings together in one handy volume the text of all major federal privacy laws. It also includes some state laws and major international documents. Overall, the volume contains more than 50 statutes and regulations.

Smith, Robert Ellis. ***Ben Franklin's Web Site: Privacy and Curiosity from Plymouth Rock to the Internet.*** **Ann Arbor, Michigan: Sheridan Books, 2000.**

Robert Ellis Smith is a lawyer, newsletter publisher, and author who has been engaged in writing about privacy for more than three decades. His book offers an impressionistic trip through

American history with an eye fixed on privacy, curiosity, and the relentless changes brought about by technology on individual rights and autonomy. He begins in colonial America and proceeds through time focused on subjects connected to privacy that characterized different periods. He covers cyberspace, databases, and the Constitution, but he also delves into privacy issues using somewhat offbeat themes such as sex, torts, mistrust, curiosity, and serenity. The book provides a good general overview of privacy in American life and law.

Staples, William, ed. *Encyclopedia of Privacy*. Westport, CT: Greenwood Press, 2007.

This two-volume encyclopedia offers a useful introduction to and discussion of virtually all privacy issues, important court cases, laws, and technologies. It is an essential reference for any library or privacy researcher.

Szoka, Berin, and Adam Marcus, eds. *The Next Digital Decade*. Washington, D.C.: TechFreedom, 2011.

This book is notable for its focus on online privacy and for its contributors, including Mark MacCarthy, Jonathan Zittrain, and federal circuit court judge Alex Kozinski. Other perspectives in this volume include a strong libertarian point of view. In the online privacy debate, libertarians arguing for little to no regulation of the Internet have had an influence on current discussions about law and regulation. The book is available free online at http://nextdigitaldecade.com/read-book-now.

Westin, Alan. *Privacy and Freedom*. New York: Atheneum, 1967.

A classic of privacy literature that offered a widely used definition of privacy as the claim of individuals, groups, or institutions to determine for themselves when, how, and to what extent information about them is communicated to others. This conception of privacy has less and less relevance in the modern and online worlds, where unknown third parties maintain increasing amounts of personal information far beyond the knowledge and control of individuals. The book looks more like a product of its time and information technology rather than a map for the future, but it deserves respect for its past influence and importance.

Zittrain, Jonathan L. ***The Future of the Internet—and How to Stop It.*** **London: Yale University Press and Penguin UK, 2008.**

Zittrain, a professor of law at Harvard Law School, argues that the innovations that led to the Internet and its rapid worldwide adoption have run their course and that the Internet is now being transmuted into an unsettling nexus for controlling speech, art, and other things. Zittrain has long been interested in online content filtering and in the chilling of free speech online as well as in digital privacy. These themes are interwoven and discussed in this important book. A chapter is dedicated to a discussion of next generation privacy issues in the Web 2.0 environment. The book is also available free online at http://futureoftheinternet.org.

Nonprint

Video

American Civil Liberties Union. ***Scary Pizza Video*** **(animated short; http://www.youtube.com/watch?v=33CIVjvYyEk).**

The American Civil Liberties Union's *Scary Pizza* video has achieved cult status. It is an animated short about a man who tries to order a pizza, only to discover that he cannot order what he wants because the pizza order taker knows too much about him, his health status, and his history. This video came out after a news story documented that certain pizza chains were selling customers' private and unlisted cell phone numbers.

American Civil Liberties Union. ***Videos*** **(many on privacy; http://www.youtube.com/user/acluvideos).**

Some of these videos are short and humorous, and others explain in short format various aspects of privacy rights. Videos most relevant to online privacy include *Monster among Us* (http://www.youtube.com/user/acluvideos#p/search/0/CFSP5gAhg04) and *Real ID—A Real Nightmare* (http://www.youtube.com/user/acluvideos#p/search/1/8XObbEwI6P4).

Electronic Frontier Foundation. ***YouTube Channel*** **(privacy shorts and how-tos; http://www.youtube.com/user/EFForg).**

The Electronic Frontier Foundation's privacy videos focus on how to protect privacy, particularly online. Subjects include how to set Facebook privacy settings (*Facebook Instant Personalization Opt OUT—Version 2*, http://www.youtube.com/watch?v=SJkoyrPFaXE), how to stop Yahoo's social networking features (*Warning. Privacy Risk for Yahoo Users. You Must Opt-Out of New Service!*, http://www.youtube.com/watch?v=nJRIRIMmrAM), and Internet architecture and policy (*Architecture Is Policy: The Legal and Social Impact of Technical Design Decisions*, http://www.youtube.com/watch?v=Kbflv-umtN8).

Google. *Privacy Channel* (http://www.youtube.com/user/googleprivacy).

Google's YouTube privacy videos discuss topics such as online cookies. The videos tend to be self-promotional and to provide a limited perspective. However, they do present how-tos on Google-specific products that may be useful to Google users and to those researching Google's activities.

Mozilla. *Firefox Channel* (videos on Web browser privacy; http://www.youtube.com/user/firefoxchannel).

These videos provide short tutorials on how to manage Web browsing privacy in the Mozilla Firefox browser. The privacy-related videos can be easily found using the YouTube search engine. Mozilla has been directly supportive of privacy by including and expanding privacy features in its browser and by supporting add-ons to its browser that provide additional privacy protections.

Sophos Labs. *Facebook Privacy Videos* (http://www.youtube.com/user/SophosLabs).

Sophos Labs offers videos on how to manage privacy settings in Facebook. The videos contain some very good tips on what is a surprisingly complex subject at both the practical and policy levels.

***Star Wars Kid* (original video from 2002;: http://www.youtube.com/watch?v=HPPj6viIBmU).**

This is the original *Star Wars Kid* video. This video was posted without permission and is one of the first major incidents of cyberbullying that has been widely reported.

Movies

***The End of America* (2008, documentary).**

This documentary is based on Naomi Wolf's book of the same name. The film reviews how the gradual loss of liberties led to repressive regimes and focuses on how liberties have been lost in the United States. There is a discussion of privacy issues in the film, particularly surveillance. In general, the film offers useful background information.

***The Final Cut* (2004).**

The Final Cut tells the story of a society where people can elect to have their entire life recorded. After their death, a film editor who specializes in lifetime video summaries makes "the final cut" telling the story of a person's life. The story explores several privacy angles and is worth seeing in conjunction with David Brin's *Transparent Society*. What rights do people have when they are filmed by others? What happens when a person with an embedded camera witnesses a crime (or is the victim of one) and inadvertently records the criminal in action? What happens to an individual who does not know that another who is recording him or that someone is recording everything? The film raises many issues relevant to privacy, online or offline.

***Gattaca* (1997).**

Gattaca tells the story of a future society that places enormous importance and reliance on an individual's genetic profile. Individuals with a "good" genetic profile (no disease, high intelligence, and so forth) are granted more and better opportunities than individuals with less desirable profiles. We already face a world where information about us recorded by third parties affects some important rights (e.g., can we fly on a commercial airplane). The prospect that genetic information could be used in the same way to determine economic and other opportunities is well illustrated by the film, which carries the idea much farther along toward a logical and scary conclusion. As the use of genetic profiles increases through medical treatment and through voluntary genetic testing activities, genetic information could be added to online and other information already being used to affect how individuals are treated.

Minority Report (2002).

The plot of this science-fiction movie focuses on the elimination of crime by the use of predictions from individuals with special powers to see into the future and predict crimes beforehand. We already face the use of predictive technology that relies on online and offline personal information to predict behaviors and responses mostly but not exclusively for advertising purposes. The movie carries the notion well beyond current practices. In addition, the advertising technologies reflected in *Minority Report* also make it an important film for privacy. In the film, billboards of the future use facial recognition technologies to identify people and personalize advertisements to them. In 2011, digital signage networks already in use are employing very similar technologies, including facial recognition and personalized ads shown to select individuals or groups. This issue and these technologies are documented in a 2010 World Privacy Forum report about digital signage networks and privacy.

Nineteen Eighty-Four. Based on the novel by George Orwell (1984).

Nineteen Eighty-Four is a dark British film based on the dystopian novel of the same name by George Orwell. It is an effective adaptation of this famous novel about a totalitarian society of the future. The hero, Winston Smith, turns into a rebel; sees the inner workings of Big Brother; and eventually learns to love Big Brother.

Sliver (1993).

Sliver is film about surreptitious surveillance. In *Sliver,* the surveillance is taking place inside peoples' private residences thanks to a network of cameras the building owner installed in the unwitting tenants' living rooms, bedrooms, and bathrooms. In real life, the technology in the film has already been used by some landlords to spy on tenants.

***The Social Network* (2010).**

Mark Zuckerberg, the cofounder of Facebook, is the subject of this film that tells how the social networking site Facebook came into being. The film is good background on a major computing and cultural shift in how people are exchanging information online. Facebook has changed certain privacy norms online. While this film is fictionalized history, it is still a behind-the-scenes look that is helpful for contextualizing this computing and social shift.

Webcasts

A number of key privacy meetings, conferences, and testimony are available online via webcasts. This is a small selection of the most important of these resources.

2010 Office of the National Coordinator Update, U.S. Department of Health and Human Services. *Webcast Archive* (http://healthit.hhs.gov/portal/server.pt?open=512&mode=2&objID=3334).

This webcast is of a two-day meeting that the U.S. Department of Health and Human Services held to update the public and policymakers on privacy and technology policies relating to online health care, health care information technologies, and the National Health Information Network. Secretary of Health Kathleen Sebelius, National Coordinator for Health Information Technology David Blumenthal, and Health and Human Services Chief Privacy Officer Joy Pritts speak on the first day's webcast, among many others. The structure, function, and privacy policies for online networked medical records are at the center of this webcast.

CSO Security and Risk Magazine. *Webcast Series* (http://www.csoonline.com/webcasts/topic/43401/data-privacy).

CSO (Chief Security Officer) magazine's website hosts a wide array of privacy-centric webcasts. The intended audience for these webcasts is chief security officers at businesses and universities, so the material is focused and technical. Others can learn as well. Webcasts include topics on data privacy, online privacy, identity management, and access management.

ComputerWorld. ***Privacy Webcasts*** **(http://www.computerworld.com/s/webcasts/topic/84/Privacy/1).**

ComputerWorld magazine hosts a growing number of privacy-related webcasts on technical topics, including, application privacy, data security, and online analytics.

Conference of the Western Attorneys General. ***Webcast.*** **July 20, 2010 (http://media.cwagweb.org/cwag/privacy_3.0.asf).**

Attorney General Rob McKenna (Washington), Commissioner Julie Brill of the Federal Trade Commission, Assistant Attorney General Shannon Smith (Washington), Professor Paul Ohm (University of Colorado Law School), and Chris Hoofnagle (Berkeley Law) appeared at the annual meeting of the Conference of the Western Attorneys General. This webcast includes a wide-ranging discussion of online privacy and includes important comments by Commissioner Brill on behavioral advertising and what she thinks the commission should do to address it.

Deloitte. ***Webcast Series on Security and Privacy*** **(http://www.deloitte.com/view/en_CA/ca/article/9215586731101210VgnVCM100000ba42f00aRCRD.htm).**

Deloitte maintains a page with links to webcasts on security and privacy issues. Webcasts include a risk-based approach to data protection.

32nd International Conference of Data Protection and Privacy Commissioners. October 2010, Jerusalem (http://www.privacyconference2010.org).

This website hosts webcasts from the annual conference of data protection and privacy commissioners from around the world. The meeting of the international data protection commissioners is an important conference where the global state of privacy is discussed at a high level and in the presence of most of the leading privacy officials.

Federal Trade Commission. ***Privacy Roundtable Webcasts.*** **2009–2010 (http://www.ftc.gov/bcp/workshops/privacyroundtables).**

The Federal Trade Commission held a series of three roundtables on privacy that included many of the nation's leading experts on privacy. The roundtables dealt extensively with online privacy and give a broad snapshot of the status of online privacy. To locate the three webcasts, click on the webcast links on the privacy roundtables page in the above Web address.

O'Reilly. ***Cloud Security and Privacy Webcast.*** **January 2010 (http://oreillynet.com/pub/e/1514).**

This webcast presents of author Tim Mather and two co-presenters talking about cloud privacy and security. The information in this webcast is technical, but it is an excellent resource on the topic.

Solove, Daniel, ***The Future of Reputation: Gossip, Rumor, and Privacy on the Internet.*** **Oxford Internet Institute, June 2009 (http://webcast.oii.ox.ac.uk/index.cfm?view=Webcast&ID=2009 0625_290).**

This webcast presents author and scholar Daniel Solove discussing privacy, the Internet, and his newest book at Oxford University.

Mayer-Schönberger, Viktor. ***Delete—The Virtue of Forgetting in the Digital Age.*** **Oxford Internet Institute, September 2010 (http://webcast.oii.ox.ac.uk/index.cfm?view=Webcast&ID=2010 0917_332).**

This webcast focuses on the topic of online privacy and on the inability to "take back" information disseminated via the Web. Mayer-Schönberger is a noted international privacy scholar, and in the webcast he talks about his recent book.

Sound Clips

Department of Health and Human Service Advisory Committees. ***Committee Audio Clips*** **(http://healthit.hhs.gov/portal/server.pt/community/healthit_hhs_gov__federal_advisory_com mittees_%28facas%29/1149).**

The U.S. Department of Health and Human Services makes available online audio files of the meetings of its committees subject to the Federal Advisory Committee Act. These files offer insight into thinking about privacy and security and health information networks. Committees represented in these sound clips include the Health IT Policy Committee, the Health IT Standards Committee, and the long-standing National Committee on Vital and Health Statistics. The last of these three committees has broad responsibilities for health data issues.

UC Berkeley. *Courses Podcasts*. Fall 2007. Search Engines: Technology, Society, and Business. http://webcast.berkeley.edu/course_details.php?seriesid=1906978492.

This podcast covers Info 141, a University of California, Berkeley, course on search engines. Lectures include detailed information about privacy and search engines.

UC Berkeley. *Courses Podcasts*. Spring 2008: Information Law and Policy. feed://webcast.berkeley.edu/rss/course-archive.php?seriesid=1906978514.

This course, Info 205: Information Law and Policy, touches on many aspects of online privacy, including electronic communications, email, and the U.S. and European Union approach to privacy protection, among other topics.

Articles

Many thousands of articles about online privacy have been published by a variety of newspapers, academic publications, and trade publications. This represents only a small selection of what is available. These articles represent significant aspects of the online privacy discussion.

Feigenbaum, Joan, David C. Parkes, and David M. Pennock. "Computational Challenges in E-Commerce." *Communications of the ACM* 52, no. 1 (2009): 70–74. http://nrs.harvard.edu/urn-3:HUL.InstRepos:4039776.

This article is a detailed and technical look at user privacy, spam, and online content. The article explores the privacy paradox involved in online shopping. While users should have more privacy because they are not physically in a store, in reality, e-commerce transactions actually provide less privacy because of increased data collection needed to authenticate the transaction. The article notes that sophisticated consumers who value privacy will often compromise it to improve their position in an ongoing transaction.

Freudiger, Julien, Mohammed Hossein Manshaei, Jean-Pierre Hubaux, and David C. Parkes. "On Non-Cooperative Location Privacy: A Game-Theoretic Analysis." In *Proceedings of the 16th ACM Conference on Computer and Communications Security*, September 9–13, 2009, Chicago, by Ehab Al-Shaer, 324–37. New York: ACM Press, 2009. http://dash.harvard.edu/bitstream/handle/1/4340686/Freudiger_Non-Cooperative.pdf?sequence=1.

This article addresses locational privacy in online mobile networks and analyzes how adversaries can track user locations by employing mobile phone nodes. The article utilizes game theory to analyze how locational privacy might be improved. Although the article is highly technical, it contains innovative ideas that are important to current and future privacy debates because locational privacy grows in importance almost daily.

Hansell, Saul. "AOL Removes Search Data on Vast Group of Web Users." *New York Times*, August 8, 2006. http://query.nytimes.com/gst/fullpage.html?res=9504E5D81E3FF93BA3575BC0A9609C8B63.

This article describes the first stages of the 2006 AOL research data breach. This is one of the most significant online data breaches to occur involving search engine data. The breach resulted when AOL researchers published a supposedly anonymous data set of its users' searches. The data set was identifiable because each user's searches were lined using a single user number. A *New York Times* reporter was able to identify a searcher by name with little effort. The AOL research data breach brought to the front pages the reality that data can still be identifiable without overt identifiers.

Helft, Miguel, and Claire Cain Miller. "1986 Privacy Law Is Outrun by the Web." *New York Times*, January 10, 2011.http://www.nytimes.com/2011/01/10/techno logy/10privacy.html.

This article discusses the issue of law enforcement requests for information stored on third-party Web servers. Google, Facebook, and Twitter are the main companies discussed in the article. The article notes that in the first half of 2010, Google received 4,200 law enforcement requests for its data about its customers. Facebook is quoted as stating that it receives 10 to 20 law enforcement requests per day for customer information. The article speculates about the Electronic Communications Privacy Act and its applicability to today's world.

Hoofnagle, Chris Jay, Jennifer King, Su Li, and Joseph Turow. "How Different Are Young Adults from Older Adults When It Comes to Information Privacy?" April 16, 2010. http://papers.ssrn.com/sol3/papers.cfm?abstract_id=1589864.

This is the first major academic article that discusses and analyzes the supposed differences in approach to online privacy by age groups. The article found that the widely held assumption that Web users in their twenties, the so-called Facebook generation, cared less about privacy than older adults was inaccurate and not supported by statistical sampling in a large survey on the topic. This article has been influential in shaping policymakers' views about privacy and about how consumers of all ages feel about the importance of online privacy.

Ledlie, Jonathan, Jeffrey Shneidman, Matt Welsh, Mema Roussopoulos, and Margo Seltzer. "Open Problems in Data Collection Networks. In *Proceedings of the 11th Workshop on ACM SIGOPS European Workshop Leuven (Belgium)*, September 19–22, 2004, edited by Yolande Berbers and Miguel Castro. New York: ACM Press, 2004. http://dx.doi.org/10.1145/1133572.1133575.

This article describes sensor networks and the powerful applications that aim to aggregate, assimilate, and interact with scores of sensor networks in parallel. This article was an early look at sensor networks, and it remains an excellent resource for understanding the relationship of sensor networks to the online world and privacy.

Malin, B., and L. Sweeney. "How (Not) to Protect Genomic Data Privacy in a Distributed Network: Using Trail Re-Identification to Evaluate and Design Anonymity Protection Systems." *Journal of Biomedical Informatics* 37, no. 3 (2004). http://www.sciencedirect.com/science?_ob=ArticleURL&_udi=B6WHD-4CGNRKR-1&_user=10&_coverDate=06%2F30%2F2004&_rdoc=1&_fmt=high

&_orig=search&_origin=search&_sort=d&_docanchor=&view=c&_acct=C000050221&_version=1&_urlVersion=0&_userid=10&md5=13638482b5439bbf64c2733175397790&searchtype=a.

It is not possible to discuss network privacy without referring to this cornerstone article by Latanya Sweeney and Brad Malin. Professor Sweeney is a leading researcher on identifiability issues in health care and otherwise. This article broke important new ground in understanding anonymous data in networks.

Mandl, Kenneth D., Isaac S. Kohane, and Allan M. Brandt. "Electronic Patient-Physician Communication: Problems and Promise." ***Annals of Internal Medicine*** **129, no. 6 (1998): 495–500. http://www.annals.org/content/129/6/495.abstract.**

The authors of this article describe the privacy issues inherent in doctor-patient communication online. While the article is older, the problems it describes are timeless and still relevant today.

Narayanan, Arvind, and Vitaly Shmatikov. "Robust De-Anonymization of Large Sparse Datasets, Security and Privacy." ***IEEE Symposium on*** **Security and Privacy, 2008. (May 2008): 111–25. http://www.cs.utexas.edu/~shmat/shmat_oak08netflix.pdf.**

This justly famous online privacy article describes how the authors used a supposedly anonymous data set that Neflix.com published on the Web and deanonymized the data. Netflix published the data as part of a contest to develop better predictive methods about movie recommendations. The authors developed a new form of statistical deanonymization that allowed them to undertake deanonymization attacks against "high-dimensional microdata" available online. This kind of information reveals online users' preferences, recommendations, and other types of transaction records. The researchers applied their then-new technique to the Netflix Prize data set, which contained "anonymous" movie ratings of 500,000 subscribers of Netflix, the world's largest online movie rental service. Using the Internet Movie Database (http://www.imdb.com) as a source of background knowledge, the authors successfully identified Netflix records of known users, relying on their apparent political preferences and other potentially sensitive information. The article led to substantial dialogue about publication of anonymous data sets of online users as well as to a lawsuit.

Turow, Joseph, Jennifer King, Chris Jay Hoofnagle, Amy Bleakley, and Michael Hennessy. "Americans Reject Tailored Advertising and Three Activities That Enable It." November 2009. http://papers.ssrn.com/sol3/papers.cfm?abstract_id=1478214.

Published jointly by researchers from the University of California, Berkeley, and the University of Pennsylvania, this article has been influential in the debate about online advertising targeted to Web users. The article describes a survey in which Americans were queried about online ads that were delivered to them on the basis of their Web browsing. The study found that online users cited a "creepiness factor" regarding online targeted ads. This is one of the first articles to explore this topic via a large survey of online users.

Ohm, Paul. "Broken Promises of Privacy: Responding to the Surprising Failure of Anonymization." 57 *UCLA Law Review* 1701 (2010). http://uclalawreview.org/?p=1353.

Statisticians have long been aware of the limits of so-called deidentified data. Law professor Paul Ohm's article brings that research to the attention of lawyers and policymakers. He concludes that it does not take much to "reidentify" or "deanonymize" individuals hidden in anonymized data. The rapidly narrowing realm of data that is truly anonymous is a growing problem for researchers.

Reports

Key Government Reports

United Nations Conference on Trade and Development. "Creative Economy Report 2010, Creative Economy: A Feasible Development Option." http://www.unctad.org/Templates/webflyer.asp?docid=14229&intItemID=2068&lang=1&mode=highlights.

The report discusses links between economies, cultures, and technologies, including online technologies. The report attempts to provide empirical evidence that the creative industries—which include the technology sectors—are dynamic drivers of trade. The report has an intriguing discussion of access to information and knowledge as key drivers of economic growth and overall development. The report did not discuss the downsides of networked technologies in repressive regimes but rather focused on the positive economic elements online technologies have the potential to bring to developing nations. The report supports the conclusion that the privacy problems now faced by technologically advanced nations will spread everywhere.

White House. "National Strategy for Trusted Identities in Cyberspace." http://www.whitehouse.gov/sites/default/files/rss_viewer/NSTICstrategy_041511.pdf.

The national strategy published in April 2011 is a controversial Obama administration proposal to establish verifiable online identities for users of the Web. The idea is to rely on public/private efforts to establish an *identity ecosystem* of technical credentials that could be used across many websites. The identity ecosystem should provide people with a variety of more secure and privacy-enhancing ways to access online services. Yet fears remain that any new identity system will increase the ability to track individuals across many Web activities and that new identities will be subject to the same problems and security lapses as existing identifiers. Identity systems and politics cut across privacy from several different directions with the potential to both solve and exacerbate privacy problems at the same time. The high-level White House involvement in this effort is noteworthy.

U.S. Federal Trade Commission. "Protecting Consumer Privacy in an Era of Rapid Change: A Proposed Framework for Businesses and Policymakers." December 2010. http://www.ftc.gov/os/2010/12/101201privacyreport.pdf.

This preliminary staff report is an analysis and explanation about the state of privacy, particularly online privacy, and what needs to be done going forward to remedy potential consumer harms arising from a lack of privacy protections. The report discusses a Do Not Track mechanism, sensitive information and how it may be defined, Fair Information Practices, online behavioral privacy, and the shortcomings of self-regulation for online privacy.

Key Nonprofit Reports, Studies, and Documents

These reports and documents either have had significant impacts on the public debate or are regarded as key privacy resources.

Gmail Letter, Coalition of Privacy Groups. "An Open Letter to Google Concerning its Proposed Gmail Service." http://www.privacyrights.org/ar/GmailLetter.htm.

This letter was written to protest Google's Gmail program when it was first launched in beta on April 1, 2004. The letter, which was written by the Privacy Rights Clearinghouse and the World Privacy Forum and signed by 31 privacy and civil liberties groups based in the United States and abroad, argued that posting advertising directly in email was violative of users' privacy. This letter is significant in that it marked the first major protest of Google's privacy practices. Prior to this time, the search giant tended to be viewed as pro-privacy.

Center for Digital Democracy. "CDD Petition to the FTC: Online Drug Marketing." http://www.democraticmedia.org/files/u1/2010-02-28-FDAcomments.pdf.

The Center for Digital Democracy (CDD) filed lengthy petitions about online activities affecting privacy with the Federal Trade Commission (FTC). These documents, some of which were filed jointly with U.S. Public Interest Research Group, provide benchmarks and a snapshot of industry personal data processing practices. Other CDD filings with the FTC addressed online search privacy, behavioral advertising, and mobile marketing. The CDD complaints appear to have had some influence on policy and legislative events. For example, after the CDD raised privacy concerns about online behavioral advertising, the FTC held a public hearing on the matter and Congress began discussing new laws in the area.

Electronic Frontier Foundation: The Clicks That Bind: Ways Users Agree to Online Terms of Service." November 2009. http://www.eff.org/wp/clicks-bind-ways-users-agree-online-terms-service.

This short report discusses what it means when users click on "I agree" buttons and other such things online. The report coined a new term—*browsewrap*—which means that if you use a site, you are agreeing to the terms and the privacy policy. This is an important report that documents a commonly found unfair practice that affects online privacy.

Electronic Privacy Information Center. "Facebook Complaint and Request for Injunctive Relief to the Federal Trade Commission." May 5, 2010. http://epic.org/privacy/facebook/EPIC_FTC_FB_Complaint.pdf.

This complaint, written by the Electronic Privacy Information Center and signed by additional privacy and consumer groups, is one of the early formal complaints about Facebook's privacy settings. Notable in the complaint was its focus on the definition of what constitutes public information, a core argument in privacy.

Electronic Privacy Information Center. "*Amicus Brief Harris v. Blockbuster.*" http://epic.org/amicus/blockbuster/default.html.

In 2007, Facebook launched its Beacon advertising program, which broadcast a user's interaction with an advertiser to the feeds of that user's friends. Beacon also broadcast information from third-party websites, such as Blockbuster. In 2008, a Facebook user filed a class-action complaint against Blockbuster for violations of the Video Privacy Protection Act, which bans the disclosure of personally identifiable rental information without written consent. The Electronic Privacy Information Center filed an amicus brief arguing for enforcement of the video privacy law in an online context.

Privacy International. "European Privacy and Human Rights 2010." https://www.privacyinternational.org/ephr.

This report provides a summary and update about the state of privacy in each of the European Union member states. It contains a resource section and a country-by-country summary of findings, with many reports in multiple languages.

Donald Carrington Davis. "My Space Isn't Your Space: Expanding the Fair Credit Reporting Act to Ensure Accountability and Fairness in Employer Searches of Online Social Networking Services." ***Kansas Journal of Law and Public Policy*** **16, no. 237 (2007). http://www.privacyrights.org/ar/mySpace-background-checks.htm.**

This report discusses ways that social networking sites are providing a way that employers can circumvent the rights that the Fair Credit Reporting Act provides for those seeking employment. While the report is a few years old, the arguments are the same today as they were in 2007, but the scope of information available online has expanded.

World Privacy Forum. "Medical Identity Theft: The Information Crime That Can Kill You." May 2006. http://www.worldprivacy forum.org/pdf/wpf_medicalidtheft2006.pdf.

This is the first report that used the term "medical identity theft," and it is also the first report to document this crime. The core argument of the report is that medical identity theft threatens profound harm for consumers because health care files can be altered as a result of the commission of a crime, and those changes can affect an individual's health care treatment. The report called for changes to the National Health Information Network to protect against this crime in the online space. Any online health network is likely to exacerbate the number and the consequences of medical identity theft.

Key Academic Studies and Reports

Online privacy issues are fertile areas for academic research and studies. There is much excellent material. Here are some key studies that have had an impact on policy and/or technology or that represent important aspects of privacy thought.

Annenberg Public Policy Center. "Americans and Online Privacy: The System Is Broken." June 2003. http://www.asc.upenn .edu/usr/jturow/internet-privacy-report/36-page-turow-version -9.pdf.

This report by Professor Joseph Turow is one of the earliest to address online privacy perceptions of users. The study questioned users' awareness of privacy policies and online data flows after "Web 2.0." One notable finding, based on a survey, is that despite adults' strong concerns about online privacy, most misunderstood the purpose of a privacy policy. The study also revealed the depth to which adults who use the Internet were fundamentally unaware of data flow, of how organizations glean bits of knowledge about individuals online, and of how they interconnect those bits, link them to other sources of information, and share them with other organizations. Turow's prognosis about the lack of consumer understanding online privacy was early and on target. Even though this study is several years old, it remains a key benchmarking study, and many believe that its conclusions remain valid.

Reidenberg, Joel R., et al. "Children's Educational Records and Privacy: A Study of Elementary and Secondary School State Reporting Systems." October 28, 2009. http://www.law.fordham.edu/assets/CLIP/CLIP_Report_Childrens_Privacy_Final.pdf.

In this study, the authors painstakingly reviewed data available about statewide longitudinal data systems across the country and found that the privacy protections for these systems were substantially deficient in most states. The report noted that "the majority of longitudinal databases that we examined held detailed information about each child in what appeared to be non-anonymous student records. Typically, the information collected included directory, demographic, disciplinary, academic, health, and family information. Some striking examples are that at least 32% of the states warehouse children's social security numbers, at least 22% of the states record children's pregnancies, at least 46% of the states track mental health, illness, and jail sentences as part of the children's educational records, and almost all states with known programs collect family wealth indicators." The report details the many ways these databases are used, disseminated, and, in some cases, outsourced. The report has far-reaching implications for the education sector and how it intersects with online privacy.

Roberts, Hal, et al. "2007 Circumvention Landscape Report: Methods, Uses, and Tools." 2009. http://dash.harvard.edu/bitstream/handle/1/2794933/2007_Circumvention_Landscape.pdf.

This report studied how governments filter and control Internet usage by their respective citizens, how those citizens were circumventing that control, and which circumvention techniques worked most effectively. This issue is of continuing interest, particularly after Egypt shut down Internet traffic in January 2011. Immediately, users found innovative ways to circumvent the shutdown through both simple and sophisticated means. This report describes the mechanisms of filtering and circumvention and evaluates 10 tools for their utility, usability, security, promotion, sustainability, and openness. While some of the report's findings may now be out of date, the broad conclusions about circumvention tools remain of interest. Online circumvention techniques are often paired with privacy-enhancing techniques.

Online Resources

General (Nongovernment) Internet Resources

World Privacy Forum. "A Patient's Guide to HIPAA." March 2009. http://www.worldprivacyforum.org/hipaa/index.html.

This guide offers numerous frequently asked questions about the complex Health Insurance Portability and Accountability Act. The audience for the guide is patients rather than for health care professionals, and the language is aimed at the average individual.

The Berkeley Blog. BCLT's Privacy Programs. http://blogs.berkeley.edu/author/choofnagle.

Chris Hoofnagle, director of law and technology programs at Berkeley Law and a well-known privacy expert, hosts the privacy blog at Berkeley, discussing topics ranging from Google and privacy to Facebook to weight loss scams. The posts are crucial reading for anyone interested in online privacy.

American Civil Liberties Union of Northern California. Bytes and Pieces (blog). http://www.aclunc.org/issues/technology/blog/index.shtml.

Technology and civil liberties policy director Nicole Ozer of the American Civil Liberties Union of Northern California publishes this blog. It focuses on privacy, technology, and digital liberties and includes ongoing discussion of online privacy issues.

Privacy Activism. *Carabella* (free online game).http://www.privacyactivism.org/carabella/quest-for-tunes.html.

Carabella is a unique resource. It is an animated online game geared toward teaching 20-somethings about privacy risks. The game is thoughtful and was created by Privacy Activism, a non-profit group in the privacy arena. Three episodes of Carabella have been posted: *Carabella on the Run* (2009), *Carabella Goes to College* (2003), and *Carrabella, the Quest for Tunes* (2002). Each game focuses on a different aspect of privacy threats, with the most recent addressing social networking.

Clinton, Hilary Rodham. "Remarks of Hilary Rodham Clinton on Internet Freedom." January 21, 2010.http://www.state.gov/secretary/rm/2010/01/135519.htm.

In this wide-ranging speech delivered at the Newseum in Washington, D.C., Secretary of State Clinton discusses the state of the Internet and the role it plays in current world affairs. Secretary Clinton touches on privacy issues, particularly in relation to oppressive regimes. In this speech, she notes, "The spread of information networks is forming a new nervous system for our planet. When something happens in Haiti or Hunan, the Berlin Wall symbolized a world divided and it defined an entire era. Today, remnants of that wall sit inside this museum where they belong, and the new iconic infrastructure of our age is the internet. Instead of division, it stands for connection. But even as networks spread to nations around the globe, virtual walls are cropping up in place of visible walls." Clinton argues that online censorship contravenes the Universal Declaration on Human Rights, which tells us that all people have the right "to seek, receive and impart information and ideas through any media and regardless of frontiers." She also noted that "with the spread of these restrictive practices, a new information curtain is descending across much of the world. And beyond this partition, viral videos and blog posts are becoming the samizdat of our day."

AppRiver. http://blogs.appriver.com.

AppRiver is a commercial company that sells messaging services. Its blog has many posts covering online privacy and security issues, including identification of many online scams, phishing expeditions, and the like.

Bureau of National Affairs. *Electronic Commerce and Law Report* (e-newsletter). http://www.bna.com/products/ip/eplr.htm.

The Bureau of National Affairs publishes an electronic newsletter on privacy and online issues. A free trial is available for this subscription-only publication. The newsletter offers extensive, comprehensive, and high-quality coverage of domestic and international privacy activities as well as e-commerce developments.

Center for Democracy and Technology. *Guide to Online Privacy.* http://www.cdt.org/privacy/guide.

The Center for Democracy and Technology maintains a guide for consumers about online privacy via its website. The guide contains tips for consumers as well as a review of relevant law. It includes an annotated list of current federal privacy laws with links to the text of the laws.

Fordham Law School, Center on Law and Information Policy. *CLIP-pings* (online newsletter). http://law.fordham.edu/center-on-law-and-information-policy/20291.htm.

Fordham's Center on Law and Information Policy (CLIP) maintains an active e-newsletter of high quality. It frequently covers the intersection between law and technology and privacy, with numerous pieces about online privacy. The Fordham CLIP site also maintains a body of privacy-related research, including groundbreaking research on educational privacy issues.

Concurring Opinions: The Law, The Universe, Everything (blog). http://www.concurringopinions.com.

The Concurring Opinions blog hosts well-known legal scholars and covers privacy, online privacy, and judicial and legislative developments. Regular contributors include Professors Frank Pasquale, Danielle Citron, Daniel Solove, and Sarah Waldeck. They are joined frequently by guest authors. The blog is a good place to find current comments on brand-new decisions of the Supreme Court and other courts on Fourth Amendment and other issues related to online privacy.

***Dark Reading* (online magazine). http://www.darkreading.com.**

Dark Reading is essential reading for keeping up to date with the security aspects of online privacy. This well-edited site includes coverage of security breaches, encryption, storage security, and other topics that overlap with privacy.

Center for Digital Democracy. Digital Destiny (blog). http://www.democraticmedia.org/jcblog.

In this blog maintained by privacy and online media expert Jeff Chester, the main topic of discussion is online privacy. The center is an important and active participant in consumer privacy activities in Washington, and Chester offers an insider's view.

European Digital Rights. *EDRI Gram* (online newsletter). http://www.edri.org/edrigram.

EDRI Gram is a free biweekly electronic newsletter about digital civil rights in Europe published by European Digital Rights, an organization with approximately 30 privacy and civil rights organizations as members from 18 different countries in Europe. The newsletter focuses on developments in all countries within the territory of the Council of Europe. Each newsletter provides a detailed and current summary of activities in Europe, often with links that identify additional resources.

Electronic Frontier Foundation. Deep Links Blog. http://www.eff.org/deeplinks/archive.

This blog is an active news and tools resource for online privacy topics and issues, with coverage of activities in the courts, in Congress, and on the Internet. It is a key resource for online privacy.

Electronic Information Privacy Center. http://epic.org.

The Electronic Information Privacy Center (EPIC) is one of the principal nonprofit organizations in Washington, D.C., focused on privacy issues. Many of the resources on its organizational website focus on online privacy and civil liberties. On its home page, EPIC maintains an active list of privacy news and policy issues. EPIC also publishes the *EPIC Alert*, a free e-newsletter on current activities affecting privacy (see http://epic.org/alert).

Federal Trade Commission. "FTC Twitter Feed." http://twitter.com/#!/FTCgov.

This is the official Twitter feed of the Federal Trade Commission, covering consumer protection and privacy matters, among other commission activities.

Facebook. The Facebook Blog. http://blog.facebook.com.

Facebook for some has been a focus of many recent privacy controversies. To keep current on the latest privacy changes to Facebook, its blog is a reliable news source and an advocate for Facebook's point of view. The archives are good for reading Facebook's official reactions to privacy concerns arising from users.

First Person Cookie Blog. http://firstpersoncookie.wordpress .com.

This blog discusses the technical aspects of online privacy. It is maintained by a Mozilla developer and includes but is not limited to technical aspects of browsers and browser privacy features.

GigaLaw. *Daily News* (online newsletter). http://gigalaw.com.

GigaLaw publishes a well-edited collection of news stories on the law and technology, which include international activities, online privacy, and other aspects of Internet law and activities.

GovInfoSecurity. http://www.govinfosecurity.com/index.php.

This active and insightful blog is a commercially operated blog that discusses the U.S. federal government's security and privacy activities with a particular focus on technology. The site also hosts webinars.

International Association of Privacy Professionals. *IAPP Daily Dashboard*. https://www.privacyassociation.org/publications/daily_dashboard.

The International Association of Privacy Professionals maintains a free daily emailed newsletter with privacy news, with an additional once-a-week newsletter on international privacy developments. The topics include online privacy as well as other areas of privacy. The Daily Dashboard website hosts a year of newsletter archives.

Institute for the Study of Privacy Issues. *ISPI Clips*. http://www.privacynews.com.

The Institute for the Study of Privacy Issues is a small organization based in Canada that offers electronic clipping service of news articles relating to privacy from the United States and Canada. A two-week trial of the subscription service is available. Many privacy organizations and chief privacy officers subscribe to this comprehensive service.

World Privacy Forum. "Internet Privacy Landing Page." http://www.worldprivacyforum.org/internetprivacy.html.

The World Privacy Forum's Internet Privacy Page contains how-to advice for consumer privacy online. Included are search engine privacy tips, online job search tips, and more.

Madisonian.net. Law, Technology, Society (blog). http://madisonian.net.

Madisonian.net is a blog about the law and how it interfaces with technology. This blog is written by law professors based in the United States, and it often contains entries about online privacy. The contributors write frequently about Facebook privacy issues and the law.

Network Advertising Initiative. "Opt-Out Tool." http://www.networkadvertising.org/managing/opt_out.asp.

The Network Advertising Initiative (NAI) is a self-regulatory group of online marketing and analytics companies. NAI maintains an "opt-out cookie" page where consumers may go and opt out of online tracking cookies. Using these cookies will not stop all tracking, but the cookies may assist in stopping certain kinds of tracking.

Patient Privacy Rights. Patient Privacy Rights Blog. http://patientprivacyrights.org.

Patient Privacy Rights, a nonprofit organization, maintains a blog with updates on medical privacy topics, a subject that increasingly involves online records and networks.

PogoWasRight.org. http://www.pogowasright.org.

PogoWasRight is a blog written anonymously. It is well known in privacy circles for its wide coverage and currency. The blog hosts information about current and past online data breaches, provides some commentary, and offers links to current articles, blogs, court cases, and other events related to privacy.

Privacy Activism. ***Blog and Twitter Feed.*** **http://www.privacy activism.org.**

The nonprofit organization Privacy Activism based in San Francisco maintains a very active Twitter feed of privacy stories and news on its home page and blog.

Privacy International. ***Twitter Feed and Resources.*** **http://www.privacyinternational.org.**

The international nonprofit Privacy International maintains an active Twitter feed on online privacy topics as well as other resources on international privacy activities.

Privacy Journal **(newsletter). http://www.privacyjournal.net.**

Published since 1974, *the Privacy Journal* is monthly subscription newsletter on privacy topics. The journal also offers other resources, including a directory of privacy professionals and a compilation of state and federal privacy laws.

Privacy Laws and Business. (newsletter and event calendar). http://www.privacylaws.com.

Privacy Laws and Business publishes an important European Union/U.K. newsletter (with other international coverage as well) on data protection as well as numerous updates via email, video, and other media. It also holds conferences and conducts extensive privacy training. There is a limited free news service, but most of the better materials are available by subscription only. Privacy Laws and Business also maintains an excellent online calendar of events.

PrivacyLives. http://www.privacylives.com.

PrivacyLives, published by privacy expert Melissa Ngo, is a blog dedicated to rounding up privacy news online. It is an excellent resource for keeping up with privacy issues, in particular online privacy issues. The website provides links to many other online privacy resources.

Privacy Rights Clearinghouse. http://www.privacyrights.org.

The nonprofit Privacy Rights Clearinghouse publishes and maintains many consumer guides about online privacy topics, including search engines, email, online job searching, and other online privacy-related topics. It is a key consumer resource for information about online privacy. Privacy Rights Clearinghouse, Chronology of Data Breaches, Security Breaches 2005-Present. http://www.privacyrights.org/data-breach. This list of security breaches offers names of organizations, locations, dates, and numbers. It has search capability and frequently asked questions about breaches. It is a unique resource.

Privacy Times **(newsletter). http://www.privacytimes.com.**

Privacy Times, published by Evan Hendricks, is a subscription newsletter on privacy topics that started in 1981. The website has limited information but does include links to other online privacy resources.

Reclaim Privacy. http://www.reclaimprivacy.org.

Reclaim Privacy, operated by volunteers, offers an online tool that helps consumers check their own Facebook privacy settings. Reclaim Privacy also maintains frequent updates about Facebook privacy news, but it is not always fully up to date.

MSNBC. The Red Tape Chronicles Blog. http://redtape.msnbc.com.

This blog site, written by Bob Sullivan, contains news about privacy-related matters, especially those issues related to privacy and technology. Articles include consumer-focused pieces, such as what happens when you buy coffee with an iPhone, what to do about Web rumor mills, and other similar topics. Articles tend to be longer and more complete than many blogs.

The Register **(online magazine). http://www.theregister.co.uk.**

The Register is an irreverently written technical magazine that has a history of being ahead of trends. It publishes many articles about online privacy and has on occasion broken significant privacy news stories. Although written in a cheeky style, *The Register* is careful with its substance and its facts.

***The RISKS Forum Digest* (moderated electronic forum/newsletter). http://catless.ncl.ac.uk/risks.**

The *RISKS Forum Digest* is an online security–focused publication in digest format, with many articles of note contributed by various authors about online privacy and other relate topics. It is published by the Association for Computing Machinery and moderated by Peter Neumann, a well-known computer scientist whose work focuses on security matters. Archives dating back to 1985 provide a rich historical resource and a rare one for the Internet.

Electronic Frontier Foundation. *Surveillance Self-Defense*. https://ssd.eff.org.

This project of the Electronic Frontier Foundation is an online tool that explains the fundamentals of data storage on computers, security threats, and how to protect data. The website also explains the complex laws that regulate government surveillance, including the Foreign Intelligence Surveillance Act. This is a key online privacy resource.

Bruce Schneier. Schneier on Security Blog. http://www.schneier.com.

Bruce Schneier, a well-known online security expert, maintains a current blog on online privacy and security issues that includes essays, audio, video, and news capsules. Schneier also publishes Crypto-Gram, a well-written and free monthly email newsletter that focuses on security and privacy.

***TechDirt* (online magazine). http://www.techdirt.com.**

TechDirt covers on all things online, including copyright, security, and privacy issues.

National Conference of State Legislatures. The Thicket (blog). http://ncsl.typepad.com/the_thicket.

The National Conference of State Legislatures (NCSL) publishes an excellent blog of state legislative news that covers online privacy among other topics. It is an excellent way of seeing news about online privacy before it is widely reported. Other NCSL online resources compile information about state legislative activities, including privacy, and the NCSL website is a good place to look for lists of state data breach laws, bills on popular topics, and the like.

***Thinkq* (online magazine). http://www.thinq.co.uk.**

Thinkq is an online magazine published in the United Kingdom dedicated to information security and with a strong focus on online privacy. To find the most recent articles on online privacy, do a key word search from the home page.

***Wired Magazine*. Threat Level Blog. http://www.wired.com/threatlevel.**

This blog consistently discusses breaking news in the area of online privacy. It is a well-researched site focusing on privacy, crime, and security online.

Kaspersky Labs. ThreatPost News Service (blog). https://threatpost.com.

ThreatPost, by the well-known security firm Kaspersky Labs, has a section dedicated to privacy that mostly covers online privacy. Posts tend to be fairly technical. The website has many other useful resources on security.

U.S. Public Interest Research Group. Consumer Protection Blog. https://www.uspirg.org/consumer-blog.

Longtime consumer advocate Ed Mierzwinski maintains the group's consumer blog, which he updates frequently with news items about online privacy and other consumer issues. Mierzwinski is an active lobbyist on Capitol Hill, and he often provides current information and insights on legislative developments.

Websense. http://community.websense.com/blogs/securitylabs.

Websense is a company that sells Web tracking tools to companies internationally. Its blog covers an array of technical online privacy topics, some of which are difficult to find elsewhere.

Government Resources

Office of the National Coordinator Update, U.S. Department of Health and Human Services. ***Event Transcripts of Dec. 14–15, 2010.*** **http://www.tvworldwide.com/events/hhs/101214.**

The full transcript of a two-day meeting on the National Health Information Network is available here. This meeting was part of an ongoing discussion of health network issues at Health and Human Services and provides a snapshot of health information technology and online health care discussions.

California Privacy and Security Advisory Board. ***Interim Privacy and Security Guidelines.*** **October 19, 2009. California Office of Health Information Exchange. http://www.ohi.ca.gov/calohi/LinkClick.aspx?fileticket=yLyFEJ10JNE%3d&tabid=56.**

The California Privacy and Security Advisory Board is a group of more than 20 stakeholders representing consumers, health plans, hospitals, doctors, and pharmacies. Appointed by the California secretary of health, the board was tasked with creating voluntary guidelines for the online transmission of health care information. The board based its guidelines on Fair Information Practices. Its guidelines went beyond the requirement of the federal Health Insurance Portability and Accountability Act, recommending that health care providers allow patients to opt in to widespread electronic exchange of records rather than mandating participation in the exchanges. The guidelines are an important example of how consent can work in an online health information exchange environment.

CHILI. ***California Health Information Law Identification Tool.*** **2008. http://www.ohi.ca.gov/chili/index.php.**

CHILI is an online interactive and searchable database of all California laws regarding health care and technology. It is an excellent health privacy law resource.

Data Council, Office of the Assistant Secretary for Planning and Evaluation, Department of Health and Human Services. ***Privacy Bibliography.*** **http://aspe.hhs.gov/datacncl/privacy/#additional.**

This website offers a bibliography that links to U.S. and foreign documents about privacy. Some old reports of significant historical interest are available online only through this website.

Department of Defense Privacy and Civil Liberties Office. http://privacy.defense.gov.

The Department of Defense (DOD) maintains one of the best-organized websites offering documents relating to the Privacy Act of 1974, a law that applies to federal agencies. In addition to DOD privacy materials, the website links to all OMB documents relating to the Privacy Act, the E-Government Act, and other guidance documents.

U.S. Government Accountability Office. "Direct-to-Consumer Genetic Tests: Misleading Test Results Are Further Complicated by Deceptive Marketing and Other Questionable Practices." July 22, 2010. http://www.gao.gov/new.items/d10847t.pdf.

This report includes an important independent investigation of direct-to-consumer (DTC) genetic tests and the advertising claims associated with those tests, some of which are sold online. To investigate advertising methods, the Government Accountability Office (GAO) made undercover contact with 15 DTC companies. The GAO found that the tests offered were not accurate predictors medically. It also found "egregious" examples of deceptive marketing. The GAO also found that some of the companies had poor privacy policies posted online, and the policies allowed additional uses of customers' genetic information. Increasingly, health and genetic activities occur online in an unregulated environment as covered by the GAO report.

Office of the National Coordinator for Health Information Technology, U.S. Department of Health and Human Services. FACA Blog. http://healthit.hhs.gov/blog/faca.

This blog is maintained by the Office of the National Coordinator for Health Information Technology (ONC), which is actively engaged in making decisions about the structure and function of the National Health Information Network. The blog contains posts related to advisory committees supervised by the ONC and updates about ONC requests for public comments, meeting dates, links to audio files and webcasts (when available), and current meeting topics. Many important aspects on online health information are being determined by the work of the ONC.

Federal Trade Commission. "Privacy Initiatives." http://www.ftc.gov/privacy.

The Federal Trade Commission oversees several federal privacy statutes, operates the federal Do Not Call Registry, and otherwise is involved in privacy oversight and enforcement in addition to its general consumer protection responsibilities. The commission maintains a Web page with information on its activities and also provides consumer advice on privacy matters, including online privacy.

Gerber, Eleanor, and Ashley Landreth. *Respondents' Understandings of Confidentiality in a Changing Privacy Environment.* Statistical Research Division, U.S. Census Bureau. September 24, 2007. http://www.census.gov/srd/papers/pdf/rsm2007-37.pdf.

The U.S. Census has conducted a considerable amount of consumer research about perceptions and understandings of privacy. This is an early look at how people understood the meaning of confidentiality of census information.

U.S. Government Accountability Office. "Information Management: Challenges In Federal Agencies' Use of Web 2.0 Technologies." July 22, 2010. http://www.gao.gov/new.items/d10872t.pdf.

This Government Accountability Office (GAO) report found that U.S. federal agencies use Web 2.0 technologies to enhance services and support their individual missions. As of July 2010, the GAO identified that 22 of 24 major federal agencies had a presence on Facebook, Twitter, and YouTube. These offerings raise complex privacy questions for federal agencies, which have a mandate of transparency and which operate under federal laws and policies that affect their online activities in ways that do not apply to other organizations.

U.S. Government Accountability Office. "Information Sharing: Federal Agencies Are Helping Fusion Centers Build and

Sustain Capabilities and Protect Privacy, but Could Better Measure Results." September 2010. http://www.gao.gov/new.items/d10972.pdf.

This Government Accountability Office report examines state-level fusion centers. Fusion centers are data centers where homeland security, terrorism, and other intelligence information is shared among law enforcement agencies at various levels of government. The collection and sharing of personal information through online government networks increases constantly, and fusion centers are relatively new institutions that have attracted a considerable amount of opposition from civil liberties organizations.

Landreth, Ashley, et al. "Report of Cognitive Testing of Privacy- and Confidentiality-Related Statements in Respondent Materials for the 2010 Decennial: Results from Cognitive Interview Pretesting with Volunteer Respondents." http://www.census.gov/srd/papers/pdf/rsm2008-04.pdf.

This Census Bureau report gives granular details about how consumers understand definitions of confidentiality and privacy. The Census Bureau has traditionally faced considerably privacy resistance from citizens and is looking to new data collection methods for the future.

U.S. Department of Health and Human Services. "Medical Identity Theft Environmental Scan." October 15, 2008. http://healthit.hhs.gov/portal/server.pt/gateway/PTARGS_0_10731_850701_0_0_18/HHS%20ONC%20MedID%20Theft_EnvScan_101008_Final%20COVER%20NOTE.pdf.

This is the first government report to acknowledge medical identity theft as an issue of significant policy concern. It follows a 2006 World Privacy Forum report that first identified the issue as a new and different type of identity theft. The medical identity theft scan is a compilation of stakeholder interviews, analysis of relevant laws, and other discussion surrounding the issue, including some consideration of how the still nascent National Health Information Network should respond to the ongoing threat of this identity crime.

U.S. Department of Health and Human Services. "Medical Identity Theft Final Report." January 9, 2009. http://healthit

.hhs.gov/portal/server.pt/gateway/PTARGS_0_10731_848096_0_0_18/MedIdTheftReport011509.pdf.

This report on medical identity theft from the department's follows up and presents a synthesis of its work in the area stemming from its information scan on the topic and from a daylong hearing on the topic.

U.S. Department of Health and Human Services. *The ONC-Coordinated Federal Health IT Strategic Plan: 2008–2012.* June 3, 2008.http://healthit.hhs.gov/portal/server.pt/gateway/PTARGS_0_10731_848083_0_0_18/HITStrategicPlan508.pdf.

The department's strategic plan for health information technology discusses online health care and lays out the federal government's approach to online health care and the National Health Information Network. It is an important reference document in the area of online medical privacy and technology.

Office of the National Coordinator, U.S. Department of Health and Human Services. *Definitions of Health Information Technology Terms.* June 2008.http://healthit.hhs.gov/portal/server.pt/gateway/PTARGS_0_10731_848083_0_0_18/HITStrategicPlan508.pdf.

This document defines the most important electronic health terms.

U.S. Department of Health and Human Services. "Personal Health Records: Understanding the Evolving Landscape." December 3, 2010. –http://healthit.hhs.gov/portal/server.pt/community/healthit_hhs_gov__personal_health_records_–_phr_roundtable/3169.

This Web page provides an archive of a Health and Human Services Roundtable meeting held on personal health records. The roundtable included a significant discussion of online health records and the privacy implications and issues related to them.

U.S. Government Accountability Office. "Privacy: Government Use of Data from Information Resellers Could Include Better Protections." March 11, 2008. http://www.gao.gov/new.items/d08543t.pdf.

This report investigated federal agencies' use of information brokers and information resellers. These companies collect, compile, and sell data from many sources, including online sources. The Government Accountability Office (GAO) published an extensive report in 2006 about the federal government's use of information brokers, and it found many privacy issues particularly relating to nontransparency. This 2008 GAO report, a follow-up to the earlier report, investigates changes since 2006. The GAO found that there were still problems but that some improvement had been seen.

U.S. Government Accountability Office. "Social Security Numbers Are Widely Available in Bulk and Online Records, but Changes to Enhance Security Are Occurring." September 19, 2008. http://www.gao.gov/new.items/d081009r.pdf.

This Government Accountability Office (GAO) investigation reviews the availability of Social Security numbers (SSNs) online and their sale in bulk. The report found "millions of records with SSNs have already been obtained in bulk or online." The report notes how they are used, with GAO research showing that some businesses send records with SSNs offshore where little is known about how they are used or protected. The report is a core document describing the online availability of SSNs.

U.S. Department of Commerce and European Commission. *US-EU Safe Harbor Documents: Documents Relating to the U.S.-EU & Swiss Safe Harbor Frameworks.* http://www.export.gov/safeharbor.

In order address different privacy approaches, the United States and the European Union (EU) negotiated in 2000 a Safe Harbor Framework, a streamlined means for U.S. organizations to comply with the EU Data Protection Directive in order to support the export of personal information from Europe to the United States. The documents that describe the Safe Harbor Framework explain the requirements and the procedures that apply. The United States and Switzerland reached a similar agreement in 2009. The Safe Harbor Framework has been controversial in many respects for a lack of oversight and compliance.

U.S. Government Accountability Office. http://www.gao.gov.

The Government Accountability Office (GAO) is a resource for high-quality reports on privacy in the government sector. To find the newest reports, use the GAO search toolbar and do a key word search for the terms "online privacy" and "privacy."

White House Office of Management and Budget. http://www.whitehouse.gov/omb/agency/default.

The Office of Management and Budget (OMB) has responsibility for overseeing some federal agency privacy operations, including those that affect the availability of online resources to the public and the rules that apply to the collection, maintenance, use, and disclosure of personal information. OMB bulletins, circulars, memoranda, privacy guidance, and other documents that relate to its information policy activities are available at the OMB website. The OMB Office of Information and Regulatory Affairs, which is responsible for information policy issues, maintains a website that focuses on information policy activities, including privacy (see http://www.whitehouse.gov/omb/inforeg_infopoltech).

Glossary

APEC The Asia-Pacific Economic Cooperation, an organization made up of 21 member economies from around the Asia-Pacific region.

APEC Privacy Framework A document setting out nine privacy principles that describe the APEC approach to privacy.

App Slang for *application*, a piece of software that operates on an iPhone, on Facebook, or another networked device or website. Applications may be created by first parties or by third parties. Facebook's *Instant Personalization* program is its own application, so it is a first-party application. *Farmville* is an example of a third-party application for Facebook. Applications, especially third-party apps, may have widely varying levels of privacy policies and features.

Article 29 Data Protection Working Party A group established by the European Union (EU) Data Protection Direction and composed of EU data protection authorities. The Working Party provides advice to the EU Commission and others.

Authentication In the context of online privacy, determining a Web user's identity to a particular degree of certainty, depending on the context. Many websites authenticate an individual's identity by asking for a user name and password. In online banking, the preference is for two-factor authentication, which means that two distinct and different elements of information will be used to determine a user's identity online. Passwords may be one form of identification; a security token that generates a random number or a biometric like a fingerprint may provide a second factor.

Behavioral targeting The practice of tracking an individual's web browsing behavior for the purpose of deciding which advertisements to display to that individual.

Behavioral tracking The practice of collecting and compiling a record of an individual consumer's online activities, interests, preferences, and/or communications over time. Use of offline data also qualifies.

CAPTCHA A test used by websites to ensure that an individual, not a computer, is typing a response. CAPTCHA tests are typically displayed as distorted numbers and letters.

CDD The Center for Digital Democracy based in Washington, D.C.

Cloud computing The sharing or storage by users of their own information on remote servers owned or operated by others and accessed through the Internet or other connections.

COPPA The Children's Online Privacy Protection Act. It can also refer to the California Online Privacy Protection Act.

Confidentiality Generally refers to the concept that personal information has or should have some degree of secrecy. The term is often used interchangeably and confusingly with *privacy*.

Consent In an online context, usually refers to agreement by an individual to the use or disclosure of personal information. Consent can be affirmative, negative, unambiguous, explicit, or otherwise, depending on the manner in which consent is obtained.

Cookie (or HTTP cookie) In the context of online privacy, refers to a small file deposited onto a computer's hard drive during a Web browsing session or sessions. Some cookies assist in website functions, such as making purchases. These and other types of cookies may be transitory. Some cookies are persistent and are used to track online behaviors over time. These persistent cookies are called *profiling cookies*, *long-term tracking cookies*, or *third-party tracking cookies*. See also *Opt-out cookie*, *Flash cookies*, and *Evercookie*.

Cybersecurity The field of securing online computers against misuse, intrusions, and attack, such as viruses, worms, hacking, and other threats that could lead to disruptions, data breaches, identity theft, or other harms.

Data breach Occurs when records containing personally identifiable information are improperly exposed, stolen, or leaked online or otherwise.

Data broker A company that collects, collates, analyzes, and sells information, including but not limited to data about identifiable consumers. Intelius, ChoicePoint, and Acxiom are examples of data brokers.

Data logging The collection and recording of detailed information about when a computer is connected to the Internet, what sites that computer visits, what search terms and other words are typed into the computer, and other usage details. Also called keystroke logging.

Data retention Typically refers to companies that provide online services, such as search engines and others, being required by law to collect and store consumer data for a defined period for possible use by law enforcement agencies.

Digital signage Refers to a form of advertising used on video screens, mobile phones, and online. It covers a wide range of technologies, from simple people counting sensors mounted on doorways of retailers to sophisticated facial recognition cameras mounted in flat video screens to interactive billboards. Digital signage may in some cases gather detailed information about identified consumers and their behaviors.

DMA Refers to the Direct Marketing Association, an industry trade association.

Do Not Call (DNC) Refers to the registry maintained by the Federal Trade Commission that allows individuals to opt out of receiving some commercial telemarketing calls. Consumers have added more than 200 million telephone numbers to the DNC list. Canada also operates a DNC registry.

Do Not Track (DNT) Refers to a proposal originally made by privacy groups in 2007 to the Federal Trade Commission to give consumers a simple way to opt out of online tracking, much like the Do Not Call list. Implementation of a DNT system is controversial and can be accomplished in many different ways.

DPA Refers to a Data Protection Authority, typically a government official or agency in a European Union member state or another jurisdiction with responsibilities for data protection.

DPI Deep packet inspection, a process of inspecting computer network traffic at a highly granular level. DPI is often conducted by an Internet service provider at the time a communication is sent or received by a user.

EFF The Electronic Frontier Foundation, an important digital privacy and civil liberties group.

Encryption A way to transform data using a cipher in order to make it unreadable except by those with a decryption key or method. Encryption can enhance the privacy and security of data that are stored or transmitted online.

EPIC The Electronic Privacy Information Center, a leading privacy group that focuses on online privacy and other civil liberties issues.

EU Data Protection Directive Refers to European Union Directive 95/46/EC on the protection of individuals with regard to the processing of personal data and on the free movement of such data.

Evercookie A highly persistent type of tracking cookie that has the capability of restoring itself even after traditional Web browser cookies are erased. These types of cookies are also called "zombie cookies."

FIPs Fair Information Practices, a set of eight privacy principles created originally by a U.S. government advisory committee in 1973 and restated influentially by the Organisation for Economic Cooperation and Development in 1980. FIPs form the basis of many international privacy laws.

Firefox A Mozilla Corporation Web browser well known for its many privacy features and add-ons.

Flash cookies A form of online persistent tracking cookie associated with the Adobe Flash program. Advertisers and some websites use Flash cookies.

FTC The U.S. Federal Trade Commission.

Geotagging The addition of precise longitude and latitude coordinates derived from GPS-enabled devices such as cameras, phones, or laptops to photographs or other objects. For example, photographs may be geotagged, as may jogging routes stored on smartphones.

GINA Refers to the Genetic Information Nondiscrimination Act, a 2008 federal statute.

Google A publicly owned company that offers numerous Web services, including its famous search engine. Many Google activities have been controversial worldwide for their privacy consequences.

HIPAA The Health Insurance Portability and Accountability Act is a federal privacy rule issued by the Department of Health and Human Services that establishes a baseline of protection that applies to health care providers and health care insurers throughout the United States.

IAPP The International Association of Privacy Professionals.

Identity theft Occurs when an individual's identity information is used to fraudulently obtain goods or services using the victim's name, credit, or other characteristics.

IP address An Internet Protocol address. These addresses are numbers assigned to computers and other devices attached to a computer network and can be used to identify and track computers as they access the Web. IP addresses can be static or dynamic.

ISP An Internet service provider.

Klout score A measurement of an individual or group's overall online influence. Klout scores can range from 1 to 100, with 100 being the highest score. Klout scores are publicly available if an individual or organization has a known Twitter handle.

Locational privacy Relates to the use of information about an individual's geographic location, obtained through GPS geotagging, location-based services, or cell phone towers.

Medical identity theft Occurs when someone uses an individual's name and sometimes other parts of his or her identity, such as insurance information, to obtain medical services or goods or uses the individual's identity information to make false claims for medical services or goods. Medical identity theft frequently results in erroneous entries being put into existing medical records and can involve the creation of fictitious medical records in the victim's name.

Modern permanent record Refers to an often hard-to-erase digital compilation of an individual's activities and transactions that typically includes online as well as offline behavior and that is maintained by any number of third parties, including websites, data brokers, and others.

NAI The Network Advertising Initiative, a self-regulatory industry trade group that develops self-regulatory privacy standards for online advertising.

NHIN The National Health Information Network, an initiative by the U.S. Office of the National Coordinator for Health Information Technology for the electronic exchange of health care information.

OECD The Organisation for Economic Cooperation and Development. The OECD has created a number of key privacy documents ratified by the United States, Europe, and other countries.

Onion routing A technique for anonymous communication over a computer network that uses a repeatedly encrypted message.

Opt in Means an affirmative choice to receive products, goods, services, or information. Often, an online opt in refers to agreeing to receive advertising or to be the subject of monitoring.

Opt out Means a choice to decline to receive products, goods, services, or information. With an opt out, a user who takes no action accepts the default choice. Opt in requires an affirmative act.

Opt-out cookie A cookie that tells online advertisers who are members of the Network Advertising Initiative to not track activities on a computer for behaviorally targeted ads. See also *Cookie*.

P3P The Platform for Privacy Preferences, a standard that allows computer users and websites to communicate privacy preferences online. The platform was not widely or earnestly adopted, but it remains as an early and important privacy-enhancing technology initiative.

PETs Privacy-enhancing technologies. These can range from the Tor onion router to Web browser plug-ins such as Ad Block Plus.

PGP Pretty Good Privacy, a well-known encryption program and one of the first made widely and freely available.

PHR A personal health record, often stored online by someone who is not a health care provider, such as Microsoft. PHRs may not be protected under health privacy laws.

PII Refers to personally identifiable information, which is information that can, directly or indirectly, identify an individual. PII includes name, address, IP address, Social Security number, and/or other assigned identifier or a combination of unique or nonunique identifying elements associated with a particular individual or that can be reasonably associated with that individual. Any set of actions and behaviors of an individual, if those actions define a uniquely identified user, is usually considered

PII because the associated behavioral record can have tracking and/or targeting consequences. There is disagreement whether and when non-unique elements constitute PII.

Plug-in A program that can be added to a Web browser. Many privacy plug-ins exist, such as AdBlocker Plus and TACO, both of which are privacy-related plug-ins for the Firefox Web browser.

PRC The Privacy Rights Clearinghouse in San Diego, California, a public interest group devoted to upholding the right to privacy and protecting consumers against identity theft and other privacy crimes.

Privacy A much-discussed and disputed term that refers, in an online context, to the rights and interests of an individual that apply to the processing of information obtained from or about that individual.

Privacy policy Refers, in its online form, to a document describing the personal data collection, maintenance, use, disclosure, and safekeeping practices by a website, person, business, or other entity. Some but not all commercial privacy policies are theoretically enforceable by the Federal Trade Commission.

Safe Harbor Refers to a program administered by the U.S. Department of Commerce that supports the export from Europe of PII to U.S. businesses qualified for the Safe Harbor.

Sensitive data Often defined as personally identifiable information about health, financial activities, sexual behavior or sexual orientation, Social Security numbers, insurance numbers, or other identification numbers. There is disagreement about the precise boundaries of sensitivity.

Social networks Web sites such as Facebook that facilitate communication between individuals and groups of people.

TACD The Trans Atlantic Consumer Dialogue, a forum of U.S. and European Union consumer organizations.

Tor An onion router that assists individuals to browse the Web privately. Tor works by incrementally building a circuit of encrypted connections through relays on the Tor network. The circuit is extended one hop at a time, and each relay along the way knows only which relay gave it data and which relay it is giving data to, thus limiting some online traffic analysis. See *Onion router.*

Traffic analysis The analysis by websites or Internet service providers of information about users browsing the Web. Traffic analysis can also refer to sophisticated statistical and other techniques used to discern Web browsing patterns of individuals, organizations, and governments.

Web anonymizers Tools that are used to hide computer's Web browsing histories. Some examples are the Tor onion router and Anonymizer.com.

Web bug An effectively invisible single pixel used to track Web users, often in conjunction with online advertising. The term was popularized in the late 1990s by Internet privacy and security expert Richard M. Smith. A Web bug is also known as *pixel tag* or *pixel gif*.

WiFi Refers to wireless Internet networks.

WPF The World Privacy Forum, a public interest group focused on privacy rights of individuals.

Index

About the Authors

Robert Gellman is a privacy and information policy consultant in Washington, D.C. A graduate of the Yale Law School, Gellman has worked on privacy matters for more than 35 years. He served half of that time on the staff of the House of Representatives Subcommittee responsible for the Privacy Act of 1974. He also served a term as a member of the Department of Health and Human Service's National Committee on Vital and Health Statistics. Gellman has testified as a privacy expert before several state legislatures and been an expert witness in court cases. In addition to online privacy, his areas of expertise include health privacy and international data protection. Gellman advises corporate clients, trade associations, federal agencies, foreign governments, and privacy advocacy organizations. His website at www.bobgellman.com offers a wealth of useful privacy resources and many of his publications.

Pam Dixon is an author and researcher. She has written seven books, published hundreds of articles, and conducted and published substantial research in the area of privacy, including pioneering work in the area of medical identity theft. She is the founder and executive director of the internationally recognized World Privacy Forum, a nonprofit, nonpartisan public interest research group, www.worldprivacyforum.org. There, she focuses on in-depth research of emerging privacy issues. She has testified before Congress and state legislators on various privacy and technology issues. A former educator, she is the recipient of a Johns Hopkins University Fellowship for outstanding teaching.